Engaging Couples

This book is a challenge to the silos in our human services that an 'atomised' focus gives rise to. They are evident in the chasm that can exist between child and adult mental health care, between competing therapeutic approaches and, most importantly for this volume, in the segmentation of support for adults who are partners as well as parents.

The contributors, all with substantial experience of providing front-line services, identify the problem their intervention is designed to address, provide a conceptual justification for the approach they have used and supply evidence for its effectiveness. Vivid illustrations bring the work to life and provide examples of best practice whose relevance can readily be transported to different settings. Unusual in bringing together approaches that encompass internal and external realities in responding to the challenges of physical constraint, emotional distress and an often-volatile social environment, the contributions are assembled to highlight a common thread that can inform services at different stages of the life course. Each chapter is accompanied by a commentary from specialists in their field who elucidate and critique the key points made by the authors and help the experience of reading the book to be one of dialogue.

Engaging Couples: New Directions in Therapeutic in Work with Families explores new ways of approaching some of the key issues of contemporary family life, including depression, living with long-term conditions, inter-parental conflict and domestic abuse to name but a few, refracting them through a lens that sees our relationships as fundamental to the fabric of our lives – the most important social capital of all.

It represents essential reading for clinicians and family practitioners of all persuasions, and those that train and support them in their work.

Andrew Balfour is Chief Executive at Tavistock Relationships, and a Fellow at St George's House, Windsor. He is a clinical psychologist, a psychoanalytic psychotherapist and couple psychotherapist. With Mary Morgan and Christopher Vincent, he co-edited *How Couple Relationships Shape our World: Clinical Practice, Research and Policy Perspectives*.

Christopher Clulow is a Consultant Couple Psychoanalytic Psychotherapist, a Senior Fellow of the Tavistock Institute of Medical Psychology, London, and a Fellow of the Centre for Social Policy, Dartington. He has published extensively on marriage, partnerships, parenthood and couple psychotherapy.

Kate Thompson is a psychoanalytic couple psychotherapist, head of Tavistock Relationship's strategic development and Couple Therapy for Depression training, Kate has worked with couples for over 20 years and specialises in the impact of mental health difficulties on relationships.

"Treating common mental disorders within the unit of the couple has been shown to be one of the most effective modes of psychological intervention. This book will ground and orient the clinician to the nuances and challenges of psychotherapy offered to couples but, beyond this, it brilliantly summarises the clinical achievements of several generations of clinicians who have created this unique and remarkable tradition to produce powerful individual change by addressing issues that concern two interlocking minds. A gem that should have pride of place on all clinicians' bookshelves."

Professor Peter Fonagy OBE, *Head of the Division of Psychology and Language Sciences, University College London, Chief Executive, Anna Freud National Centre for Children & Families, National Clinical Advisor on Children's Mental Health, NHS England*

"At a time when policy-makers tend to look for simple answers to overly-simplified 'what works' questions, this volume makes a very refreshing and instructive read. It showcases the highly complex and deeply humane work of the Tavistock team as they go below the surface of couple relationships across the life cycle."

June Thoburn CBE, *Emeritus Professor of Social Work, University of East Anglia, UK*

"The contributors to this text demonstrate ways of broadening the application of their approach to a number of potentially stressful relationship problems encountered at various stages in the life cycle. This will be a very useful text for a range of community-based services looking for specialist help in dealing with family relationship problems."

Mervyn Murch CBE, *Emeritus Professor, School of Law and Politics, Cardiff University, UK*

"Tavistock Relationships has occupied a leading place in the world of couple mental health for more than 70 years. This marvelous book, written by some of the superstars of couple psychoanalysis, provides a wonderful insight into the pioneering work of this remarkable institution. Anyone with an interest in promoting the mental health and wellbeing of couples and families will benefit hugely from these chapters."

Professor Dr Estela Welldon, *Founder and Honorary Elected President of the International Association for Forensic Psychotherapy*

"*Engaging Couples* is a most engaging book. It offers the clinician a rich tapestry of the history, science and art of psychoanalytic couple therapy as practiced and researched by probably the finest collection of couple therapists in the English speaking analytic world. From theory to practice, from parenting to old age, this volume examines many of the issues couple therapists face. In celebrating 70 years of Tavistock Relationships, this volume also enriches the ideas behind the work so many of us cherish. At the same time it presents an agenda for future development. This book is essential reading for all analytic couple therapists, novice or veteran. Bravo to the editors and contributors for ushering in the next 70 years of one of the most enduring and celebrated institutions in psychoanalysis."

David Scharff, *Co-Founder, International Psychotherapy Institute, and Chair, Couple and Family Psychoanalysis Committee of the International Psychoanalytic Association*

Engaging Couples

New Directions in Therapeutic Work with Families

Edited by Andrew Balfour, Christopher Clulow, and Kate Thompson

LONDON AND NEW YORK

First published 2019
by Routledge
2 Park Square, Milton Park, Abingdon, Oxon OX14 4RN

and by Routledge
711 Third Avenue, New York, NY 10017

Routledge is an imprint of the Taylor & Francis Group, an informa business

© 2019 editorial and individual chapters, Andrew Balfour, Christopher Clulow, and Kate Thompson; individual chapters, the contributors

The right of Andrew Balfour, Christopher Clulow, and Kate Thompson to be identified as the author of the editorial material and of individual chapters, has been asserted in accordance with sections 77 and 78 of the Copyright, Designs and Patents Act 1988.

All rights reserved. No part of this book may be reprinted or reproduced or utilised in any form or by any electronic, mechanical, or other means, now known or hereafter invented, including photocopying and recording, or in any information storage or retrieval system, without permission in writing from the publishers.

Trademark notice: Product or corporate names may be trademarks or registered trademarks, and are used only for identification and explanation without intent to infringe.

British Library Cataloguing-in-Publication Data
A catalogue record for this book is available from the British Library

Library of Congress Cataloguing-in-Publication Data
Names: Balfour, Andrew, editor.
Title: Engaging couples : new directions in therapeutic in work with families / edited by Andrew Balfour,
Christopher Clulow, and Kate Thompson.
Description: Milton Park, Abingdon, Oxon ; New York, NY : Routledge, 2018.
Identifiers: LCCN 2018021159 (print) |
LCCN 2018021831 (ebook) |
ISBN 9780429445071 (Master eBook) |
ISBN 9780367000028 (hbk) |
ISBN 9780367000042 (pbk) |
ISBN 9780429445071 (ebk)
Subjects: LCSH: Couples therapy.
Classification: LCC RC488.5 (ebook) |
LCC RC488.5 .E645 2018 (print) |
DDC 616.89/1562–dc23
LC record available at https://lccn.loc.gov/2018021159

ISBN: 978-0-367-00002-8 (hbk)
ISBN: 978-0-367-00004-2 (pbk)
ISBN: 978-0-429-44507-1 (ebk)

Typeset in Times New Roman
by Integra Software Services Pvt. Ltd.

Printed and bound in Great Britain by
TJ International Ltd, Padstow, Cornwall

Contents

About the editors and contributors viii
Foreword xv
Editors' preface xviii
ANDREW BALFOUR, CHRISTOPHER CLULOW AND KATE THOMPSON

Introduction: policy and practice contexts 1
SUSANNA ABSE

1 Being a couple: psychoanalytic perspectives 15
ANDREW BALFOUR AND MARY MORGAN

Commentary on Chapter 1 29
DAVID HEWISON

2 Couples becoming parents 34
CHRISTOPHER CLULOW

Commentary on Chapter 2 48
MARGUERITE REID

3 Adopting together 53
JULIE HUMPHRIES AND KRISZTINA GLAUSIUS

Commentary on Chapter 3 67
JOHN SIMMONDS

4 Working with couples in groups   71
   LUCY DRAPER

   Commentary on Chapter 4   84
   PHILIP A. COWAN AND CAROLYN PAPE COWAN

5 Let's talk about sex . . .   90
   MARIAN O'CONNOR

   Commentary on Chapter 5   104
   JANICE HILLER

6 Couple Therapy for Depression   109
   KATE THOMPSON

   Commentary on Chapter 6   124
   JEREMY HOLMES

7 Mentalization-based couple therapy   130
   VIVEKA NYBERG AND LEEZAH HERTZMANN

   Commentary on Chapter 7   144
   STANLEY RUSZCZYNSKI

8 Working with couple violence   150
   ANTHEA BENJAMIN, PARMJIT CHAHAL, STEVE MULLEY AND ANTONIA REAY

   Commentary on Chapter 8   164
   DAMIAN MCCANN

9 Working with the fractured container   169
   AVI SHMUELI

   Commentary on Chapter 9   183
   CHRISTOPHER VINCENT

10 Living together with dementia ANDREW BALFOUR AND LIZ SALTER	189
Commentary on Chapter 10 JANE GARNER	203
Index	209

About the editors and contributors

Susanna Abse is a couple psychoanalytic psychotherapist and executive coach and has worked in private practice with couples and individuals since 1991. She was CEO of Tavistock Relationships from 2006 until 2016, and now coaches other senior managers. She is a member of the British Psychoanalytic Council and serves on their Executive Board. She has published widely on couple therapy, parenting, and family policy, and how these areas need to be at the heart of progressive welfare provision. She is a Series Editor for the *Library of Couple and Family Psychoanalysis* and became a Senior Fellow of The Tavistock Institute of Medical Psychology in 2017.

Andrew Balfour is Chief Executive at Tavistock Relationships. He originally studied English Literature before training in clinical psychology at University College London. He went on to train as an adult psychoanalytic psychotherapist at the Tavistock & Portman NHS Trust while working in a staff post there. Subsequently, he trained as a couple psychotherapist at Tavistock Relationships (formerly Tavistock Centre for Couple Relationships). For more than ten years he was Clinical Director and in 2016 took on the leadership of the organisation. He has published widely and teaches both in Britain and abroad. With Mary Morgan and Christopher Vincent, he co-edited *How Couple Relationships Shape Our World: Clinical Practice, Research and Policy Perspectives* (Karnac, 2012).

Anthea Benjamin is a UKCP registered integrative arts psychotherapist, adolescent therapeutic counsellor, group analyst and supervisor. She has worked extensively with children, adolescents, adults, families and groups for over fifteen years in various settings including schools, community projects and the NHS. She currently works as a therapist at Tavistock Relationships delivering training, running groups for couples and working within The Safer Family's Project. Anthea has a special interest in working with looked after children and adults who have been in the care system or adopted, exploring issues of identity, particularly with those who have been placed trans-racially or via intercountry processes.

Parmjit Chahal is Head of Service for a statutory children's safeguarding service in the London Borough of Harrow and is the Harrow Children's Services strategic lead for domestic abuse. Parmjit was behind the development of a couple's response to domestic abuse leading to the London Borough of Harrow supporting and funding the first pilot of the couples approach with Tavistock Relationships. The devastating consequences of children being exposed to domestic abuse is well documented, Parmjit therefore believes that developing initiatives that work with both parents is central to safeguarding children from exposure to domestic abuse.

Christopher Clulow is a Consultant Psychoanalytic Couple Psychotherapist, past Director of Tavistock Relationships (1987–2006) and a Senior Fellow of the Tavistock Institute of Medical Psychology, London. He has published extensively on marriage, partnerships, parenthood and couple psychotherapy, most recently from an attachment perspective. He is a Fellow of the Centre for Social Policy, Dartington, a Series Editor for the *Library of Couple Psychoanalysis*, a member of the editorial board of *Couple and Family Psychoanalysis* and the *International Review of Couple and Family Psychoanalysis*, and an editorial consultant for *Sexual and Relationship Therapy*. He maintains a clinical and training practice from his home in St Albans and in London.

Carolyn Pape Cowan, adjunct professor of psychology, emerita at the University of California, Berkeley, is co-director of three longitudinal preventive intervention studies, and has published widely in the literatures on couple relationships, family transitions, and preventive intervention. She is co-editor of *Fatherhood Today: Men's Changing Role in the Family* (Wiley, 1988) and *The Family Context of Parenting in the Child's Adaptation to School* (Lawrence Erlbaum, 2005), and co-author of *When Partners Become Parents: The Big Life Change for Couples* (Lawrence Erlbaum, 2000). She is a Senior Fellow of the Tavistock Institute of Medical Psychology.

Philip A. Cowan, professor of psychology, emeritus at the University of California, Berkeley, served as director of the Clinical Psychology Program and the Institute of Human Development. He has authored numerous scientific articles and *Piaget with Feeling* (Holt, Rinehart & Winston, 1978), co-authored *When Partners Become Parents: The Big Life Change for Couples* (Lawrence Erlbaum, 2000), and co-edited four books and monographs, including *Family Transitions* (Lawrence Erlbaum, 1991) and *The Family Context of Parenting in the Child's Adaptation to School* (Lawrence Erlbaum, 2005). He is a Senior Fellow of the Tavistock Institute of Medical Psychology.

Lucy Draper is based at Tavistock Relationships, where she is programme manager for both Parents as Partners and the Harrow Safer Families Project, a mentalization intervention with couples who have experienced domestic violence. Originally a teacher, she worked for many years as a children's centre manager, where she became particularly interested in groupwork with parents. Having trained as a group analytic psychotherapist, she has specialised in groups for young parents, for same sex parents, and for people with a personality disorder. For the past few years, her main focus has been on work with parental couples in groups.

Jane Garner is a consultant in old age psychiatry and for many years led a team in north London. She holds a number of honorary positions at the Royal College of Psychiatrists, including Deputy Chief Examiner and Secretary of the Old Age Faculty and is also a founding member and honorary secretary of the older adult section of the Association for Psychoanalytic Psychotherapy in the NHS. Her specialist interests include: psychotherapy with older adults; institutional abuse; continuing care in dementia, and the use of psychodynamic ideas in psychiatric practice. With Sandra Evans, she edited *Talking Over the Years: A Handbook of Dynamic Psychotherapy with Older Adults*. She is currently retired from clinical practice.

Krisztina Glausius is Head of Clinical Services at Tavistock Relationships and was Co-Project Lead on the Adopting Together Service. She is a couple psychoanalytic psychotherapist who has worked extensively with couples on issues around parenting. Having facilitated a number of Parents as Partners couples groups she now teaches and supervises this work. She has also worked as a senior research psychotherapist on Tavistock Relationship's randomised controlled trial of a mentalization-based intervention aimed at highly conflicted separated parental couples. She has been part of various mentalization-based intervention projects within Tavistock Relationships working with high conflict couples, and is involved in both time-limited and open-ended psychoanalytic work with couples.

Leezah Hertzmann is a couple and individual psychoanalytic psychotherapist at the Tavistock and Portman NHS Foundation Trust and in private practice. Previously at Tavistock Relationships, she developed several mentalization based interventions for conflictual parents and couples. Leezah was co-principal investigator of the successful evaluation of one of these interventions, and in 2015 was awarded the British Psychoanalytic Council Award for Innovation. Leezah teaches and publishes widely, and one of her particular interests is in psychoanalytic theory and technique with lesbian and gay individuals and couples. She is a member of the British Psychoanalytic Council special advisory group on sexual diversity.

David Hewison is a consultant couple psychoanalytic psychotherapist and Head of Research at Tavistock Relationships. He is the co-author (with Christopher Clulow and Harriet Drake) of *Couple Therapy for Depression: A Clinician's Guide to Integrative Practice* (2014), based on the model of couple therapy he developed as an evidence based treatment for depression in the NHS. He is a Jungian training analyst at the Society of Analytical Psychology, and he teaches internationally and publishes widely on individual and couple therapy and research. He has a particular interest in links between psychoanalysis and Jungian analysis, and in understanding creativity and imagination.

Janice Hiller is a consultant clinical psychologist who worked in adult mental health before becoming head of an NHS Psychosexual Service in North East London for many years. She joined the faculty of Tavistock Relations as academic tutor in psychosexual studies from 2012–2017. Janice has taught on training courses, organised and presented at conferences, and published on a range of topics. These include sexual arousal and desire difficulties, pain disorders, psychosexual development, and neurobiological aspects of sexual responding. She was joint editor and contributor to *Sex, Mind and Emotion* (Hiller, Wood and Bolton, 2006). Her private practice is in North London.

Jeremy Holmes was for 35 years consultant psychiatrist/medical psychotherapist at University College London (UCL) and then in North Devon, UK, and Chair of the Psychotherapy Faculty of the Royal College of Psychiatrists 1998–2002. He is visiting professor at the University of Exeter, and lectures nationally and internationally. In addition to over two hundred peer-reviewed papers and chapters in the field of psychoanalysis and attachment theory, his books include *John Bowlby and Attachment Theory* (2nd edition, Routledge, 2014) and *Attachment in Therapeutic Practice* (Sage, 2018, with A. Slade). He was recipient of the Bowlby-Ainsworth Founders Award in 2009. Music-making, gardening, Green politics and grand-parenting are gradually eclipsing his lifetime devotion to psychoanalytic psychotherapy and attachment.

Julie Humphries is Director of Studies at Tavistock Relationships and was Co-Project Lead on the Adopting Together Service. She is a couple psychoanalytic psychotherapist who also teaches and supervises on the organisation's clinical training programme. Her previous roles at Tavistock Relationships include Programme Head of the Psychodynamic Training, and supervisor and trainer on IAPT Couple Therapy for Depression courses. Apart from adoption, Julie has an ongoing interest in working with violent couples, and in understanding and working with domestic violence. Before training at Tavistock Relationships she was a senior lecturer in sociology, and researched and published in the areas of domestic violence and mental health.

Damian McCann is a couple psychoanalytic psychotherapist working as head of learning and development at Tavistock Relationships. He is also a consultant systemic psychotherapist working in a Child and Adolescent Mental Health Service and is an associate of Pink Therapy where he taught on the Diploma in Relationship Therapy for Gender and Sexual Diversities. He has a particular interest in working with same-sex couples, and his doctoral research was concerned with understanding the meaning and impact of violence in the couple relationships of gay men.

Mary Morgan is a psychoanalyst, couple psychoanalytic psychotherapist and Fellow of the British Psychoanalytical Society. At Tavistock Relationships she is the Reader in Couple Psychoanalysis and is a member of the IPA Committee on Couple & Family Psychoanalysis. She has published many papers in this field, taught and set up trainings in several parts of the world. Her book *A Couple State of Mind: Psychoanalysis of Couples and the Tavistock Relationships Model* is published in late 2018.

Stephen Mulley is a dance movement psychotherapist and occupational therapist, based at Tavistock Relationships. Along with the Safer Families Project, he is part of the team delivering Parents as Partners, a group-based intervention for parental couples supporting partners to strengthen their relationship with one another and improve outcomes for their children. Prior to joining Tavistock Relationships he worked in many different NHS mental health services and specialities, including acute, community and rehabilitation settings.

Viveka Nyberg is a lecturer and visiting clinician at Tavistock Relationships, where she was previously on the faculty staff. She is a graduate member of the Tavistock Institute of Medical Psychology and a senior member of the British Psychotherapy Foundation. She has lectured in the UK and abroad and has a private practice in London. She is on the editorial board of the journal of *Couple and Family Psychoanalysis*. Her publications include, with Molly Ludlam, *Couple Attachments: Theoretical and Clinical Studies* (Karnac, 2007), and, with Leezah Hertzmann, "Developing a Mentalization-Based Treatment (MBT) for Therapeutic Intervention With Couples (MBT-CT)" in *Couple and Family Psychoanalysis*, 2(4) 2014.

Marian O'Connor is Programme Head of the Diploma in Psychosexual Therapy at Tavistock Relationships where she was previously Head of Professional Development and Training. She is a consultant couple and psychosexual therapist, a supervisor and teacher so it reads – a supervisor and teacher. She has lectured on psychosexual issues in UK and abroad and has a private practice in Central London.

Antonia Reay is a counselling psychologist with 15 years experience. She works as a member of the Safer Families Team and as a group worker, supervisor and trainer on Tavistock Relationship's Parents as Partners Project. Before this she spent 11 years working in a specialist Primary Care Psychology Team in Tower Hamlets for parents with under five year olds. Prior to that she worked at the Henderson Hospital Therapeutic Community and at HMP Holloway. She has a private practice working with individuals using dynamic interpersonal therapy.

Marguerite Reid is a consultant child and adolescent psychotherapist who has more recently trained as a couple psychoanalytic psychotherapist. She co-founded the Perinatal Service at Chelsea and Westminster Hospital, where she specialised in perinatal mental health problems. Her doctoral research was in the area of perinatal loss and the mother's experience when she gives birth to the next baby. She has taught in the UK and abroad, and co-founded the Infant Observation Course in Izmir, Turkey where she has taught for many years. She has published in the area of perinatal mental health, and now works in private practice in South Kensington, London.

Stanley Ruszczynski is a psychoanalyst, a psychoanalytic couple psychotherapist and a full member of the British Psychoanalytic Association. He is a consultant adult psychotherapist (and past Clinical Director, 2005–2016) at the Portman

Clinic (Tavistock and Portman NHS Foundation Trust, London), which offers psychotherapeutic treatment to patients disturbed by their criminality, violence or damaging sexual behaviours. He was Deputy Director of Tavistock Relationships between 1987–1993. He has a private clinical and organisational consultancy practice, has authored many book chapters and articles, and edited and co-edited five books, including *Psychotherapy with Couples*, with James Fisher *Intrusiveness and Intimacy in the Couple*, and with David Morgan *Lectures on Violence, Perversion and Delinquency* (Routledge, 2007).

Liz Salter is a couple and individual psychodynamic counsellor and has worked for 15 years counselling individuals and couples who have been affected by life threatening and long term health conditions. She originally trained as an adult and mental health nurse and completed her MA at Tavistock Relationships, which focused on the influence of attachment styles in couples diagnosed with cancer. Since 2013 she has worked with Andrew Balfour developing and delivering the 'Living Together with Dementia' intervention.

Avi Shmueli is a psychoanalyst and couple psychotherapist, having initially trained as a clinical psychologist and completing a research doctorate at University College London. He has worked in the National Health Service, the Anna Freud Centre and was a staff member at Tavistock Relationships for many years. He now works in private practice and supervises the work of Tavistock Relationship's Divorce and Separation Consultation Service. Committed to psychoanalysis as a theory for understanding the mind and as a mode of clinical practice, he has pursued its different applications, including to empirical research and the fields of family and criminal law.

John Simmonds is Director of Policy, Research and Development at Coram BAAF, formerly the British Association for Adoption and Fostering. A qualified social worker, he is currently responsible for Coram BAAF's contribution to the development of policy and practice in social work, health, the law and research. His recent research has focused on unaccompanied asylum seeking children in foster care, undertaken with the Universities of York and Bedfordshire, a study of 100 women adopted from Hong Kong into the UK in the 1960s with the Institute of Psychiatry, and a government funded study on Special Guardianship with York University. He sits on the Adoption Leadership Board and was awarded an OBE in the New Years Honours list 2015.

Kate Thompson is Head of Strategic Development and Project Lead for Couple Therapy for Depression Training at Tavistock Relationships. Currently supervising the Parents as Partners and Safer Families Project, she has also written and created trainings around the impact of unemployment on couples. Her specialist interests also include working with couples and depression, running groups for couples with a child on the autism spectrum and, as a psychoanalytic couple psychotherapist, mentalization-based therapy for Tavistock Relationship's Parents in Dispute service. Kate is a regular contributor to *Couple and Family Psychoanalysis*, has written widely on the uptake of Couple Therapy for Depression within the NHS, as well as a series of popular blogs on relationship matters for Open University Press.

Christopher Vincent is a psychoanalytic couple psychotherapist registered with the British Psychoanalytic Council (through the Tavistock Institute of Medical Psychology). He is a consultant visiting lecturer at the Tavistock Relationships and maintains a private practice in Hayling Island, Hampshire. He has a special interest in the interface between psycho-social research methods and psychoanalysis particularly as this applies to the support and treatment of couples where one partner has a chronic illness.

Foreword

For nearly three quarters of a century, Tavistock Relationships has occupied a unique and remarkable role in the landscape of British mental health.

Extraordinarily, this visionary, impactful organisation developed from the most humble of origins, founded by a woman who, at the time of its inception, had undertaken absolutely no psychological training whatsoever.

During the Second World War, amid the horrors of the Blitz, the bombs of the *Luftwaffe* destroyed not only countless numbers of buildings across Great Britain but, also, shattered the security of innumerable marriages and families. With hundreds of thousands of soldiers slaughtered overseas, with countless numbers of civilians killed or injured or traumatised on the Home Front, and with millions of children evacuated far and wide, the Second World War wreaked havoc upon the very foundations of domestic life.

While fire fighters attempted to extinguish the flames which blazed on London's streets, Mrs. Enid Eichholz – a bold woman of Anglo-Jewish origin – began to do likewise with troubled marriages. In fact, as the war ended, she encountered many bereaved wives, post-traumatically distressed husbands, and delinquent children who had suffered the consequences of parental abandonment. Through her work at the Family Welfare Association – a charity designed to help the poor – Eichholz eventually began to create a series of offices in which social workers, known, initially, as 'secretaries', could engage spouses in an early version of talking therapy, in an effort to ease their marital miseries.

With support from leading psychoanalytical practitioners at both the Tavistock Clinic and the Tavistock Institute of Human Relations in London, such as Dr. John Bowlby, Dr. John Sutherland, and, most especially, Dr. Archibald Thomson Macbeth Wilson, Mrs. Eichholz's small endeavour began to grow. Known initially as the Marriage Guidance Council and, subsequently, as the Marriage Guidance Committee and, not long thereafter, as the Marriage Guidance Centres Committee, this project would eventually be restyled as the Family Discussion Bureaux, and then as the Family Discussion Bureau (without an 'x'). Before long, Mrs. Eichholz's small institution became a formal member of the wider Tavistock family, and would come to be known thereafter as the Institute of Marital Studies (quartered in the Tavistock Clinic itself), and then as the Tavistock Institute of Marital Studies. Several further name changes ensued: the Tavistock Marital Studies Institute, then the Tavistock Centre for Couple Relationships and, finally, in 2016, Tavistock Relationships.

During the early days, the application of psychoanalytic ideas to the study of the couple relationship generated considerable scepticism among more traditional Freudian practitioners. Many psychoanalysts regarded clinical work with the couple as a dilution of the purity and intensity of multi-frequency work with individuals. But as the Tavistock tradition of marital psychotherapy developed and prospered, and as the organisation began to publish its ground breaking contributions, suspicion soon gave way to admiration and, thanks to the pioneering vision of its successive leaders – Enid Eichholz (later known by her married name, Enid Balint), Lily Pincus, Douglas Woodhouse, Janet Mattinson, Christopher Clulow, Susanna Abse and, most recently, Andrew Balfour – the organisation has become truly seminal.

When I began my own clinical training at the Tavistock Marital Studies Institute many years ago, I had to endure the loneliness of being the *only* registered student during my first year. At that time, literally no one else had applied to study! But now, Tavistock Relationships regularly attracts hundreds of trainees who constitute a veritable community of ambassadors, applying the fruits of psychoanalytic couple mental health work in a creative variety of settings and contexts.

To celebrate its seventieth anniversary, Tavistock Relationships has commissioned a wonderful book, which documents its philosophy and its outreach. *Engaging Couples: New Directions in Therapeutic Work with Families*, explores the tradition of Tavistock Relationships and provides a compelling account of the innovations that have developed within its welcoming walls. Readers of this carefully conceived text will learn a great deal about not only the fundamentals of couple psychoanalytic theory and technique but, also, about the application of such thinking to many diverse arenas, including adoption, sexuality, divorce, depression, and forensic mental health. Moreover, the book explores several new avenues of application, such as parenting intervention programmes, as well as the increasingly indispensable work on supporting couples struggling with dementia. Moreover, this compendium also chronicles the creation of landmark dialogues instituted by Tavistock Relationships with government organisations and committees, which have come to influence public policy about family well-being.

As the supra title of the book proclaims, those of us who work in this field have the privilege of meeting *engaging* couples and, then, of *engaging with* these couples. Indeed, as we encounter our couples, we often find that the members of an intimate pairing become increasingly engaging, not only to their psychotherapists but, most fundamentally, to one another. Those who immerse themselves in the chapters contained herein will have the opportunity to study precisely how one works with a couple in distress and, moreover, how one discovers the truly compelling and intriguing nature of coupledom, especially when one becomes more adept at understanding and deciphering the secret, unconscious meanings communicated by the couple itself.

The practice of couple psychotherapy requires clinicians with sensitive skins and with sturdy spines who can survive the often-tumultuous experience of facilitating treatment of partners in painful, often violent, conflict. Those couples who stay the course and who commit themselves to this sometimes-taxing process will benefit from the compassion and the insight and the durability of the psychological practitioner, and will often find themselves, in consequence, privileged to be in a healthier, more robust, and more creative domestic situation. In fact, couples who do embark upon this work will, in many instances, be less likely to inflict severe psychopathology upon their children, will often suffer from fewer physical illnesses, and will frequently enjoy a greater quality of life. Couple psychotherapy has the capacity to alter the very fabric of our communities.

In 2009, my fellow couple psychoanalytic colleagues, Susanna Abse, Christopher Clulow, David Scharff, and I launched 'The Library of Couple and Family Psychoanalysis' – a monograph series conceived to publish the best contributions to this field. On behalf of my co-editors, it gives me very great pleasure to welcome the arrival of this well written, skilfully edited, and profoundly invigorating classic which offers us not only a study of the intricate detail of couple mental health work but, also, of its grand panorama.

I certainly could not imagine a more useful birthday present for Tavistock Relationships or a more impactful gift for the generations of students and practitioners to come.

Professor Brett Kahr
Series Co-Editor, 'The Library of Couple and Family Psychoanalysis'
London, November 2018

Editors' preface

Andrew Balfour, Christopher Clulow and Kate Thompson

After 70 years of the Tavistock approach to 'engaging couples', what does it mean to claim to offer 'new directions'? Over this time, Tavistock Relationships has contributed to the conceptual, clinical, and technical development of couple psychoanalytic psychotherapy, and applied this specialism to practice in the broader field of mental health services. What, though, makes this book any different from the scores of others on psychotherapy that you might invest your time in reading, and what might be its relevance beyond the consulting rooms of specialist practitioners? Why be interested in 'engaging couples'?

Alongside the development of couple psychotherapy, Tavistock Relationships has established a plurality of new approaches, reaching people who, historically, have not had access to such psychological help. Consider, for a moment, how much our systems of health and social care are focused on the individual in isolation. If you think about it, this holds true right across the lifespan: from maternity services that rarely include the parental couple as the locus of care, to services for people with long term conditions, such as dementia, that focus on the individual patient alone, without considering their partner or family who are living with the realities of chronic illness alongside them.

This book is a challenge to the silos in our human services that this 'atomised' focus gives rise to. These are evident in the chasm that exists between child and adult mental health care, they contribute to the neglect of our relationships in treating illness and depression, and they limit opportunities to strengthen the relational environment of the older couple at one end of the lifespan and of children at the other. The work described in this book explores new ways of approaching some of the key issues of contemporary family life, including depression, living with long-term conditions, inter-parental conflict and domestic abuse to name but a few, refracting them through a lens that sees our relationships as fundamental to the fabric of our lives – the most important social capital of all.

What you will see as you read on, is that such 'new' approaches are about developing established therapeutic models to fit different circumstances, tackling some of the problems of our modern world from fresh angles. Previous generations of colleagues did radical things, and close study of the innovative thinking of our analytic forbears can be humbling. In claiming an analytic lineage for the diversity contained within Tavistock Relationships' wide 'family' of approaches, we need to recognise that some 'children' will resemble their 'parents' more obviously than others; that the next generation, whilst sharing the same genes, will also be different. To pursue this metaphor, it is true that, after all, offspring are their own people, responding and adapting to the circumstances of their generation. That said, their capacity to make use of what is of value from parental figures will strengthen and enable them to adapt to the unique features of their lives. This, we hope, is what the reader will encounter in this book – not an attempt to re-invent wheels or make manic claims for our own originality, but evidence of our best efforts to learn from the past to engage with the present; addressing troubling, contemporary problems, not from a position of preconception, but in a psychoanalytic spirit of enquiry, meeting them with open minds about how to understand and respond effectively.

At the heart of the psychoanalytic model is the recognition that we are not free agents, making conscious choices about what we will do and how we shall be; rather, we are driven by unconscious forces. Modern neuroscience confirms just how much of our minds remain outside conscious awareness: brain changes can be detected that show the movement of the body towards a particular goal before we have any conscious awareness of having 'decided' to perform that action. This is a picture of our minds as driven by a significant degree of unconscious determinism, which challenges popular beliefs around conscious free-will. In his book *A Children's History of the World*, E.H. Gombrich uses the image of a lighted taper falling down the well of human history, illuminating as it falls different layers of the past, plunging downwards into deeper strata, until finally going out, consumed by darkness as by an infinite regress of time. This image could be extended to the human mind, whose area of depth is in the layers of our minds that we are consciously unaware of but which nevertheless exert their influence on our everyday lives. These influences can be discerned, perhaps most of all, in the ways in which we find ourselves repeating familiar, sometimes destructive, behaviour with others, and especially with those who are closest to us.

Curiosity about ourselves, and the wish to understand and find meaning in our lives, may represent a fundamental human need that drives our potential for growth and emotional development and our striving to find ways of living better, more meaningful lives. This is not the exclusive preserve of psychotherapy or therapists. However, because so much is outside our conscious awareness, our attempts to make sense of our feelings and behaviour are at times defeated and we may be in need of help to extend our understanding of ourselves and others. It can be painful, sometimes threatening, to seek such understanding, to think about our motivations, the sources of our actions and behaviour. Such curiosity or thinking can be defended against and denied. Yet, the psychotherapeutic approach suggests that the act of seeking to understand and of feeling ourselves understood can itself be therapeutic and lead to change, offering an enlargement of the area in our minds where we have some choice or freewill in terms of what we think, do and feel in our closest relationships, and so to be less driven by unconscious enactments and defeating patterns of behaviour.

In a world of competing models of psychological therapy, where the success of one can threaten the extinction of others, it can be difficult to make space for a plurality of approaches. This is true even of those we describe here, which, although rooted in a common conception of mind, are adapted to different uses and aims. Under such conditions of competition it can be difficult to retain a mind that is open to seeing similarities and recognising differences where they exist. Such struggles are, to some degree at least, familiar to all of us in our relationships, as couple therapists know from their daily work. These conflicts can also be played out within services, where competition over resources is the order of the day. At the risk of joining the clamour of competing voices for the merits of one therapeutic modality over another, this book describes, using examples from diverse settings, how the couple relationship offers a uniquely important locus of intervention. It is the site for the inter-generational transmission of mental health and should be at the forefront of our therapeutic efforts, at the centre of thinking in health and social care, throughout the lifespan, from cradle to grave. As you will read, the research and clinical evidence is now clear – intervening to help couples offers a chance to free the adults involved from damaging, repetitive cycles and the possibility of transforming the psychological inheritance of future generations.

Each chapter of the book reflects a new iteration of a tradition of 'applied work' that reaches back to Tavistock Relationships' beginnings in 1948, when the war had brought profound challenges to families across the country and around the world. From the opening chapter, which gives an account of the lens psychoanalytic couple therapists use to understand the internal dynamics of couple relationships, making sense of the 'better and worse' experiences that are intrinsic to being a couple, a broadly chronological path is taken in charting the challenges of parenthood for couple relationships, problems surrounding sexuality and mental health that can occur at any time during a relationship, the challenges of working with couples who act out in communicating their internal experience through violence, separation and divorce, and the trials and sometimes unexpected rewards of ageing for couples when physical and mental capacities are depleted by the erosion of time. We have encouraged contributors to open chapters with a clinical vignette, not so much to demonstrate a way of working but to provide an immersive experience of the phenomena they go on to elucidate. In this way we hope to have been able to engage feelings as well as thoughts in considering the complexity of family relationships and the challenges of responding therapeutically.

The opening chapter gives an account of the unconscious dimensions of couple relationships, offering an approach to understanding intriguing and often apparently inexplicable aspects of our lives, such as why we choose the partners we do, why difficult patterns may be repeated in our couplings, and the links between childhood experience and adult relationships. In this chapter, Andrew Balfour and Mary Morgan describe how these ideas, which help us to understand relationships, translate into psychotherapeutic work with couples, taking the reader into an account of the model of psychotherapy that is currently practised at Tavistock Relationships. In his response to this chapter, David Hewison takes up the importance of evidence-based practice, discussing key issues in outcomes research in this field and outlining the evidence base for the effectiveness of couple psychotherapy.

The sense of being a couple provides a foundation for starting a family. In considering aspects of what is involved for couples in becoming parents, Chapter 2 explores the opportunities for early intervention to mobilise the resources of couples as they come into and develop their parental roles and responsibilities. Christopher Clulow examines the reciprocal relationship between how parenthood changes couples and how couples impact on children. In exploring the implications for therapeutic practice, he describes the potential for group programmes for parental couples as well as couple-focused therapy to improve the well-being of families. Margaret Lawson Reid, in responding to this chapter, underlines the risks that a traumatic birth can pose to the mental health of new parents and the need for perinatal services to pick up on distressing affective and relationship fall-out that can follow from it, especially when the consequence can be a child with special needs.

While Clulow's chapter assumes a biological connection between parents and their offspring, Chapter 3 considers the particular stresses and strains on couples who become parents through adoption. Julie Humphries and Krisztina Glausias examine specific areas that can have a defining impact on the experience of adoption from the couple's perspective, and describe an innovative service that has learned from this experience and translated it into therapeutic action. John Simmonds, in responding to the Adopting Together Service, comments on the surprising lacuna of those working in the adoption field when it comes to engaging with the relationship between adoptive parents. If this is an avoidance, it may well be one with which adoptive parents collude, for they are in the impossible position of having to present the best of their relationship at a time when their feelings about not being able to conceive their own child, and their exposure to infertility treatments, may have exposed them to the worst. Given the challenges posed by many children placed for adoption he argues that strengthening the parental dyad is especially important in managing the triadic dynamics that children bring to family life.

Once the arrival of children has created a family the complexities of managing competing commitments increases, along with other stresses on parents that can prove challenging for even those best placed to meet them. Chapter 4 describes a group intervention to support parents and examines the phenomenon of a group dynamic on couple relationships, exploring the question of difference for couples by comparing the benefits of joining a heterogeneous versus homogeneous group for a same sex couple. Parents as Partners, a semi-structured group intervention, first introduced by Philip and Carolyn Cowan, who provide the response to this chapter, and Marsha Kline Pruett and Kyle Pruett in California, saw the introduction of this integrated model as a means of supporting the couple to benefit families, as opposed to more traditional parenting classes that habitually focused on the parent–child dyad, neglecting the centrality of the couple relationship. While the Cowans provide a description of the far reaching evidence base for this psychodynamic, attachment and psychoeducational group approach, Lucy Draper outlines its British incarnation, which has provided a sense of relief for countless couples as they discover that they are not alone in managing the complexities of the transition to parenthood.

While children are the natural consequence of sexual activity, sexual behaviour is a defining feature of adult couple relationships with or without their presence. It may be particularly important in connecting and sustaining couples in the early stages of their relationship, but its significance can endure well into old age. The centrality of sex in the lives of couples is underlined by Marian O'Connor in Chapter 5, and this makes her curious about why attending to sexual functioning is so often avoided by couples and clinicians alike. She suggests that oedipal anxiety, envy and fear of intrusion beset this intimate area of therapy and outlines an integrated way of working within a psychosexual framework that combines educational and behavioural interventions whilst grappling with cognitive distortions, concluding with a helpful description of the process of making a psychosexual assessment. Janice Hiller's response points to information from advances in neuroscience that deepen and enhance therapeutic skills, and outlines a biopsychosocial model of sexual responsiveness. She points out that, despite developments – including pharmacological advances – inadequate understanding of how bodies function sexually continues to threaten couple intimacy.

As with problems around sexual intimacy, mental ill-health can threaten the couple relationship at any stage of life. Chapter 6 focuses on depression and its impact on the couple dynamic. Couple Therapy for Depression, an innovative, integrated model, was designed specifically to address relational issues often concealed within a diagnosis of depression and seeks to harness the relationship as a valuable resource for recovery and relapse-prevention. This evidence-based model combines psychodynamic, cognitive, behavioural, emotionally-focused and systemic therapies. In this chapter Kate Thompson illustrates, in a detailed case study, the considerable therapeutic skill needed to move between the competencies required in practising the model. Offered predominantly to date within the NHS, Jeremy Holmes, in his response, takes a quizzical look at the 'new' world of evidence base and data analysis from an attachment perspective. He describes couples as hidden regulators of one another's feelings and traces the developmental origins of depression and their role in couple functioning.

In the same way that traditional psychoanalytic approaches have been influenced by, and needed to adapt to, the mental health challenge of depressive disorders, so too have adjustments been required to provide effective help for those challenging couples who have difficulty containing labile emotional states that can trigger violence, addictive behaviours and other forms of acting out. In Chapter 7, Viveka Nyberg and Leezah Hertzmann describe the mentalization based approach to working with such couples that has been pioneered at Tavistock Relationships, and consider how its theoretical underpinnings relate to those informing other psychoanalytic interventions with couples. At the heart of this approach is deploying interventions that generally eschew interpretation of the transference in favour of techniques that encourage curiosity about each individual's own experience and that of their partner. Responding to this chapter Stanley Ruszczynski offers a nuanced response that questions some of the distinctions drawn between the two approaches, except, perhaps, in the attention paid to the couple relationship as an object in its own right.

Strengthening the couple relationship to benefit the welfare of children is central to all chapters in this book. Working with couples who choose to stay together despite violence and abuse is a controversial and difficult task. Anthea Benjamin, Parmjit Chahal, Steve Mulley and Antonia Reay describe the development of new ways of harnessing mentalization based therapy to work with these couples, to help them to begin to be curious about their own internal emotional states and those of their partners and children. They describe a promising innovation, still in its early stages, that can lead to an easing of relational tension in critical cases of entrenched situational violence, often working in the face of trans-generational trauma and attachment rupture. The chapter outlines the therapeutic team's emphasis on safety and assessment as well as the importance of working alongside social services, and openly shares some of the therapeutic dilemmas encountered in this effort to restore mentalization when thinking and relating has been replaced by violent acting out and chaotic family dynamics. Damian McCann's response reminds us of current social sensitivity around working with couples where there is violence by exploring the differences between the more traditional perpetrator – victim approach, with the distinctions that can be drawn between coercion, control and situational couple violence. He casts the net wide to include an examination of treatments offered for domestic violence in other countries and elaborates on the crucial thinking around risk, responsibility and collaboration between professional workers supporting these couples.

Violence signifies the breakdown of containment in a couple's relationship, and it is to the 'fracture' of containment that Avi Shmueli turns in Chapter 9 when addressing the therapist's role in helping couples on the cusp of separation and divorce. Building on his earlier conceptualisation differentiating between three domains of divorce, he offers a post-Freudian theoretical basis that makes sense of such fractures in terms of a non-alignment between past and present unconscious fantasy. Commenting on his argument Christopher Vincent shares some clinical dilemmas arising from working on the boundary between preconscious and conscious experience, the site where much conflict occurs between separating couples. He concludes with two profound questions facing clinicians as they review their models of practice and the prospect of their own therapeutic hopes being fractured.

The final chapter investigates the often-neglected area of dementia in later life. Andrew Balfour and Liz Salter describe the development of an intervention for couples living with dementia designed to assist communication and understanding, using shared involvement in everyday activities as a basis for enhancing emotional contact between the partners. The aim of this approach is to support the resilience of the couple, helping them to hold onto emotional meaning and shared activity in the face of challenges and pressures towards withdrawal and loss of contact that can be so characteristic of the situation. Although the use of video-taped interactions between the partners may make this intervention look far from psychoanalytic, it is rooted in the importance of promoting containment, emotional contact and understanding, and draws on attachment-informed approaches developed in parent-infant psychotherapy applied to the caring dyad at the other end of life. In her response, Jane Garner considers the social and humanitarian consequences of neglecting the experience of the dementia sufferer and espouses a relational view of their needs in dementia care settings. The profound need for radical change in this most neglected area of end of life care is the final, poignant note on which we end.

It is not possible to assemble a book like this without drawing on the experience of couples with whom we have worked. They are our best teachers, who guide and inform our understanding of the dynamics of couple relationships and how best to offer help when they are in trouble. So they are the hidden contributors to this volume, to whom we owe an enormous debt of gratitude. Each of the case examples that follow is an amalgam of different couples made into composite 'cases', to give a picture for the reader which protects confidentiality, whilst retaining fidelity to the authenticity of the experience of the couples involved. The focus is always on illustrating themes, themes that feature in many relationships and are often dynamic in nature, and these are not dependent on describing personal details. In managing this process we have been helped by the Ethics Committee of Tavistock Relationships, and we wish to acknowledge their invaluable contribution.

We are also, of course, indebted to the authors who have contributed to this volume, recognising the time and discipline that will have been involved for them in sharing their knowledge and experience through the printed word. As editors we have felt privileged to work with them, and thank them for their forbearance with us as we coaxed and commented on the drafts they produced in reaching the final product. The three of us editors have enjoyed working together as a team and have learned much in the process of putting this volume together. We would like to thank Fong McGeorge and Katie Torres for their invaluable help in preparing this book ahead of and during the publication process. We would also like to express our appreciation and support to Oliver Rathbone and his staff at Karnac Books, who contracted with us to produce the book, and to Russell George and his colleagues at Routledge who took over the brief when their parent body, Taylor & Francis, bought Karnac Books.

To conclude, our purpose is to draw to the attention of a wide readership the importance of the couple relationship as an untapped resource that research shows can contribute to the well-being of adults, children, and the communities of which they are a part. More particularly, this book describes ways in which this resource might be tapped into, and provides evidence of how this might be done effectively. Our hope is that it will provide an informative, engaging and useful text for practitioners from many backgrounds whose job it is to support family members in managing creatively the range of predictable and unpredicted challenges that change relationships during the course of a lifetime.

The 'plural approach' to developing diverse interventions to help couples, which we survey across the different chapters and responses in this book, requires rigour in describing and differentiating between models and techniques, and exposing them to proper evaluation. These different approaches are linked to, but separate from, the core analytic model used by Tavistock Relationships, which remains at the heart of its clinical practice and invigorates the wider applications the organisation is striving to develop. Innovation, accessibility, and social relevance should not be restricted to the many 'new' therapies which proliferate these days. Some of the approaches described in this book have reached the stage of having clearly articulated treatment manuals and models, and, like our core psychoanalytic model, have been subjected to rigorous evaluation. Others are work in progress. They reflect not only the experience of the authors of the chapters, but also many others besides, following the rich lineage of our forebears in this field in becoming part of a long tradition of applied psychoanalysis, whose conceptions of mind support the diversification of approaches needed to address contemporary psycho-social problems facing couples and families in our time. To this end we hope that Tavistock Relationships will continue over its next 70 years to support both specialist and first responder mental health services through developing sharing and applying its core ethos, while also adapting and being responsive to the challenges posed by a rapidly changing environment.

Introduction
Policy and practice contexts

Susanna Abse

"Where there is an open mind, there will always be a frontier."
Charles F. Kettering[1] (cited in Boyd, 2002, p.216)

Relationship problems dominate our landscape. Whether watching a television soap opera or looking at the underlying reasons for intergenerational disadvantage, one cannot avoid the centrality of the couple relationship. Yet, despite this, interventions designed to work with difficulties between couples have been slow in coming. Gurman and Frankeal's (2002) millennium review of the history of couple therapy, describes how, despite couple and marital problems being at the heart of much clinical practice, the development of couple therapy has lagged behind other modalities such as individual and family therapy. The reasons for this are multifarious but are deeply concerning given the overwhelming need. A review by the charity Relate, using data from the *Understanding Society* survey found that 1 in 5 (18%) of the population are in relationships which could be described as 'distressed' (Sserwanja & Marjoribanks, 2016). In the UK this amounts to 2.87 million people.

Policy perspectives – then and now

The breakdown of relationships exacts an enormous cost to public health, so innovation and research are vital in this area (Meier et al., 2013). Links between relationship distress and a vast range of problems have now been identified – children's mental health, heart disease, depression, post-natal depression, loneliness in old age, poverty, housing, drug and alcohol abuse to name a few. Given this, the fact that couple interventions have largely been the poor cousin to other psychological therapies is curious. Is it because difficulties between couples are so ubiquitous that they have seemingly become both everyone's problem and no one's?

In UK policy terms it has been a long, hard struggle to get governments to take the issue of relationship distress seriously and fund services. Over decades, there has been a sense that the intensely personal minefield of adult relationships has been too tricky to tackle. The political, in this instance, to turn a phrase upon its head, being simply too personal. Indeed, it is notable, for instance, that in the UK until this last decade the provision of help for couples almost completely stood outside the remit of psychological therapies within the NHS. Couple therapy or counselling has been largely provided by the voluntary sector, often by volunteers with little professional training or status.

However, since the Second World War successive governments *have* provided small scale funding for the core marriage counselling agencies in the UK, and Tavistock Relationships has historically benefited from these modest grants. For this organisation, founded in 1948, such funding allowed a small, expert staff group to undertake a series of action research projects alongside the development of a clinical methodology based on psychoanalytic principles.

Over the decades, there has also been a growing evidence base that clearly shows the important role that healthy, stable adult relationships can play in improving outcomes for children (Acquah et al., 2017). This evidence has led to a greater interest from policy makers. Yet real policy and practice shifts that would make supporting couple relationships centre stage in family health and social care interventions still remain a long way off.

The last Labour administration (1997–2010) had an admirable focus on supporting families, but this focus, implemented through fiscal measures and the development of children centres and parenting education, overlooked interparental relationships. This limitation was, no doubt, linked to two concerns. Firstly, that any focus on marriage would stigmatise single parent families, and secondly, the belief that support for couples would be seen as a marriage agenda which flew in the face of influential feminist policy makers who equated marriage with patriarchy (Abse, 2014).

It was in 2009, late in the Labour years, when the Brown government began to see that support for children needed to include a focus on adult relationships. Concern was growing about the general failure to make significant shifts in improving the economic and social circumstances of children with lone parents. The links between family relationships and poverty began to be acknowledged in government policy, with a specific focus around how family breakdown increased economic disadvantage (Cabinet Office, 2007). The influential report, *Breakdown Britain* published by the Centre for Social Justice (Social Justice Policy Group, 2006), a conservative think tank with a strong interest in the links between marriage, family breakdown and poverty, helped to influence the wider agenda, so that family separation, inter-parental conflict and poverty now became recognised as having significant impacts on children's outcomes.

In 2009, Gordon Brown, then Prime Minister, and Ed Balls, Secretary of State for Education, organised a government summit to discuss policy on couple relationships. As a result, a package of measures was launched to improve support for parents and children facing family breakdown, and this was embedded within the government's wider child poverty strategy. Alongside these measures, the government published *Support for All: The Families and Relationships Green Paper* (DCSF, 2010), which was to drive early and holistic multi-agency support to families with complex problems and which cited couple relationships as part of this holistic approach. At last it looked as if the need for relationship support for couples was to be properly enshrined in wider family support.

These measures were never enacted, the Labour government fell, and austerity, brought in by the new Conservative-led coalition government, led to the rapid shrinking of family and children's services. However, despite the onslaught of cuts to services, Cameron's government did prioritise the centrality of marriage and the couple relationship. In an atmosphere of decline in government support, the need for family stability was even more clearly highlighted as the key weapon in combating child poverty. Fiscal approaches such as tax credits were considered no longer affordable; families, it seemed, had to become more resilient and self-reliant, and not look to the state for support. As a result, the Cameron government emphasised the importance of both relationship support and parenting as key components in improving children's life chances, and signified a commitment to investing £7.5 million a year (Cameron, 2010). This modest increase in funding was a boon for the relationship support organisations; in an atmosphere of shrinking funding, the sector was, for the first time, prioritised for money and Tavistock Relationships took advantage of this funding to rapidly develop new intervention and evaluation projects.

In reality, however, this funding was seen by many as a drop in the ocean in relation to the scale of the problem. The costs of relationship breakdown, annually estimated by the Relationships Foundation's Cost of Family Failure Index (2010), were running above £40 billion. In this context, an annual funding envelope of £7.5 million, though welcome, was not a serious shift in policy. Moreover, the focus increasingly narrowed away from the universal field of couple support to a narrower focus on the impacts of inter-parental relationships on children.

This focus on the important links between couple functioning and children's adjustment had been an extraordinarily long time in coming. In 2008, Tavistock Relationship's strapline – "*Supporting Couples; Strengthening Families; Safeguarding Children*" – indicated that the organisation was seeing this as the strongest direction of travel. But resistance to the idea that children's mental health and general outcomes were being affected by the relationship between their parents is still expressed by many to this day. The unhelpful disconnection of relationship support from the NHS and services working with children acts as a considerable bar to achieving whole family help. Children's mental health, for instance, continues to be largely treated as a problem that can be addressed in isolation from couple difficulties, despite clear evidence that family relationship problems are the biggest presenting issue in child and adolescent mental health services (Wolpert et al., 2016).

The Department for Work and Pensions, currently the government department responsible for family policy, has, unsurprisingly considering its remit, narrowed this focus further to support those families most disadvantaged by worklessness.

In its most recent policy report, *Improving Lives: Helping Workless Families* (DWP, 2017), relationship conflict is identified as a 'root cause' of poverty via direct impacts on an individual's capacity to be engaged in work. Funding outcomes may well become focused on getting parents into work rather than more nuanced achievements around relationship quality or inter-parental collaboration. A somewhat reductionist policy argument seems to be promoting the idea that if services can fix relationships, then parents will become more productive members of the workforce, thus leading to better economic circumstances for children. Whilst the move away from technocratic, fiscal support to families is welcome, the complexity of family dynamics may well scupper this latest approach to improving family stability.

This narrowing of focus on worklessness may also continue to limit and hold back the field from further development. Couples move in and out of relational distress and, indeed, in and out of work. The 'just managing' families identified by Theresa May (2016) in her first statement as prime minister are likely to miss out on accessing help, tipping them into 'not managing'. Moreover, in the context of an underdeveloped field, funding interventions and services that focus only on workless families are likely to mean that important opportunities for development and research, not least in the area of early intervention, may be missed.

History and methodology

Despite the funding challenges, Tavistock Relationships has been leading the field since its inception in 1948 as the Family Discussion Bureau. Its original task was to research the psychological and emotional aspects of marriage and its impact on family life, particularly in the context of the trauma and distress that families were experiencing post war. Relationship breakdown, violence between partners or between parents and children, alcoholism and homelessness were rife at this time, and to add to this mix returning traumatised soldiers plus post war austerity increased the pressure on families. Divorce rates soared to a rate six times higher than pre-war (Clark, 1990). In this context the Family Discussion Bureau set about trying to find better ways to help families in distress by bringing together the traditions of family casework and insights from psychoanalysis.

The earliest relationship support intervention started in the UK and USA in the 1920s and 1930s, when clergy and social work marriage counsellors 'told their clients how to make their marriages work better' (Barker, 1984, p.11). Marriage counsellors, at that time and for many years after, offered simple advice and practical information. They provided sorely needed education on sexual matters and advice on how to manage the seemingly uncomplicated practical problems of everyday life. These interventions were short-term and didactic, and were often driven by a moral and normative approach to marriage and gender roles.

Moreover, it was not until around 50 years ago that counsellors and therapists began to routinely see couples together in conjoint sessions. One study estimated from the case records of the three largest marriage and family clinics in the United States that in the 1940s only 5% of marriage counsellors' cases were couples seen conjointly, with this proportion rising to 9% during the 1950s and to 15% in 1960 (Michaelson, 1963). This approach of working with partners separately was also true in the UK, and, indeed, in the early clinical work of Tavistock Relationships. Nowadays, however, couples are generally treated together, and a central tenant of the approach taken by the organisation is that couples have a *shared* problem and need to work on it together, as best they can, in order to bring about effective change.

Most interventions offered to couples are still short term and often have a strong behavioural focus. The approach taken by the staff of the original Family Discussion Bureau was different. From early beginnings, the organisation began to investigate the unconscious aspects of marital problems. Consultation with psychoanalysts from the Tavistock Clinic, together with the seminal work of Henry Dicks (1967), informed the development of a new methodology which focused on shared unconscious aspects of a couple's difficulties.

Over time, Tavistock Relationships has developed a rich theory about couple relating which has been influenced by the diverse theoretical orientations of an eclectic staff. This combination of Jungian, British Object Relations, Kleinian and post-Kleinian thinking including that of Winnicott, Bion and Meltzer, has led to a rich 'marriage' of ideas, which is informed by the clinical practice at the heart of the organisation's endeavours. In recent years, attachment theory and findings from neuroscience have also been influential and have led to new applications and services, often targeted at complex and challenging problems.

The psychoanalytic approach developed by Tavistock Relationships has had worldwide impact and influence, but it is also true to say that 'deep' work with couples, which combines intrapsychic understanding with interpersonal dynamics, has not been largely taken up in the mainstream; whilst some of the early applied projects (Ruszczynski, 1993, p.14) were influential in the wider field of social work, more formal research and the wider development and influence of couple psychotherapy remained a challenge in an environment of very constrained funding.

As the new century dawned, it was clear that the psychoanalytic approach, so central to the way Tavistock Relationships approached its work, was increasingly out of favour. Cognitive behavioural therapy, and other manualised interventions such as parenting programmes, had gained ground in part because of the failure of psychoanalytic approaches to develop an evidence base but also because funding was becoming available for services that could be offered cheaply and quickly to a wider population. Couple psychotherapy was a non-manualised approach, training and treatment took years rather than weeks, and the trend was towards brief interventions with specific outcomes and aims. In this environment, Tavistock Relationships began to struggle; new developments were needed that could use the knowledge and expertise embedded in the organisation and adapt it for this new world where evidence based, manualised interventions, or packages of specialised trainings, were increasingly in demand.

One important aspect of the work of Tavistock Relationships has been the study of the unconscious impacts and dynamics of the 'helping relationship' (Mattinson, 1975). This focused on detailing how the difficulties and struggles of the client can deeply affect the 'worker'. This phenomenon, known in psychoanalytic terminology as the countertransference, is taken very seriously. Because of this perspective, case supervision is central to all of the interventions undertaken at Tavistock Relationships. Countertransferential feelings experienced by the therapist can be closely examined in supervision, as this is seen as a key way to advance understanding of the unconscious dynamics at play in the case. The more recent interventions described in this book, even when using a methodology quite different from the standard psychoanalytic 'frame', continue to emphasise and employ this way of working.

Unconscious pressures and emotional impacts on the therapist/worker are understood to be an inevitable part of the work; without paying attention to these impacts the relationship between workers and clients can go awry. Processing the feelings experienced by the worker helps come to a clearer understating of what is going on the relational field. Internalised patterns of relating that have been introjected from the past experiences of the couple can quickly come alive in the relationship between worker and client. Without supervision, it can be hard for therapists and other practitioners not to fall into re-enacting roles that pertain to events long gone, but which are still echoing in the relational ether. This focus then on the way relational patterns and experiences can come alive between worker and client, and most crucially between partners, is a central part of the ethos of these new interventions and gives them a sophistication and depth that goes beyond the bare bones of the how and what of what is being delivered.

Another aspect of the shared philosophy of the interventions is the relational aspect of the methodology used. The underlying assumption is that human joy and suffering largely has its origins in human relationships, and in order to ameliorate suffering an attuned, reflective and robust relationship with another human being is needed. Good interventions, therefore, are by definition services provided through, or in the context of, such relationships. This is, perhaps, quite a different philosophy from the more mechanistic parenting interventions or therapies that emphasise teaching and behaviour change.

Tavistock Relationship's core theory starts from the premise that the relationship of long term partnerships is deeply influenced by the early lives of each member of the couple (Ruszczynski, 1993). Couples bring stories to the consulting room of broken promises, squabbles over domestic life and disputes about money or child rearing, and these stories, rich with archaic content, are re-enacted in front of the therapist. Psychoanalytic couple psychotherapists work not only with the transference relationship from each partner to their therapist but also particularly with the transference relationship *between* the partners. As a result, the therapist must treat the relationship itself as the 'patient'. This stance is based on an underlying assumption that presenting issues such as jealousy, depression or anger, though expressed perhaps by only one partner, are in some way shared issues. Distress or disturbance in one partner is understood to resonate with the other partner too. This fundamental stance encourages the therapist to investigate and explore the couple's relationship as a whole, rather than the individual pathology of each partner, and this enables an understanding of the *shared* aspects of the presenting difficulties.

Developments in attachment theory also brought new thinking into the organisation (Clulow, 2001; Fisher & Crandell, 1997), which enriched and complemented the psychoanalytic methodology. Attachment theory has triggered an explosion of research into family relationships, and offered a new and evidenced conceptual basis for thinking about couples. The organisation began to think of ways to classify couple attachment and this focus brought new partnerships with academics and clinicians engaged in more formal research endeavours that were to have great value in the subsequent decade.

These rich theoretical perspectives and advancements have enabled the sophisticated development of a treatment methodology that is now shared with many couple psychotherapists, not only in the UK but across the English-speaking world. This secure theoretical base has also been the fulcrum from which the organisation has been able to progress new ways of working. Grounded in an understanding of unconscious processes, Tavistock Relationships has been able to develop applications of its theory in innovations and advancements, some of which are described in this book.

Strategy and ethos

When the Family Discussion Bureau was established in 1948, it defined its task as threefold:

- to provide a service for people seeking help with marriage problems;
- to devise techniques appropriate to such a service and evolve a method of training caseworkers;
- to find out something about problems of inter-personal relationships as they reveal themselves in marital difficulties (Astbury, 1955).

The strategy of linking clinical work, research and training has continued to be a fruitful way for the organisation to develop new work. Meeting with couples, studying the dynamics of their relating, theorising and schematising interventions and evaluating their impacts has provided a useful framework for innovation. In an atmosphere of highly restricted funding, income generating service delivery can become the main focus, leaving risky new developments to be side-lined. By combining service delivery with service development and evaluation, Tavistock Relationships has managed to maintain itself as a centre of innovation and study, something that is exceedingly rare in the field.

In 2009 a strategic decision was made to more clearly reconnect the organisation to its charitable purpose by focusing on the 'wicked problems' society was facing. The organisation's values were refreshed, and the importance of family stability and the emotional security it provided as the bedrock of well-being for society was more clearly articulated. Further, this renewed commitment to social justice and the stronger focus on the needs of children meant that the organisation had to recognise that new ways of reaching people needed to be found, and these ways need not rely exclusively on couples presenting themselves at a designated centre ready and able to engage in couple therapy. Some of the studies undertaken in the first decade of this century clearly indicated that many people felt fearful of going to therapy, and new, creative ways of engaging couples were needed (Walker et al., 2010).

Tackling 'wicked problems' effectively needs high level skills and a clear underpinning methodology, both of which the organisation possessed. These attributes meant that Tavistock Relationships had the capacity to focus on acute and chronic issues rather than, as some other relationship support organisations did, on early preventative approaches. It had the expertise that allowed it to develop services where others feared to tread, for example with high conflict and violent relationships, whether before or after separation and divorce, as the services described in these chapters attest.

Research and evaluation

Research can take many forms. For Tavistock Relationships the development of psychoanalytic theory, as applied to couples, was for many years the main research focus. Its methodology was the single case study, an approach famously employed by Freud and which is still used to this day. Single case studies require in-depth observation and investigation over time; it is therefore a method well suited to the practice of long term therapy. Understanding gathered from the close analysis of the couple's life histories and ways of relating have provided extraordinary insights into couple difficulties. However, in a context increasingly hostile to psychoanalysis and increasingly focused on 'scientific', quantitative research methodologies, the organisation needed, if it was to regenerate and grow, a different kind of approach.

Innovation is exciting, but without reflective practice and evaluation new ideas generally die. Whilst a considerable body of literature outlining the organisation's approach to therapy had been amassed, little formal evaluation of outcomes had been undertaken. At the turn of the century the organisation began exploring how to develop its research capacity (Clulow et al., 2002), and later in that decade its first formal research study of couple psychoanalytic therapy was completed (Balfour & Lanman, 2012).

The organisation was beginning to develop the confidence to use formal evaluation measures more widely, and in 2007 it began to administer psychometric measures to all its clients in order to evaluate outcomes pre-and post-therapy. In 2016, the data gathered from more than 7,000 patients was published (Hewison et al., 2016), this being the largest naturalistic study of couple therapy outcomes ever undertaken. Results showed significant positive outcomes in both general mental health and relationship quality. Furthermore, it was now indisputable that couple psychotherapists were working with a population who were considerably distressed and in need of psychological help: over 70% of patients were shown to be suffering from clinical levels of depression. This study is an important landmark in several ways: it strengthens the evidence for psychoanalytic approaches, it shows that the power of large scale naturalistic research, and it puts to bed the idea that couple distress is somehow distinct from other mental health issues so can therefore be ignored by psychological services and left to lightly trained volunteers or generalist front line practitioners.

Building on the routine outcome research, and responding again to the need to gain an evidence base for the organisation's latest interventions, in 2011 the organisation took the brave step of embarking on a small scale randomised control trial. The trial was to evaluate a new mentalization based approach for parents where there was high post separation conflict (Hertzmann et al., 2017). The aim of the therapy was to improve the co-parenting relationship in order to relieve children of the burdens imposed by this kind of family conflict, and the research was able to show some positive results in this respect (Hertzmann et al., 2016).

The experience of conducting this randomised control trial was, however, challenging. The formal protocols involved were costly and demanding, and stretched the organisation to its capacity. Much innovation is conducted by organisations like Tavistock Relationships, working on the front line, often small in size and without the capacity to undertake such formal evaluation. Further, the rigours and demands of randomised control trials can lead to manipulations or limitations to treatment that are inimical to routine clinical practice, leading to a real question as to whether randomised control trials are really the 'gold standard' research tool for psychological and social interventions? Randomised control trials, it seems, work best with therapies that define problems and outcome in terms of uncomplicated symptoms, which may well be unrealistic in the context of family based treatments. In contrast, large scale outcome studies from routine clinical practice have the advantage both of size and of being properly linked to the realities of everyday practice, where outcome is not understood solely in terms of symptom reduction.

As government commitment to funding relationship support increased, several initiatives over the last decade have attempted to map the evidence base for couple interventions. These attempts have highlighted the paucity of good UK research in the field and some of the evaluations conducted by government bodies have not made a serious contribution to this impoverished landscape. Starting with a study commissioned by the Department of Education of the interventions offered by the four main relationship support organisations in the UK – Relate, Marriage Care, One plus One and Tavistock Relationships (Spielhofer et al., 2014) – government has produced a series of reports which have shown positive results, but these have been conducted without the time or rigour that would produce an unassailable evidence base.

Responding, to this concern Tavistock Relationships published an international evidence review (Abse et al., 2015). This was a broad look at all the evidence across interventions that encompassed not only couple therapy but also parenting interventions and pre-marital preparation. The review was able to identify a wide range of interventions that had undergone convincing evaluations, which showed positive outcomes for couples. However, the policy focus on children now demanded research that could show the outcomes which were flowing down to the children of those participant couples. Research was now needed that could go beyond the routine assertion of most couple therapists that children's symptomology is relieved by their parents engaging in therapy. Fortunately, a long-standing relationship with two American academics, Professors Philip Cowan and Carolyn Pape Cowan, was to reap incredible rewards. They, light years ahead of their time, *had* developed couple focused parenting programmes and gained this evidence base; showing outstanding outcomes for children (Cowan & Cowan, 2009). Moreover, in 2011, Tavistock Relationships was funded by government to trial this approach in the UK.

But on the whole there was little evidence which could show the benefits of couple interventions for children, and this woeful lack of evidence was highlighted in the Early Intervention Foundation's report *What Works to Enhance Inter-parental Relationships and Improve Outcomes for Children* (Gordon et al., 2016), which indicated that owing to the paucity of funding, the UK evidence base was sparse and largely at a very early stage.

Tavistock Relationships, in response to this concern, began to collect data on parents' appraisals of their children's well-being within its routine service. It will take some time to amass a substantial body of data, but in time this could provide a further rich naturalistic study of the whole family impacts of couple therapy.

Innovation: past, present and future

The needs of couples are as long as a piece of string, and whilst good couple therapy should be able to address a wide variety of symptoms and presentations the need for briefer more focused therapeutic interventions has grown. Because of the focus on early intervention and social justice, applications of couple psychoanalytic therapy to specific populations of parents were to the forefront of new developments. Innovations have included work with post separation conflict, domestic violence in families with children and a specific service designed to support adoptive couples. But beyond this focus on parents there have been at least two other significant developments.

One initiative has involved new thinking around modifications of technique in therapy with couples who are particularly challenging. At Tavistock Relationship's clinics in central London, where trainees and senior staff offer long term therapy to thousands of couples each year, there has been an increasing number of patients who present with complex difficulties. Some of these couples find conventional psychoanalytic interpretive approaches unhelpful. Where couples have difficulties with affect regulation, conventional interpretation can raise the emotional 'temperature' to the point where it is difficult to create a contained space for useful work. As a result, Tavistock Relationships has developed an application of mentalization based approaches to these couples who present in borderline states of mind (Abse, 2013). This new approach combines Mentalization Based Therapy (Bateman & Fonagy, 2004) with the psychoanalytic approach to couples described above. Nyberg and Hertzmann (2014) have argued that all psychoanalytic couple therapists should be trained in these methods as a specific model either for working with severely dysregulated couples, or where one of the partners suffers from borderline personality disorder.

A further development in the organisation has been the creation of a psychosocial intervention for couples where one is suffering from dementia. This treatment programme, which is delivered to couples in their homes, again draws on a psychoanalytic theory of couple relating but combines it with Video Interaction Guidance and other pragmatic approaches drawn from the field of parent–infant psychotherapy (Balfour, 2014).

This example brings us to the sticky problem of how innovation gets into the mainstream. The growing population of people with dementia should, in theory, make an intervention designed to strengthen the relationship between couples very attractive to funders everywhere. If one can improve the relationship between partners and make life a little better for the partner/carer then, in theory, the move to residential care is likely to be postponed. A more rewarding relationship between couples in this situation benefits everyone. As a result, this exciting and ground-breaking development received considerable interest from a wide variety of organisations and even commissioners, but getting it into the mainstream remains a challenge.

All too often, it seems, innovation programmes are funded as 'pilots', and 'roll out' remains just a dream. Usually the funding is too short-term or limited, whereas it takes years to refine an intervention and then years to develop the evidence base. Getting funding to cover that time is hugely challenging, particularly outside the mainstream of health or academic funding. Moreover, it is clear that innovations scale or spread most rapidly and effectively when the diffusion strategy is devised and implemented from the outset, with potential adopters identified right from the start. One of the challenges, therefore, is to devise innovations that can be delivered by practitioners who are not necessarily skilled in working with couples, let alone familiar with a psychoanalytic methodology. This is something that has now begun to be addressed in recent developments.

There is also, of course, the narcissism involved in invention. Who wants the second-hand ideas of others – why not devise our own? This is another challenge to the problem of scaling, which every inventive organisation has to manage, and which, perhaps, can be done best via respectful partnerships with end adopters, though of course the risk of 'acquisition' or, indeed, stealing is unfortunately real.

Conclusion

The demand for couple treatments is growing, and whilst there are exciting and positive signs that this locus of intervention is about to have its heyday, there are serious challenges ahead. Considerable resistance remains to acknowledging and valuing this kind of approach as it challenges current ways of working that are individualistic, treating the person without reference to his relational context. Individual interventions are far easier to schematise and evaluate, as outcomes can be closely aligned to symptoms. In family based treatments, how do you decide what, and, indeed, who to evaluate? Moreover, treating couples is challenging, and requires considerable skill and expertise alongside particular personality traits in the practitioner. A further challenge is the relative absence of interest and expertise in academics and clinicians based within UK universities. These are the people who can access serious research funding, so it is vital that this interest within the academic world develops. Despite all these challenges, however, the acknowledgment of the social, emotional and societal costs of couple distress can no longer be ignored. Tavistock Relationships has led the way in UK couple treatments for seventy years, and the expertise within the organisation is likely, in my view, to be in considerable demand in the coming years.

Note

1 Charles Franklin Kettering (29 August, 1876–25 November, 1958) was an American inventor, engineer, businessman, and the holder of 186 patents. A founder of DELCO, the Dayton Engineering Laboratories Company, Kettering's innovative work brought him more than 200 patents, the most notable of which is the electric automobile self-starter. His conviction that new ideas can best be developed through a cooperative team effort was applied to a wide variety of problems—everything from explaining why grass is green to understanding how paint dries. Included in his interests were a broad range of social and political problems, issues like world hunger and political instability.

References

Abse, S. (2013). Further thoughts on working with borderline couples. *Couple and Family Psychoanalysis*, 3(2): 178–87.

Abse, S. (2014). Labour needs to use family policy to support and strengthen relationships. *New Statesman* [Electronic Version]. Retrieved from www.newstatesman.com/politics/2014/04/labour-needs-use-family-policy-support-and-strengthen-relationships

Abse, S., Casey, P., Hewison, D., & Meier, R. (2015). *What Works in Relationship Support – An Evidence Review*. London: Tavistock Centre.

Acquah, D. et al. (2017). *Inter-parental Conflict and Outcomes for Children in the Contexts of Poverty and Economic Pressure*. London: Early Intervention Foundation.

Astbury, B.E. (1955). Foreword. In: K. Bannister et al. *Social Casework in Marital Problems*. London: Tavistock.
Balfour, A. (2014). Developing therapeutic couple work in dementia care – the living together with dementia project. *Psychoanalytic Psychotherapy, 28*(3): 304–20.
Balfour, A. and Lanman, M. (2012). An evaluation of time-limited psychodynamic psychotherapy for couples: a pilot study. *Psychology and Psychotherapy: Theory, Research and Practice, 85*(3): 292–309.
Barker, R.L. (1984). *Treating Couples in Crisis*. New York: Free Press.
Bateman, A. W., & Fonagy, P. (2004). *Psychotherapy for Borderline Personality Disorder: Mentalization Based Treatment*. Oxford: Oxford University Press.
Boyd, T.A. (2002). *Kettering: A Biography*. Washington DC: Bear Books.
Cabinet Office. (2007). *Reaching Out: Think Family Analysis and Themes from the Families at Risk Review*. London: Cabinet Office, social exclusion task force.
Cameron, D. (2010, December). *Speech on families and relationships*. Speech. Retrieved from www.gov.uk/government/speeches/speech-onfamilies-and-relationships
Clark, R. (1990). Economic dependency and divorce: implications for the private sphere. *International Journal of Sociology of the Family, 20*(1): 47–65.
Clulow, C. (Ed.) (2001). *Adult Attachment and Couple Psychotherapy: The 'Secure Base' in Practice and Research*. London: Brunner-Routledge.
Clulow, C., Evans, C., Shmueli, A., & Vincent, C. (2002). Is empirical research compatible with clinical practice? *British Journal of Psychotherapy, 19*(1): 33–44.
Cowan, P.A., & Cowan, C.P. (2009). How working with couples fosters children's development: from prevention science to public policy. In: M. Schulz, M, Pruett, P. Kerig, & R. Parke (Eds.), *Strengthening Couple Relationships for Optimal Child Development* (pp. 211–28). Washington, DC: APA Publications.
Department for Children Schools and Families (DCSF) (2010). *Support for All: The Families and Relationships Green Paper*, Cm: 7787, London: DCSF.
Department of Work and Pensions (DWP) (2017). *Improving Lives: Helping Workless Families*. Policy Paper. London: DWP.
Dicks, H.V. (1967). *Marital Tensions*. London: Routledge & Kegan Paul.
Fisher, J.V., & Crandell, L.E. (1997). Complex attachment: patterns of relating in the couple. *Sexual & Marital Therapy, 12*(3): 211–23.
Gordon, H., Aquah, D, Sellers, R., & Chowdry, H. (2016). *What Works to Enhance Interparental Relationships and Improve Outcomes for Children*. London: Early Intervention Foundation for the Department of Work and Pensions.
Gurman, A.S., & Fraenkel, P. (2002). The history of couple therapy: a millennial review. *Family Process, 41*: 199–260.
Hertzmann, L., Target, M., Hewison, D., Casey, P., Fearon, P., & Lassri, D. (2016). Mentalization-Based Therapy for parents in entrenched conflict: a random allocation feasibility study. *Psychotherapy, 53*(4): 388–401.
Hertzmann, L. Abse, S., Target, M., Glausius, K., Nyberg, V., & Lassari, D. (2017). Mentalization-Based Therapy for parental conflict – parenting together; an intervention for parents in entrenched post-separation disputes. *Psychoanalytic Psychotherapy, 32*(2): 195–217.
Hewison, D., Casey, P., & Mwamba, N. (2016). The effectiveness of couple therapy: clinical outcomes in a naturalistic United Kingdom setting. *Psychotherapy, 53*(4): 377–87.

Mattinson, J. (1975). *The Reflection Process in Casework Supervision*. London: Tavistock Institute of Human Relations.

May, T. (2016). www.gov.uk/government/speeches/statement-from-the-new-prime-minister-theresa-may

Meier. R, Scholl, P. Coleman, L. Burridge, S., & Abse, S. (2013). "Relationships: the missing link in public health". A report by the Relationship Alliance in association with the All Party Parliamentary Group for Strengthening Couple Relationships.

Michaelson, R. (1963). *An Analysis of the Changing Focus of Marriage Counseling*. Unpublished Doctoral Dissertation, University of Southern California.

Nyberg, V., & Hertzmann, L. (2014). Developing a Mentalization-Based Treatment (MBT) for therapeutic intervention with couples (MBT-CT). *Couple and Family Psychoanalysis*, *2*(4): 115–35.

Relationships Foundation (2010) Counting the Cost of Family Failure Briefing Note 2 Retrieved from: www.relationshipsfoundation.org/wp-content/uploads/2014/02/Briefing_Note_2.pdf

Ruszczynski, S. (Ed.) (1993). *Psychotherapy with Couples: Theory and Practice at the Tavistock Institute of Marital Studies*. London: Karnac

Social Justice Policy Group (2006). *Breakdown Britain*. London: Centre for Social Justice.

Spielhofer, T., Corlyon, J., Durbin, B., Smith, M., Stock, L., & Gieve, M. (2014). *Relationship Support Interventions Evaluation*. London: Department for Education.

Sserwanja, I., & Marjoribanks, D. (2016). *Estimating Levels of Couple Distress Across the UK*. London: Relate Research Report.

Walker, J., Barrett, H., Wilson, G., & Chang, Y.S. (2010). *Relationships Matter: Understanding the Needs of Adults (Particularly Parents) Regarding Relationship Support* Research Report-RR233 Department of Children Schools and Families.

Wolpert, M., Jacob, J., Napoleone, E., Whale, A., Calderon, A., & Edbrooke-Childs, J. (2016). *Child- and Parent-reported Outcomes and Experience from Child and Young People's Mental Health Services 2011–2015*. London: CAMHS Press.

Chapter 1

Being a couple

Psychoanalytic perspectives

Andrew Balfour and Mary Morgan

At first sight this may seem an extravagant claim, but we hope that, as you read on, you too will come to feel that a psychoanalytically-informed approach to working with couples offers a way of understanding some of the core mysteries of our lives.

What draws us together to form couples? Why do we choose this person, rather than that person as a partner? Why do we get stuck in familiar, unhappy patterns of experience in our closest relationships? How may these patterns replay early conflicts in our lives? These questions, and others, will be explored in this chapter, which is divided into two parts. The first will outline what we know about couple relationships, taking the reader through the key ideas about how couple relationships work. The second describes how these ideas are translated into the model of couple psychotherapy that has been developed and is currently practised at Tavistock Relationships.

The questions we have raised are ones that we all might wonder about. They have been around since the inception of Tavistock Relationships 70 years ago and they continue to preoccupy the minds of clinicians and writers to this day. In post-war Britain it was recognised that families needed support, both material and psychological. It became clear, and has been further established since, that the couple relationship is at the centre of family life; what today we might call a 'creative couple relationship' provides the conditions in which children thrive (see Chapter 2). The early work of Tavistock Relationships also showed that an enduring intimate couple relationship could provide the conditions in which each partner can continue to grow psychologically.

An attitude of curiosity or research mindedness has always been central in the clinicians at Tavistock Relationships. In order to help couples, it is necessary to understand the couple relationship, and the early therapists, while offering 'family casework' to the couples they saw, also learnt from them, drawing on psychoanalysis and developing a model of theory and practice that today has a national and international influence (see Morgan, in press).

So, what have we discovered over the last 70 years about the couple relationship? And do we have a model of psychotherapy that is effective in helping couples?

What have we learnt about the couple?

- We are drawn together for unconscious as well as conscious reasons, and the relationship we establish can be developmental and defensive.
- We need intimacy, but what this means to each couple can be very varied.
- For a relationship to develop there needs to be a capacity to tolerate separateness and difference, as well as closeness and intimacy.
- Love, hate and curiosity are all intrinsic to a relationship.
- We need to relinquish an idealised 'in love' state and move to a more reality-based relationship to enable a deeper, enduring love.
- Couple relationships can provide the conditions in which individual partners, separately and together, continue to grow and develop.

Couples are drawn together for unconscious as well as conscious reasons

This was one of the early discoveries of Tavistock Relationships clinicians. They observed that each partner, disowning parts of the self with which they were not comfortable, could 'find' and recognise these disavowed aspects of themselves in the other. This is like an unconscious version of the idea that opposites attract – whereby one partner, at an unconscious level, selects another who has a capacity for feelings that they find difficult to know about in themselves. Why would this be an attraction? The early pioneers in this field realised that one of the opportunities that the adult intimate relationship provided was that, within the safety of the relationship, it was possible to make contact again with these lost ('split off') parts of the self. Someone ill at ease or even frightened of their more aggressive or assertive self, for example, might be attracted to this denied part of themselves in the partner they chose. Over time, it may be possible to 'get to know' this part of the self, lived with in the other, and eventually, as it becomes experienced as less threatening, to 'take it back' into the personality. In this way, the individual develops and becomes more whole by virtue of this opportunity provided by the relationship. Importantly, there is an idea of complementarity to such unconscious partner choice, such that there is a 'fit' between the partners whereby each recognises in the other their capacity to hold and express feelings that they find difficult to encompass, or know about, in themselves. In the example just given the other partner may be afraid of vulnerability and over time, as it is expressed in the relationship by their partner, find this less frightening so that gradually it can be brought back into the self.

The early clinicians also encountered many relationships that were not working positively in this way. The partners were drawn together for similar reasons but, instead of the other partner containing the troubling part of the self, the other who was carrying a 'double dose' (both their own feelings as well as the extra 'dose' of their partner's feelings too) exaggerated that part of the self, making it more, not less frightening. The couple then present in a polarised way, one partner carrying, for example, an excess of aggression, the other an excess of vulnerable feelings. Each partner remains frightened of this troubling part of the self and cannot take it back, so the need for the other to carry it is further intensified. Understanding this kind of defensive arrangement threw light on why some couples were very unhappy together but could not separate. In a situation such as this, where each partner is holding aspects of the other's self, the couple are 'joined together' in a psychological system. Whilst this may be experienced as unhappy, any movement towards separation threatens the emotional equilibrium on which each individual has relied. Often, this is the presenting situation of couples seeking help for relationships in which they and their children are suffering, where greater closeness and intimacy cannot be tolerated nor can the partners separate and move on in their lives.

A couple's need for intimacy

Being part of a couple requires intimacy, and for most a sexual relationship; for some it involves discovering and expressing their sexuality. Couple relationships provide the conditions for intimacy that are different from a mother–baby intimacy or intimacy between friends, but this can be hard for a couple to negotiate and maintain.

Sex, we are discovering, is a complex thing. Many couples have a good, exciting sexual relationship at the beginning but it changes over time. Others have problems from the outset, with painful sex, loss of erections, premature ejaculation or different levels of sexual desire. Having children usually means less time and energy for sex, and often when the children are older and making fewer demands and there is more time for sex, desire has diminished or even disappeared. Recent ideas suggest that part of sexual excitement is to do with having our own sexuality discovered and elaborated by another (Target, 2007), but with the familiarity of a long-term partnership it can be difficult for desire to be maintained, and there is a significant body of literature on this important area (see Benioff, 2017; Clulow, 2009, 2017). Ageing also brings challenges for the couple's sexual and emotional life together, with changing bodies and health requiring adjustments that can be difficult to make. For some, the capacity to adjust to losses and functional limitations enables them to sustain intimacy into old age (Balfour, 2009). They are more accepting of such changes and maintain a satisfactory sexual relationship, even if it may not be felt to be as exciting as it once was. For others, these changes are threatening to the relationship and to the sense of self: the need to feel desired and to be sexually potent feels central to who they are. If these changes cannot be managed in the relationship, either partner may seek sexual validation outside it.

We know sexualities to be complex too. While the most common sexual orientations are heterosexual, bi-sexual, gay and lesbian and transsexual, there are other ways people experience their sexuality, for example pansexual or polyamorous. Others reject the idea of gender as binary, choosing not to be identified as masculine or feminine. Sexuality is also fluid, someone may feel themselves to be heterosexual yet after several years of married life meet someone of the same gender and discover or develop their same sex orientation, or move between more than one sexual orientation. It is easy to draw distinctions between couples with different sexualities, such as heterosexual or same sex couples, but within any couple the way they express and live out their sexuality is not only unique but also can be challenging for the couple.

Separateness and difference

Later in the history of Tavistock Relationships, in the 1990s, there was a lot of interest in what might be described as 'narcissistic relationships'. We started to understand more about problems for the individuals in the relationship feeling separate from each other and allowing the other to be different from the self. Indeed, whether we can see the 'other' and know about their unique centre of gravity and different perceptions, or instead re-create in our minds a version of them which is in our own image, shaped by our own pre-conceptions, is a fundamental question in terms of how much room there is for development in our relationships. It is not easy being with another person in an intimate relationship, and there is a part of all of us that would find it easier if the other simply agreed with us or saw the world in the same way as we do.

For some couples this may be an ordinary problem. They might argue about their different ways of seeing things, but then find a way of accepting the other's difference. For others it can be much more serious, the other's difference feeling like a threat. Instead of the partners in the couple having the sense that their different thoughts or views can come together to produce something new or shared, the thoughts and feelings of one are experienced as threatening to annihilate the other. Taking on the other's point of view then feels like it can only be done by giving up one's own view entirely. It can feel that the other's commitment to their beliefs is an intrusive attack on one's own beliefs or way of seeing things. Such couples may avoid the problem by convincing themselves they have no differences and form a 'comfortable' kind of fusion (Morgan, 1995). Usually these fused relationships become quite claustrophobic and break down. For such couples, there is no belief that their difference can come together in a creative way.

Love, hate and curiosity

Wilfred R. Bion (1967) described the links in emotional intimate relationships as those of L, H, & K, standing for Love, Hate and the desire to Know. We now understand that all of these are important in the couple relationship. Relationships are not just about love. We hurt and disappoint each other as well as love each other. Love is important, and might be thought of as the container for both hate and curiosity.

Those in a relationship soon discover that these different emotions cannot be avoided. The other frustrates us, says and does things we do not like or understand, and this can give rise to hate. Yet many couples feel there is no room for hatred in their relationship and so it goes underground. It can then be acted out in destructive behaviour or have an on-going insidious effect on the relationship. Couple therapists, by helping the couple become aware of their hostile feelings and revealing how these can be contained within a relationship that is fundamentally loving, can reconnect a couple with lively, including sexual, feelings (Grier 2009; Hewison, 2009).

In the beginning of a relationship there is excitement in getting to know someone new, physically and emotionally, and in having them interested in getting to know oneself intimately. We know that relationships that develop are based on mutual curiosity in the other and in the relationship, and receiving curiosity in the context of a loving attitude can be a very gratifying experience. This is very different to the state of mind we described above, in which knowing the other's mind is felt as a threat.

Disillusionment

We know that many couples come together because they 'fall in love'. Discovering aspects of themselves in the other, as described earlier, may be part of this. Finding someone who is intensely curious about us and who helps us become curious about ourselves may also be part of this powerful experience. The recreation of the earliest intimacy between mother and baby, to which the 'in love' state has often been compared (Clulow & Boerma, 2009), can also be extremely powerful emotionally and physiologically. Sexual excitement is usually central too. Couples feel something rather magical has happened – that they have found their other half, their 'soul mate'.

This mental, emotional and physiological state of being cannot last forever, at least not with the same intensity. The 'in love' state wanes with the couple's experience of familiarity and getting to know the good and bad aspects of each other, and the self as seen through the other, though there may continue to be surges of feeling that recapture it. This inevitable change need not necessarily be a negative one, because it can give way to a deeper connection between the partners. However, for some couples the loss of the experience of being in love can feel devastating, experienced as if it is the same thing as the loss of the relationship; they may feel there is something fundamentally wrong with the relationship if it cannot be sustained.

A creative couple relationship

If it is not the 'in love state' that sustains a relationship then what is it? As the early clinicians at Tavistock Relationships discovered, couple relationships can provide the conditions in which partners continue to grow and develop, because, under 'good enough' conditions, they offer the potential to reintegrate disowned parts of the self, discovered in the other. In this way, things that have gone wrong in the past, perhaps in the individuals' early years, can be worked through and changed within the context of the new relationship.

This is not the only creative potential of the couple. One idea that has been developed in recent years is that of the 'couple state of mind' (Morgan, 2001, 2018), a concept that applies both to the couple and the couple therapist, for whom it is essential. Drawing on the work of Britton (1989), who describes the development of a 'third position' in which one can both observe oneself and be oneself, a couple state of mind is the capacity to be oneself in a relationship and observe oneself in that relationship. If there is a capacity for intimacy, separateness and curiosity, enabling the development of a 'couple state of mind', the couple can be creative together in a way that they cannot be separately. This means that when there are difficulties in the relationship, such as conflict over differences, painful losses or change, the couple can come together to find a way forward. There is a trust in their relationship as a container in this process (Colman, 1993) enabling each partner to develop more successfully within it than they would do alone (Colman, 1993; Morgan, 2004; Ruszcynski, 2004). There is a considerable literature which evidences this, from the early days of Tavistock Relationships, for example, showing the importance of relationships for people with learning disabilities, who together were able to support and sustain mutually enhanced levels of independent functioning, to recent studies indicating the significant physical and mental health impacts of couple relationships, supporting resilience throughout the lifespan (Kiecolt-Glaser & Newton, 2001).

Some couples establish this capacity as part of the ordinary process of psychic development in becoming a couple. For those who do not, it is very hard for them to 'see' their relationship and what they are *creating together*; they tend to view what is going on between them as one of them doing something to the other. We know such couples can be helped by the process of couple psychotherapy, in which the therapist, by holding a couple state of mind and addressing their relationship, can help the couple to take this position themselves, and eventually, as an outcome of therapy, to internalise such a state of mind of their own. But this process can take time and may be resisted by partners who feel more comfortable blaming each other. We shall now discuss such issues associated with practising couple psychotherapy in more detail.

What is our model of couple psychotherapy?

The approach developed at Tavistock Relationships not only offers a framework for understanding our relationships, it also offers a method of harnessing this understanding in the service of psychotherapeutic intervention with couples. Why intervene at the level of the couple, with both partners and their therapist working together in the room? Why not simply work with people in individual therapy, effecting individual change that then leads to changes in relationships?

The very early pioneers of psychotherapy with couples did just that – they worked individually with each partner, and it was only the therapists who then met together to think about the couple and their relationship. However, the model of couple therapy subsequently developed at Tavistock Relationships works *in vivo* with the dynamics of the couple's relationship as this unfolds in their interactions when they are together with the therapist. This approach takes the couple's relationship itself as the patient, so to speak, without losing sight of the fact that this is made up of two individuals. Couple psychotherapy offers us the chance of understanding something of the unconscious forces that are driving us in our relationships, enhancing our capacity to think about ourselves, giving us greater choice about how we behave and therefore – potentially – offering a way out of repeating cycles of negative interaction.

Whilst in recent years, there has been progress in tackling the stigma of mental health, there are still taboos about seeking psychological help as a couple, and often couples will wait until difficulties are entrenched before taking the step of coming to therapy. By the time they do, their experience may be one of being in familiar, repetitive cycles of conflict in which they feel trapped. Often the intensity of emotion will escalate during arguments, leaving them feeling bruised and damaged from the way in which they argue as much as by the content of the fights themselves. What is striking is how difficult it can be for couples in the grip of such problems to achieve a perspective, a vantage-point, for thinking reflectively about their relationship and their role within it, even though outside the stress of this each partner may be capable of considerable thoughtfulness.

The enacted nature of couples' presentations in therapy

An important aspect we have explored in recent years is the way in which couples experience their problems and how they bring them into therapy. Problems are often expressed as complaints, or 'facts', about the other partner and what they are perceived to be doing; there can be an atmosphere of blame and mistrust and a lack of space for thinking about and reflecting on what is happening. Instead, there may be a quality of certainty to each partner's views and a difficulty in taking any perspective, or thinking about what the couple is creating together in the relationship. Fisher (1995) suggests that verbal communication in couple therapy is often experienced as a form of action: one partner being felt to be doing something to the other partner, not merely communicating about something: 'the couple relationship frequently produces sessions that resemble enacted dreams' (p. 166).

What do we mean by 'enacted' in this context? The term 'enactment' describes the acting-out in the interaction with the other of a mental scenario, rather than the associated thoughts or feelings being communicated verbally and symbolically, ways that would render them as food for thought and understanding between the partners. In a classic paper on individual analysis, Freud wrote: 'for instance, the patient does not say that he remembers that he used to be defiant and critical towards his parents' authority; instead, he behaves in that way to the doctor' (Freud, 1914, p. 150). In couple therapy, partners may express their core difficulties and feelings, their internalised unconscious beliefs and expectations of relationships, towards each other in this kind of way – giving the other *the experience* of something that they find difficult, for example, rather than talking to them *about* it. Such enactment[1] is not an occasional phenomenon, it is centre stage and often is simply *how* the couple functions with each other much of the time.

'Enactment' can help the therapist know about the couple's deeper unconscious levels of functioning, through witnessing and experiencing these as they are played out in transactions between the partners and with her. In other words, the therapist makes use of her experience of the transference[2] of the couple to her and links this to her understanding of the 'transference' between the partners. Such an approach can help the couple to move from a way of being with one another which is dominated by the enactment of their problems, to a position of being more able to think about them. Couples may then achieve a perspective from which they can observe and think about their relationship and its dynamics and what they are creating together, so enhancing the possibility of reflective communication and understanding between them. By addressing the couple's relationship in this way, helping the couple to 'see' their relationship, the therapist may help them to find a way out of their troubled patterns of interaction and, over time, to internalise a couple state of mind themselves.

How couple psychotherapy is a unique intervention

The setting of couple psychotherapy, which, of course, comprises the two individual partners plus the therapist, offers a uniquely important, 'triangular' frame. In the process of the session the therapist moves between a focus on the couple relationship and each of the individual partners in a dynamic way, engaging at one moment more with one, then with another, in endeavouring to hold a couple state of mind throughout the pushes and pulls of the therapeutic work. The advantage of this setting is that it offers dynamic opportunities for getting hold of enactments in different permutations of coupling in the room as the therapeutic work goes on. This is important in so far as the couple can witness their relationship difficulties being enacted not only between them, but also enacted with, and hopefully contained by, the therapist. This can enable the couple to get some perspective on their dynamic, which they are normally just 'in' together. In this way, the 'triangular' setting of the therapy allows them to experience different combinations of who is 'in' the couple and who is 'outside' it, shifting over time. The toleration of such a position of being linked to but outside the couple is also particularly significant for couples with problems in sharing psychic space, as Britton (1989) has described. We shall return to these themes in the case illustration that follows. However, first, we need to make some remarks on the place of history within couple psychotherapy.

The place of history in therapeutic work with couples

It has been well said that if we do not understand our history, then we are doomed to repeat it. Whilst this may be true of countries and societies on the world stage, it is just as relevant as an observation of our individual histories. Our history, if it is not to some extent understood and worked through, is likely to live on in an unprocessed way in our inner worlds, and thence to be repeated and enacted in our contemporary lives, most of all, within our closest relationships.

Links to the couple's individual and relationship histories will be made during the therapy, providing a sense of continuity that can be helpful in the process of integrating them with their present experience. However, the integration of the past with the present often occurs at a more meaningful level when the history feels alive in the present, when there can be thinking in the therapy about the contemporary impacts of each partner's history as it has been internalised and played out within the relationship and in the room with the therapist.

For example, the therapist may live out with the couple the experience of madness and chaos that both partners share in their experience of growing up with disturbed parents. In terms of such direct experience in the room with the couple, the therapist does more than just learn about the 'historic' account of what happened, she has a chance to know directly what this experience of growing up has meant to them, how it has affected their internal worlds and how they position themselves in relation to it. Is one or other of them, for example, at times still the careful son or daughter managing and looking after their disturbed parents? Are they at other times the son or daughter who provokes or pushes the other to hold and express strong feelings (felt as akin to 'madness') that are difficult for them to know about in themselves? Is there a need to sustain a sense of being different from the 'mad' parent, perhaps one partner requiring the other to hold the more angry and 'irrational' feelings and states of mind, which are felt to be too threatening in the self? Although the actual 'there and then' account of what happened in their personal histories is important, the therapeutic work takes place in the area of the current experience of the couple. The focus is how their internalised histories shape each partner's inner world, and how these are then lived out, or enacted, in the current relationship, and re-created, in the everyday transactions that make up their lives together:

> Tom tells the therapist that he and Jane had had an argument. He had tried to persuade their son not to wear what he saw as a 'feminine' outfit to a birthday party, worrying that he would alienate himself from his peer group. It had quickly turned into an argument, and Tom had insisted more and more firmly that their son must not wear the clothes. Their son then had a

tantrum. Jane came in saying she understood Tom's anxieties, of course she did. But could he not see that he was taking up a rigid position with their son, which was not going to help? Their therapist felt some agreement with her position as she was talking: forcing a change in their son's apparel would cloak, but not alter the underlying problem. The therapist hesitated, as all three in the room knew that Tom had considerable anxieties in this area. His mother had, metaphorically speaking, 'dressed' him as a girl, treating him, he felt, like a longed-for daughter throughout his childhood and frowning on any 'boyish' activities he had wanted to undertake, disallowing these and controlling him. Yet the therapist felt constrained from opening up this link – she felt that then she would be conveying it was 'his' problem and that he would feel that all the difficulty was being located in him. In the meantime, Jane continued in her 'helpful' vein, but the quality, which at first had conveyed an understanding of Tom's anxieties, now seemed less shared. She could not believe that Tom was not able to see what he was doing, she said. Her parents had tried to impose things on her, at one point trying to control everything – her clothes, her friends – all to fit her with their religious faith. It had been completely counter-productive; she had refused to take on their faith at all.

As Jane went on, her position, as she expressed it, became more absolute– his position was completely mistaken and rigid, 'how could he not see it as she did?' seemed to be her underlying message. Indeed, the implication was that he had to see it as she did. Whereas her sympathy had at first been with Jane, the therapist became aware that, under the guise of arguing for a liberal position with their son, Jane's position had now become rigid: seeking to impose her way of seeing it on Tom, so that he should have the same views as her. There was no room for the nuances in his position, for example his anxiety about the difficulties he saw unfolding for their son when the boys at school might reject him for being different from them. Tom, in turn, insisted on 'standing his ground'.

The situation developed into one in which there was no fluidity, or give and take, no room for knowing about their differences on the one hand or any shared parental anxiety on the other. Instead there was a sense that, for each of them, there was a desperate need to get something through to their partner, which the other would not take in, and at the same time needing to protect themselves from having the other's point of view pushed into them. Here, it seemed that the need for protection of the self from intrusion, or from an impenetrable other, was being played out between them.

At this point the therapist felt that the couple were enacting a scenario in the session where there was room for only one mind in an intimate relationship. Not only were they showing their struggle with sharing psychic space, as, defensively, they turned the situation into a fight in order to escape the risks of greater openness and intimacy, but they were also managing to give the therapist a taste of this experience. For her part, it was difficult to find any place to stand from which to talk to them that would not put her between the couple, experienced as taking sides, as being lined up with one or other partner, wiping out the other one. Initially this was what happened when the therapist put her observations into words. Hostility was evoked when she was felt either to be pushing them to submit to her way of seeing things or failing to take in their experience. Putting into words what one of them felt was at the cost of negating the other.

Now there was an enactment in the room involving three rather than two, the couple and the therapist who tried to find a space within the session where she could step back and think with them about what was happening. Eventually, finding a position where she could speak to them about how they were reacting to her seemed to give them some room to think. From this perspective, they began to be able to see that it was no longer just the two of them enacting the dynamic in a linear way, but a three-way affair where, within the triangular configuration in the room, each had witnessed the other playing out an aspect of this relationship with the therapist. For each partner, witnessing the same thing happening with her that they were familiar with in their battles with each other was important, giving them a perspective on something that they were otherwise just 'in' together.

The therapist's attempts not to push back, but to consider their complaints, without either disagreeing or agreeing with them, provided the experience of containment in the heat of the session. It became possible to talk to them about their feeling that they had no common ground, but how they did, in fact, have shared anxieties, about being able to get through to each other, or having things pushed into them. They became interested in these observations, linking the dynamic enacted between them with an interpretation of their phantasy of the danger of 'psychic takeover' in their relationships, and how they shared aspects of this experience in their respective childhoods where each of them had experienced intrusive parental figures who had sought to 'clothe' them in their own beliefs, in ways that had threatened the development of their sense of self. The struggle, enacted between them in the consulting room, represented a contemporary version of these core difficulties for each partner. Working with the transference situation opened a space in which the couple could begin to think about themselves, allowing, at least temporarily, a way out of the enactment that had such a grip on them.

Concluding thoughts

As described at the beginning of this chapter, being part of a couple in an enduring and satisfying relationship is not easy. We are faced with the re-emergence of our past as this intersects with that of our partner, creating tension and misunderstanding. We struggle with how to manage the range of feelings that arise in an intimate relationship. We have to bear the loss of our idealised image of our relationship and make room for something new to emerge, which might not be what we expected. And we have to find room for intimacy, for expressing our sexuality, and managing our separateness and difference from each other.

Some of the key elements of contemporary thinking about the couple relationship and the specificity of psychotherapeutic work with couples have been outlined in this chapter. The example of Tom and Jane illustrates that at the heart of this approach is the way in which the therapist works with the couple's enacted experience. In the process of the work the couple may witness their dynamic being played out not only between them, but also enacted with, and ultimately contained by, their therapist. What is important is the therapist's capacity to take in and not 'refuse entry' to the couple's projections, to contain feelings that the partners have not been able to be receptive to in each other, or to bear in themselves. As the experience of containment becomes more established in the work, the couple may gradually 'take back in' such feelings, having less need to project them, or to see them as belonging only to their partner.

This highlights the significance of the 'triangular setting' of couple therapy, where the partners experience different permutations of 'coupling' in the consulting room, including with the therapist who will often be 'outside' the couple. Witnessing the therapist tolerate this position can be important. If such shifts of perspective can be explored and thought about with the couple, they may be helped to develop their own observing capacity and to reflect on their relationship. Over time, each partner might begin to extend a curiosity and openness to thinking about the experience of the other – to move towards thinking about the meaning of their relationship dynamics and how each contributes to them, internalising what has been termed a 'couple state of mind' (Morgan, 2001, 2018). Such a state of mind allows the emergence of their relationship as a 'third entity' (Ruszczynski, 1998) to which both partners relate, which may become a creative resource (Morgan, 2004) and fulfil a containing function for them.

For couples whose everyday experience of their relationship can be an oppositional, lonely one of entrenched difficulties, it can be very powerful to begin to see that their problems may be a conscious manifestation of underlying common or *shared unconscious anxieties*; that they have been drawn together for powerful, thinkable, *shared unconscious reasons*. If this understanding can be achieved through the therapeutic work, the couple may begin to recognise that the repeating negative patterns of interaction in their relationship have a deeper meaning that reflects overlapping aspects of their inner worlds. If couples can be helped to give up the positions of certainty and blame that pervade their relationship what may look like small gains in the session can have significant long term effects. If couple therapy can help to enable such psychological development, it has the potential not just to improve the mental health and well-being of the adult partners involved, but also of their children – and, as they grow up and have children of their own, of those yet unborn generations to come.

Notes

1 'Enactment makes it possible to know in representable and communicable ways about deep unconscious identifications and primitive levels of functioning which could otherwise only be guessed at or discussed at the intellectual level' (Tuckett, 1997, p. 214).
2 'Transference' is the process by which one displaces onto the other feelings and ideas which derive from previous figures (or 'object relationships') in one's life. Classically, the concept refers to the patient-analyst, but it can encompass any relationship, most significantly for this discussion, the adult couple relationship.

References

Balfour, A. (2009). Intimacy and sexuality in later life. In: C. Clulow (Ed.), *Sex, Attachment and Couple Ppsychotherapy: Psychoanalytic Perspectives* (pp. 217–36). Library of Couple and Family Psychoanalysis. London: Karnac.

Benioff, L. (2017). Discussion of "How was it for you? Attachment, sexuality and mirroring in couple relationships". In: S. Nathans & M. Schaefer (Eds.), *Couples on the Couch: Psychoanalytic Couple Psychotherapy and the Tavistock Model*. London: Routledge.

Bion, W. R. (1967). Attacks on linking. In: *Second Thoughts* (93–110). Maresfield Library. London: Karnac.

Britton, R. (1989). The missing link: parental sexuality in the Oedipus complex. In: J. Steiner (Ed.), *The Oedipus Complex Today: Clinical Implications*. London: Karnac.

Clulow, C. (Ed.) (2009). *Sex, Attachment and Couple Psychotherapy: Psychoanalytic Perspectives*. London: Karnac.

Clulow, C. (2017). How was it for you? In: S. Nathans & M. Schaefer (Eds.), *Couples on the Couch: Psychoanalytic Couple Psychotherapy and the Tavistock Model*. London: Routledge.

Clulow, C., & Boerma, M. (2009). Dynamics and disorders of sexual desire. In: C. Clulow (Ed.), *Sex, Attachment and Couple Psychotherapy: Psychoanalytic Perspectives* (pp. 75–101). Library of Couple and Family Psychoanalysis. London: Karnac.

Colman, W. (1993). Marriage as a psychological container. In: S. Ruszczynski (Ed.), *Psychotherapy with Couples*. London: Karnac.

Fisher, J. (1995). The impenetrable other: ambivalence and the oedipal conflict in work with couples. In: S. Ruszczynski & J. Fisher (Eds.), *Intrusiveness and Intimacy in the Couple*. London: Karnac.

Fisher, J. (1999). That which couples bring to therapy. In: *The Uninvited Guest: Emerging from Narcissism Towards Marriage*. London: Karnac.

Freud, S. (1914). Remembering, repeating and working-through. *S. E.*, *12*: 145–56. London: Hogarth.

Grier, F. (2009). Lively and deathly intercourse. In: C. Clulow (Ed.), *Sex, Attachment and Couple Psychotherapy: Psychoanalytic Perspectives*. Library of Couple and Family Psychoanalysis. London: Karnac.

Hewison, D. (2009). Power vs love in sadomasochistic couple relationships. In: C. Clulow (Ed.), *Sex, Attachment and Couple Psychotherapy: Psychoanalytic Perspectives*. Library of Couple and Family Psychoanalysis. London: Karnac.

Kiecolt-Glaser, J. K., & Newton, T.L. (2001). Marriage and health: his and hers. *Psychological Bulletin*, *127*(4): 472–503.

Morgan, M. (1995). The projective gridlock: a form of projective indentification in couple relationships. In: S. Ruszczynski & J. Fisher (Eds.), *Intrusiveness and Intimacy in the Couple*. London: Karnac.

Morgan, M. (2001). First contacts: the therapist's "couple state of mind" as a factor in the containment of couples seen for consultations. In: F. Grier (Ed.), *Brief Encounters with Couples: Some Analytical Perspectives* (pp. 17–32). London: Karnac.

Morgan, M. (2004). On being able to be a couple: the importance of a 'creative couple' in psychic life. In: F. Grier (Ed.), *Oedipus and the Couple* (pp. 9–30). London: Karnac.

Morgan, M. (2018). *A Couple State of Mind: Psychoanalysis of Couples and the Tavistock Relationships Model*. London: Routledge.

Ruszczynski, S. (1998). The 'marital triangle': towards 'triangular space' in the intimate couple relationship. *Journal of the British Association of Psychotherapists*, *34*(31): 33–47.

Ruszczynski, S. (2004). Reflective space in the intimate couple relationship: the 'marital triangle'. In: F. Grier (Ed.), *Oedipus & the Couple*. London: Karnac.

Target, M. (2007). Is our sexuality our own? A developmental model of sexuality based on early affect mirroring. *British Journal of Psychotherapy*, *23*: 517–30. doi:10.1111/j.1752-0118.2007.00048.x

Tuckett, D. (1997). Mutual enactment in the psychoanalytic situation. In: J. L. Ahumada, J. Olagaray, A. K. Richards & A. D. Richards (Eds.), *The Perverse Transference and Other Matters: Essays in Honor of R. Horacio Etchegoyen*. Northvale, NJ: Jason Aronson.

Commentary on Chapter 1

David Hewison

Balfour and Morgan's excellent summary of the developments in therapy with couples from a psychodynamic perspective shows how fruitful this area of clinical intervention is. They suggest that we now have a good understanding of what contemporary couple relationships are all about, what makes some of them successful and why others lead to disappointment and break-up. They address the nature of psychodynamic couple therapy and focus on two principal ways in which it helps couples: the first is that the couple are seen together, so that their relationship is lived out in the sessions with the therapist and not simply described, as it would be were both partners in individual therapy; the second is that the way in which therapists attune themselves to what happens in the therapy and to the stories that are brought allows the idea of 'enactments' to bring a helpful perspective to what happens between all actors in the therapy. These elements of psychodynamic couple therapy widen the kinds of understanding that can be brought, helpfully, to the couple's relationship. In my comments I want to pay particular attention to the evidence that psychodynamic couple therapy works.

Psychodynamic couple psychotherapy is based upon the fundamental concept that we all have an unconscious, hidden from us, which influences what we do, feel, perceive and think in relation to ourselves, our personal histories, and our intimate relationships with others. As such, although it shares features with other models of couple therapy – such as the importance of the therapeutic relationship, the need for emotional expression, the value of each partner being able to reflect on and respond to what they hear in the sessions, an overall idea of what 'good' and 'bad' couple relationships look like – it nonetheless brings something very particular to each encounter with couples seeking therapy. This is a rigorous attention to the ways in which complex unconscious material can be made more conscious, and how the new meaning that this brings to the couple interaction is itself therapeutic. Couples are not told what to do, how to structure conversations between them, or what thoughts to get rid of; they are listened to in a highly specialised way. The case example of Jane and Tom shows just how this might be done (it will be different with each couple), and just how alert the therapist is to the unconscious that is at play between the couple and in the sessions. One of the things the case example does not do is show just how effective such interventions are across a wide range of couples.

At the very end of 2016, in the highly-respected clinical research journal *Psychotherapy*, Tavistock Relationships published the largest study of the outcomes of couple therapy in an ordinary clinical setting to date, analysing the results of 439 couples and comparing them with other ordinary setting studies (Hewison et al., 2016). We showed that psychodynamic couple therapy is a very effective form of intervention for people who are in the 'clinical' range for both individual and relationship distress. In fact, there is no couple intervention that is better.

The study is important for a number of reasons. The first is that there are powerful debates in the psychotherapy and commissioning fields about which therapies should be funded and which should not. The second is that the evidence used for these decisions is not of a kind that psychodynamic therapies specialise in, and so are being excluded from consideration despite their long history of working well and creatively with couples in the way that Balfour and Morgan describe. The third is that the provision of psychodynamic couple psychotherapy is still very much a private/voluntary sector activity, and new evidence of its effectiveness is vital in helping spread awareness of its value.

Over the last few decades, pressures on health care funding have led to an appreciation that not every promising intervention can be afforded for everyone who might make use of it, and that there has to be some kind of process for deciding who should get what in order to manage the limited pot of money available to meet growing demands. In the US this process has been led by Insurance Companies; in the UK by the National Health Service (NHS) and the National Institute for Health and Care Excellence (NICE). Psychological therapies, despite their obvious differences with medical and pharmaceutical interventions, have had to go through a similar process of being recognised as being 'efficacious' for specific disorders found in the relevant diagnostic manuals. This has proved to be highly problematic for psychotherapies generally, leading to a distorted understanding of which therapies work and which do not (Wampold & Imel, 2015). Therapies were dealt with as though they were a variety of drug: a specific thing that could be prescribed for *that* condition, in *this* dose, and always worked in *exactly* the same way, just as aspirin does for a headache. As we have seen in Balfour and Morgan's chapter, this model is a long way away from the highly individualised practice of psychodynamic couple psychotherapy. The same is true for the humanistic, existential, systemic and family therapies, to name just a few. The therapies that most appeared to resemble a drug (specific, repeatable, aimed at symptom-removal) grew in prestige as a result. It led to a situation where highly structured cognitive and behavioural therapies began to be privileged by institutional purchasers, because they could be tested just like a pharmaceutical product.

This then led to a distortion in the kinds of evidence that were acceptable. Drugs are tested by highly structured trials that follow particular rules of treatment and comparison. To see if a drug works it has to be compared with something else – most usually, no treatment. Participants with the condition to be treated are divided between two comparison groups in a random way that ensures that they are broadly similar. Each is given an intervention, one of which is the drug of interest and the other an identical-looking pill with no active ingredient. Any resulting differences between the groups are evidence of the efficacy of the drug, as all other influencing factors have been controlled-for. This Randomized Controlled Trial (RCT) methodology has been of immense value in medicine, determining which treatment or intervention to prescribe. It has shown that the cognitive and behavioural therapies work better than no therapy for a variety of diagnostic conditions. These therapies are officially 'efficacious', having had their results repeated in another RCT. The distortion that this methodology and certification has brought with it, however, is that it has become assumed that therapies that have not been put through an RCT study do not work: 'no RCT-evidence of working' has mistakenly been taken to mean 'evidence of not working', despite the fact that the majority of therapies have not had an RCT and yet people are just as helped by them (Barkham et al., 2010).

In part this distortion is a reaction to the kind of evidence that is prevalent in psychodynamic writing: illustrative case studies. These follow the brilliant example of Freud who would show how his developing theories matched his developing clinical practice and thereby confirmed as 'true' his ideas. This 'argument from authority' fell out of fashion as 'evidence-based practice' favouring larger-scale data-analysis over individual case examples became the preferred methodology. There is some substance to this shift, yet it does not justify the under-commissioning of psychodynamic therapies. In fact, there is evidence of bias against the psychodynamic model even when it has RCT, larger-scale data-analysis (Fonagy, 2015). Psychodynamic researchers have shown that it is misrepresented as unscientific, not given equal weight in commissioning guidelines (though its results are the same), excluded from representation on guideline committees, misused in studies as a neutered comparison treatment, and unfairly evidenced in meta-analyses combining studies (Abbass et al., 2017). Perhaps this bias is because each new RCT test of psychodynamic therapy shows that it works, and that it works as well as any other therapy. In psychotherapy research generally, the focus is now moving onto the effectiveness of individual therapists, and away from fruitless comparisons between different therapy modalities.

What does this mean for the model of intervention outlined by Balfour and Morgan? The question of how to judge the value of psychodynamic couple psychotherapy is an old one. Historically, it has been assessed by two main outcomes: first, the coherence of its case-study based literature, which showed how this variant of psychoanalytic practice was based in the traditional requirements of the field and how its developing theory and technique were explained in accounts of particular couple therapies; and second, in its continued acceptability to couples seeking help for their distressed relationships. These are clearly linked, but different, kinds of approach. The brilliance of a therapeutic theoretical model is useless if people do not feel helped by it. In a sense, the development of theory outlined by Balfour and Morgan shows us that the psychodynamic couple psychotherapy model is capable of evolving and changing as more experience is gathered and ideas are shared amongst a professional community and tested in ordinary clinical setting with couples. The model is alive and adaptive to new forms of couple relating.

Over the years, beginning in 1955 with Bannister and colleagues' account of interventions into troubled marriages, psychodynamic couple psychotherapy has been described in a very similar format in books and journal papers, with theory and technique exemplified and supported by extracts from particular sessions or case study reports of whole therapies (Morgan, in press; Ruszczynski, 1993). This has been a very fruitful activity for the field, allowing improved understanding of the nature of the unconscious dynamics between partners in a couple, and between them and their therapist(s), and an improved understanding of the kinds of technical adjustments needed to fit this style of couple therapy to different kinds of couples. These publications have been fascinating, valuable and thought-provoking, enabling couple therapists to reflect on their practice and develop their professional understanding of what they are doing. This has, in turn, led to a specialist professional training for the modality in line with those developed for the treatment of individuals and groups, matching European standards that have emerged over this time.

The work of Tavistock Relationships in collecting outcome and satisfaction data from couples consistently since 2007 has provided much material to understand statistically and clinically, and it is clear that the psychodynamic couple psychotherapy developed and delivered by the organisation is an effective way of treating individual and relationship distress. The research has shown that men and women get similar amounts of benefit from this therapy, regardless of ethnicity or sexual orientation. The current debates in the psychotherapy field are now exploring what makes one therapist's outcomes different to another's, even when they have the same training and work in the same clinic. The focus is on the amount of 'deliberate practice' that a therapist engages in: identifying clinical weaknesses and poor technique and working deliberately on these to see results improve (Rousmaniere et al., 2017). Work already done on psychodynamic individual therapy from this perspective may indicate ways forward for improving the already impressive outcomes from psychodynamic couple therapy (Hilsenroth & Diener, 2017).

References

Abbass, A., Luyten, P., Steinert, C., & Leichsenring, F. (2017). Bias toward psychodynamic therapy: framing the problem and working toward a solution. *Journal of Psychiatric Practice*, 23: 361–365.

Barkham, M., Stiles, W. B., Lambert, M. J., & Mellor-Clark, J. (2010). Building a rigorous and relevant knowledge base for the psychological therapies. In: M. Barkham, G.E. Hardy, & J. Mellor-Clark (Eds.), *Developing and Delivering Practice-based Evidence. A Guide for the Psychological Therapies* (pp. 21–61). Chichester: Wiley-Blackwell.

Fonagy, P. (2015). The effectiveness of psychodynamic psychotherapies: an update. *World Psychiatry, 14*: 137–50.

Hewison, D., Casey, P., & Mwamba, N. (2016). The effectiveness of couple therapy: Outcomes in a naturalistic United Kingdom setting. *Psychotherapy, 53*: 377–387.

Hilsenroth, M. J., & Diener, M., J (2017). Some effective strategies for the supervision of psychodynamic psychotherapy. In: T. Rousmaniere, R.K. Goodyear, S.D. Miller, & B.E. Wampold (Eds.), *The Cycle of Excellence: Using Deliberate Practice to Improve Supervision and Therapy* (pp. 163–88). Chichester: John Wiley & Sons.

Morgan, M. (2018). *A Couple State of Mind: Psychoanalysis of Couples and the Tavistock Relationships Model*. London: Karnac.

Rousmaniere, T., Goodyear, R. K., Miller, S. D., & Wampold, B. E. (Eds.) (2017). *The Cycle of Excellence. Using Deliberate Practice to Improve Supervision and Therapy.* Chichester: John Wiley & Sons.

Ruszczynski, S. (Ed.) (1993). *Psychotherapy with Couples: Theory and Practice at the Tavistock Institute of Marital Studies*. London: Karnac.

Wampold, B. E., & Imel, Z. E. (2015). *The Great Psychotherapy Debate: The Evidence for What Makes Psychotherapy Work* (2nd edn). New York: Routledge.

Chapter 2

Couples becoming parents

Christopher Clulow

Where to begin?

While there are many routes to parenthood there is only one coupling that generates life. All children have two biological parents, and most grow up with both of them. Nevertheless, in most families there are many couplings that sustain new life and promote its development. Some children have more than two adults who act as parents, and some have only one. Even for those who are parenting on their own there may be other kinds of partner (for example, a grandmother or other relative) who share with them different aspects of being a parent. In any of these scenarios, and however families are structured, it is fair to assume that what goes on *between* those parenting children will form an important part of the social and emotional environment in which children grow up and develop.

What goes on between parents is influenced by their own developmental experiences and the support of those around them. Romantic love may spark the passions, but the capacity to sustain a loving relationship has little to do with the intoxication of being in love. Perhaps this fact is most clearly recognised in cultures where partnerships are seen as the coming together of two families, with family members other than the couple having a say in the prospective arrangement. And it may also be recognised by those in gay and lesbian relationships who feel the absence of community support for the choices they have made. Most tested of all, perhaps, is the love between partners who already have children from other relationships; establishing themselves as a couple can be a fraught business when the web of allegiances is complex and pulls partners in different directions.

When things go wrong between parents where do we as therapists look to identify and make sense of their problems? If we begin with the couple relationship as the progenitor of life do we focus on the meanings the partners ascribe to their relationship, and to the intercourse that resulted in the mixing of fluids transporting that one in hundreds of millions of sperm that successfully penetrated and fertilised the ovum resulting in their child? Were they both up for this outcome, or was the motivation to become parents ambivalent and less equally shared between them? How might they interpret any damage or disability arising from their intercourse? What if they have had to rely on others to accomplish this miracle, leaving them with the social but not biological responsibility of parenthood? How do their stories shape the physical and emotional environments that transform cells into people?

Or should we look outside the couple and consider the influence of extended family, of friends and community (including the professional community of health and other service providers) when considering what pressures can affect a couple's experience of becoming parents? Conversely, is our attention to be drawn to parents as individuals – to their unique genetic, temperamental and psychological endowments that, blended with those of others, form the legacies passed on from one generation to the next? What determines the emotional as well as physical environment that facilitates her or his development, and supports those tasked with bringing up baby?

In deciding where to look in diagnosing and addressing distress, how influenced are we therapists by our sense of time? If the where of our attention is *here*, do we focus on the *now*? If it is *there*, do we focus on the *then*? In other words, is there a question not only of where but when to begin in thinking about intervening? When biology is not alone in shaping the experiences of hatching, matching and despatching, what other events or processes might mark the time at which the seed of subsequent distress first took root? Or does this question take us down a cul-de-sac? Is the notion of time as a linear concept a reliable guide to thinking about the more circular concept of life cycles, when the moment of now, in marking the point connecting past and future, constitutes both an end and a beginning? Are we defined by time, our past shaping our future in some predetermined developmental line, or do the unknowns of the future have the power to shatter history and transform the people we thought ourselves to be? Is time, whether circular, repetitive or relative, no more than a human construct designed to locate ourselves in an otherwise unbounded infinity of being in the world? Does it allow for the joker of chance to upend the continuities we seek to establish and confirm in the ways we survey the past and anticipate the future?

The notion that we are authors of our own stories, bounded by space and time, perhaps affords too little attention to what goes on beyond the limited horizons of consciousness. Psychoanalytically orientated therapists are particularly interested in looking beyond those horizons, following Freud's assertion that the unconscious is essentially timeless in its capacity to conflate past and present in generating felt experience (Freud, 1915). The stage is then set for current roles and relationships to be allocated on the basis of scripts and dramatic scenarios that essentially belong to the past: historical confusions affecting temporal bearings, resulting in geographical confusions affecting spatial orientation.

In the end we, as psychotherapists, have little choice but to begin where and when those who consult us decide that we should, even, as in the case of Tom and Tessa, if we think their concern is displaced and they have left things quite late.

Tom and Tessa have a school-age child in his latency years. He has learning and speech difficulties attributed to a traumatic birth, and there have been recent concerns about his behaviour at school. When he was a toddler Tessa asked Tom to leave as she was no longer in love with him. He reluctantly agreed to go and they lived apart. Despite his devastation at their relationship ending they managed to set up a contact routine that allowed him regular access to their child and them to remain on reasonably friendly terms. This had ended two years previously when a proposed change of arrangement from Tessa had the impact of making Tom believe she was obstructing contact. He consulted a solicitor who suggested mediation. She refused to mediate with him over the issue and so he went to court to enforce contact. The court asked for a child welfare report. She was very angry about this, feeling he had acted in a way that portrayed her as a bad parent in the eyes of the professionals involved in helping their son. Tom likewise felt a sense of injustice, thinking he was perceived by those in their child's school and social network as the abandoning partner, when she had been the one to instigate the break.

Both parents were advised by the court to seek professional help for their relationship as co-parents because of concerns that the problems between them were adversely affecting their son. They were seen by two therapists who worked together with couples. When they went to meet the couple for their appointment Tom and Tessa were sitting at opposite ends of the waiting room, turned away from and avoiding eye contact with each other. Tessa, a petite and attractive young woman, looked both intense and buttoned up, giving the impression she was ready to explode. Tom conveyed a more sociable, perhaps placatory attitude, getting up to greet the therapists and making small talk on the way to their consulting room.

A shaming aspect of their situation was that their relationship, and the difficulties associated with it, had been in full professional view. Their son's needs meant a network of professionals was already involved with the family and now the family justice system had joined it in a way that cast doubt on their competence. They were being scrutinised by outsiders. They felt they were living under a cloud of criticism not only from a support network on which they depended but also from the courts and, perhaps most importantly, from each other. That made each of them wary and apprehensive about any contact between them, especially when this was likely to increase their exposure to public scrutiny. Public scrutiny exacerbated their fear that they would be judged and blamed.

This was the challenge for their therapists: how to help a couple who were uneasy about being seen together and ambivalent about having to depend upon each other and an array of professionals with whom they were involved and who they feared might be critical and shaming? The irony that they had joined this network was not lost on them.

In what way, it might be asked, do Tom and Tessa's problems relate to their becoming parents? They are out of time in the sense that their child was born years before this consultation took place, although Tessa's dissatisfaction with Tom was temporally very closely connected with them becoming parents. They are also out of time in that there is little history to contextualise their problem, except in the broadest of terms: a traumatic birth, a damaged child, a broken relationship, blame slowly replacing friendliness between them as parents, the ensuing mistrust prompting a court action that made a difficult relationship between them worse. And all this happening in front of a cast of professionals witnessing and becoming increasingly concerned about the potential consequences for their child of them as his parents not getting on.

It was because of such clinical experiences that staff of Tavistock Relationships first became interested in the transition to parenthood. The 'out of time' quality of these encounters featured then as it does now. It was not that there was a high incidence of couples seeking help around the time they became parents, although some did. It was more a growing awareness of how the solutions they adopted to manage this family change affected their relationship in subsequent years, the impact of which could be felt much later on and sometimes not until their children left home. We became curious about how parenthood changed couples, whether being a couple contributed to the well-being of children, and what implications there might be for therapeutic practice.

Does parenthood change couples?

Six decades of research has revealed a vigorous debate about the nature and severity of the impact of parenthood on couples. Whether the language of 'crisis', 'transition', or 'big life change' is used, most studies show that children fundamentally change the relationship between their parents for better and for worse (Belsky & Kelly, 1994). On the credit side of the equation is the sense of fulfilment and satisfaction that children bring to couples, providing tangible confirmation of their creativity together and usually realising their deepest hopes and dreams. Re-entering the world of childhood through their own children, re-experiencing the joys and pains of growing up, these are treasured experiences offering parents a second chance to relive and even redeem their past. On the debit side there is a clear and consistent tendency for relationship satisfaction to fall when children arrive (especially for women and particularly in the pre-school years), for this to level out when children go to school, sometimes dipping again in the adolescent years and then generally recovering as children leave home (Twenge et al., 2003). This shallow 'U' or 'W'-shaped graph charts a predictable, if generalised, trajectory of the way parents say children have affected how satisfied they feel as a couple.

In trying to understand why this might be, attention has focused on the experiences of women becoming mothers, including why depression is so commonly a part of that experience, and the experiences of men becoming fathers, often including their sense of exclusion resulting in a turning away from family involvement. A raft of explanations has been offered encompassing biological predispositions at one end of the spectrum to changing socio-cultural norms at the other – defining the roles and responsibilities of women and men in relation to children and the social status (more frequently lack of status) accorded to the actual work of bringing them up. Importantly, mid-range studies have indicated that the impact of children on their parents' relationship with each other must be understood not only in relation to prevailing circumstances but also by taking account of developmental history, which provides the lens through which current experience is interpreted. Together, these factors affect whether parents feel supported by each other, which, in turn, impacts on their experience of becoming parents.

Perhaps of most significance is how parents manage the conflicts that inevitably accompany the arrival of children. In a booklet aimed at those working with young families I coined the acronym 'SHAME' as a mnemonic for common sites of conflict between young parents: *S*ex, *H*ousework, *A*ctivities, *M*oney and *E*mployment (Clulow, 2009). These are important issues that couples have to negotiate about in their own right, but they are also capable of containing historically rooted dynamic conflicts:

- *Sex*: While sex is less frequently referred to in research than clinical writings its significance is apparent to therapists who have worked with men who feel they have lost their partners' to their babies and women who experience their partners' sexual advances as another infantile claim on their bodies. In these circumstances partners can be converted from lovers into rejecting mothers or needy children.
- *Housework*: Arguments over who does what about the home can assume the guise of parental control, to be either resisted of complied with. Becoming parents can then feel like being either the contrary child in relation to a demanding parent, or the overburdened parent with a truculent child.
- *Activities*: Giving up a lifestyle that marked the time before parenthood involves loss as well as gain, requiring partners to adjust to their changed circumstances. The freedom to continue separate activities can generate competitive feelings about fairness if they are pursued at the expense of one or other partner, and may revive unresolved sibling rivalries.
- *Money*: Household finances have huge significance as the symbol of emotional as well as material resource, including who is seen to have control of the family purse, who is dependent on whom for payments, whether there is enough to go around for family members and who must go without if there is not.
- *Employment*: Employment can resonate with money in reviving feelings about having to depend on one's partner and no longer being financially self-sufficient, affecting the dynamics of couple relationships in this regard. Employment outside the home is also an important marker of identity and status for parents as individuals, and it can become the main factor that

lures partners away from family life or, in its absence, locks them into domestic and dyadic definitions that can undermine self-confidence.

These five sites of conflict (which are by no means comprehensive, perhaps the most important omission being conflict over parenting styles),is what individuals can so easily feel when their performance and experience as parents falls short of the expectations and standards they had set for themselves, especially when their shortcomings are exposed to public view.

Do children destabilise partnerships, in the sense of making them vulnerable to breakdown? The answer to this question is an unequivocal 'no', especially if partners are well supported and come from families that managed conflict constructively. However, children are definitely no cure for an ailing partnership. What research tells us is that while children do not break up partnerships (it is their absence in the forms of non-arrival or death that are more likely to do this), they may expose and enlarge any cracks that already exist in the relationship. This is particularly likely to be the case if children suffer from disability or other conditions that make more than the usual demands on the care resources of their parents. For parents more generally, it is the fall in satisfaction during the parenting years that constitutes the main challenge to their relationship, and this can mostly be accounted for by conflicts arising from pre-existing problems, unconfirmed expectations of parenthood and changes in the quality of communication between them.

It can take time for parents to appreciate that their relationship as a couple is changing. Just as the major concern during pregnancy is with the baby being born safe and well, so the early months of parenthood are about surviving sleepless nights, crying babies, lack of space, interrupted conversations and all the other demands that the new arrival brings. While mothers may be the first to register dissatisfaction with their partners when things are not going well, the fundamental changes affecting them as a couple may take years rather than months to be noticed and acknowledged between them.

> Had they been seen closer to the time of their son's birth Tom and Tessa might have been able to share their feelings about what was happening to them, especially in the light of the trauma surrounding that time; years later we can only speculate about what caused their relationship to break down. Even in the best of circumstances the demands of a young baby shift the locus of intimacy for parents and may disappoint their expectations of parenthood, exposing them to their own needs for help and support – the baby in the nursery evoking the baby within the parents. A traumatic birth, a damaged baby, and the accompanying mistrust of those who were supposed to prevent such an outcome complicates the process of becoming parents, disappointing expectations, increasing the burden of care on them and cautioning against trusting others. Such an experience may also generate anger with those who failed to provide adequate care and raise

questions about who is to blame. Is it me? Is it you? Was it the midwife, the doctor, the nursing staff? If they can be directed outwards such feelings may unite the couple, but when partners turn on each other their relationship may be unable to withstand the burden of grief that each feels about their child being damaged. This burden can be unbearable if one or other of them feels held in some way responsible for the damage.

How do couples affect the well-being of children?

Clinicians know that if things are going well between adults the outlook for their children is good. If things are going badly, children (like their parents) may suffer in terms of health, behaviour, emotional well-being and the capacity to learn. This assumption is well supported by research (Cowan & Pape Cowan, 2009; Reynolds, 2001; Rodgers & Pryor, 1998; Schulz et al., 2010). Whether parents are living together or apart, children suffer if they are exposed to and involved in damaging arguments between their parents. On the other hand, the experience of parents getting on well together boosts the security of children in ways that can benefit their own children when they, in turn, become parents.

Research associations do not amount to explanations, and it is a mark of scientific advance that we now have evidence about processes that explain outcomes. For example, while it had widely been assumed that couple relationships impacted *only indirectly* on children (by supporting or undermining each partner in their role as a parent), refined research techniques have now established a *direct* link between the quality of the co-parenting relationship and outcomes for children (Harold & Leve, 2012). This work has allowed clinical awareness (and, indeed, common sense) to be reinforced by research evidence in understanding how couple relationships affect family process, which, in turn, sharpens the focus of and provides an evidence base for intervention programmes.

Inter-parental conflict that affects children badly originates from the way their parents behave and how their children process the significance of the conflict. When it spills over from the way parents behave with each other and affects the relationships with their children it compromises their children, drawing them into taking sides, to compensating for what might be missing in the parental couple or to becoming the scapegoat sacrificed in the service of holding their parents together. Children may then be recruited into roles, responsibilities and even identities that are alien to their needs, desires and sense of self. Intervention in these circumstances is likely to be directed at helping parents bound their conflict, preventing spill-over that can be so damaging for their children.

Children are not passive in this process, and will be anxious to make sense of what is happening between their parents given how important that relationship is for their emotional security. When families operate at a high level of emotional intensity a row between parents has much less significance than when it bursts unannounced into the apparent calm of families operating with low expressed emotion. Frequent conflict dulls its impact; it is unexpected conflict that will put children on high alert. In making sense of conflict children frequently believe they are somehow responsible for what has gone wrong and either blame themselves or, fired up by a sense of injustice, blame others in managing their feelings. The content of their parents' arguments is clearly relevant to this process (especially when it concerns them), and in the absence of information, as when the arguments are cold, children are inclined to fill in the gaps for themselves. When the war is hot, the problem for children may be one of information overload, triggering defences against emotions that threaten to overwhelm them. In either circumstance intervention might involve working directly with children to access their thoughts and feelings about what is going on.

The relationship between parental conflict and emotional security has intergenerational implications. For example, an American study found that securely attached new parents who reported low levels of conflict between their own parents were less susceptible to a decline in relationship satisfaction than insecurely attached parents who reported high levels of conflict in that relationship. They also showed more positive parenting styles. When securely attached fathers reported low conflict between their parents and their insecurely attached partners reported high conflict, the outcome was very similar. But when the position was reversed (with securely attached mothers reporting low and insecurely attached fathers high levels of parental conflict) the negative impact on relationship satisfaction was the same as if both partners were insecurely attached and had reported high conflict between their own parents (Cowan & Pape Cowan, 2005). In commenting on this the researchers speculated that the level of conflict between partners in new families may be of less importance than whether they acted together to escalate or reduce it, and that gender stereotypes might influence such affect regulation. The attachment security of the father (which was associated with low reported levels of parental conflict) emerges then as a key factor in escalating or damping down relationship conflict.

Children are conceived and develop under the psychosocial arc of their parents' relationship, which forms an important aspect of their environment. D.H. Lawrence (1915) captured this image beautifully in his depiction of three generations of the Brangwen family, using the image of a rainbow, the eponymous title of his book, as the factor releasing young Anna Lensky from her sense of responsibility for keeping her parents together after her mother and stepfather made up following an argument between them:

> Anna's soul was at peace between them. She looked from one to the other, and she saw them established to her safety and she was free. She played between the pillar of fire and the pillar of cloud in confidence, having the assurance on her right hand and the assurance on her left. She was no longer called upon to uphold with her childish might the broken end of the arch. Her father and mother now met to the span the heavens, and she, the child, was free to play in the space beneath, between.
>
> (p. 88)

Or, to put it in the colloquial language of psychoanalysis: 'The acknowledgement of the child of the parents' relationship with each other unites his psychic world' (Britton, 1989, p. 86).

Uniting the psychic worlds of children and parents is the capacity for reflection, a capacity that is honed or blunted by the ways in which relationships play out within families. Especially important in this regard is the developing capacity for self-reflection. Being able to experience and observe oneself and others, without intruding upon their intimacy or taking up a position of detached isolation, is a mark of social maturity. It comes from learning about living in a world that exists beyond the exclusive dyad of mother and infant, an education that is facilitated by the way parents operate together in managing a relationship environment that is no longer binary. It is how contemporary psychoanalysts think relationally about what Freud described as the process of resolving the Oedipus complex.

> An unusual feature of the consultation offered to Tom and Tessa was that they were seen by two therapists – a couple for a couple. There is no information about the relationship between the parents of either partner, so we have no way of knowing how integrated or divided their psychic worlds might have been as a consequence of their own childhood experiences. What the consultation did offer was two people working together to try and help Tom and Tessa with their problems. The fact there were two of them may have helped each partner feel supported; neither of them had to compete for the ear of their therapist. At a less conscious level they would have absorbed an experience of a coupling between professional 'parents' in the service of helping them, which may have been novel. If this was the case, the experience might have been as therapeutic as anything the therapists said.

Learning, or, perhaps more accurately, ingesting from the environment, begins before birth. The developing foetus is biologically joined to its mother and physically sustained by her. Whatever substances course through her body course through the body of her unborn child, be they nourishing or toxic. Because affective states and bodily biochemistry are interlinked, a mother's emotional experiences will be communicated to her developing infant through neuropeptides such as cortisol. Cortisol is necessary for the development of the embryo, but highly elevated (or reduced) levels, especially early in pregnancy, are thought to affect the foetus' own stress response system. Other neurohormones, such as testosterone, are believed to act on developing brain structures during a critical period in early pregnancy in ways that can affect gendered play in early childhood.

While such ingestion appears to be the function of a dyadic relationship – that between a mother and her unborn baby – the influence of others in the mother's social environment may also be significant. We know that in infancy and early childhood high levels of parental conflict, especially violent conflict (like high levels of parental neglect), can affect brain development by 'pruning' neural networks via dissociation, disrupting the endogenous opiate system that affects the capacity to be comforted and reducing the corpus callosum (the tract of nerve fibres that regulates exchanges between the right and left hemispheres of the brain allowing perceptions and memories to be integrated). It may be no great leap to infer that, at least through the mediating pathway of the endogenous opiate system, these effects might operate pre-natally as well.

There is some evidence that how a mother represents her foetus – her fantasies about her baby and so the web of expectations surrounding him or her – is more linked with how she represents her partner during pregnancy than with how she represents herself or her mother (Ammanti et al., 1992; Diamond & Yeoman, 2007). Likewise, the capacity of parents to include others while maintaining their relationship (defined as how they envision post-natal triadic relationships) assessed before the birth of their first child can predict the quality of triadic play interactions between parents and infants at four months (Von Klitzing et al., 1999). Post-natal research has shown that infants demonstrate clear capacities to co-ordinate their attention and affective responses between their parents simultaneously, displaying an emergent 'triangular capacity', and that even by three months they can show a capacity to share and respond to their parents affects and states of mind in triadic ways, for example, by appealing to one parent if the other shows a 'still face' in an experimental setting (McHale et al., 2008).

These findings suggest how the parental couple and their management of triangular relationships may be registered internally by the emerging infant as he or she slowly enters their social milieu. It is not that dyadic relationships are unimportant in this process – an infant's primary attachment figure remains the primary source of emotional security – but that this and the infant's developing experience is affected by the capacity of parents to hold each other as well as their child in mind.

What are the implications for therapeutic practice?

> Tom and Tessa's therapists responded to and focused on their implicit communication that they feared being criticised and shamed as parents if they expressed what they were feeling. First, they encouraged Tessa to express her anger towards Tom for initiating court proceedings, despite how difficult it was for Tom to hear that she hated him for this. They also encouraged Tom to express his fear of being edged out of his son's life, and for the anger they thought might conceal the pain he had felt about losing his partner, something they thought he might be expressing in terms of fearing losing his son. Trading these difficult feelings in a safe and non-judgemental setting reduced their paranoia and permitted some expression of positive intent, paving the way for them to say that their motive for

agreeing to come to the consultation was the hope they might find a way to leave their hurt with each other behind so this did not impact on their son. The therapists validated and reinforced their shared wish to do the best for him and related to them as parents with executive strengths. They stayed in the present, and, rightly or wrongly, did not use the consultation to explore the impact on them of their son's traumatic birth.

Tom and Tessa finally agreed that direct communication between them – for example Tessa providing Tom with details of their son's life that he might not be aware of, and Tom letting Tessa know what they did on contact visits and how that was working out – might not only be helpful in reducing the feeling of alienation between them but also help their son link up what could otherwise be his experience of leading parallel and separate lives with each of his parents. By his parents communicating with each other, and conveying information that his language impairment disabled him from doing for himself, it could be said that they would be helping him integrate not only the experience of having two parents but also his internal psychic space, a space that might otherwise become fractured.

Tom and Tessa ended their consultation saying the encounter had been helpful. Their therapists observed the tension between them lessening in the course of the meeting, despite – indeed, because of – some of the difficult things they had said to each other. Presumably these could be expressed because the consultation was experienced as a safe environment in which they both felt supported and encouraged, not blamed or judged. The outcome was that they agreed to communicate more than they had been doing over contact arrangements, allowing them both to feel involved and important as parents. Whether this intent was translated into practice is not known, but at the time it indicated progress.

The key to managing conflict, in whichever site or context it occurs, is constructive communication. This is easier medicine to prescribe than to take, because there is always the fear that there may be negative side effects – consequences – associated with sharing grievances and disappointments. The fear that conflict will escalate into a damaging war that will be emotionally destabilising, or that major concessions may have to be made to maintain a relationship depended on for emotional security, can be disabling. Couple psychotherapy works in these circumstances because it provides a place of safety in which highly charged emotional issues can both be engaged with and reflected upon, detoxifying fantasies that this will be damaging and thereby loosening the grip of defences that prevent change. This is the assertion that therapists make about some of the mechanisms accounting for therapeutic effectiveness, as, indeed, do many couples identifying what has been helpful to them from the service they have received. The quality of the relationship established with couples is almost certainly more important in this process than therapist technique.

The main difficulty is that couples tend not to seek help, if they do at all, until problems have become entrenched. Given the evidence for the importance of the transition to parenthood in the life course of a family the argument for preventive, as compared to reactive, intervention is a strong one. While this has been accepted and acted upon at policy and practice levels in terms of supporting partners in taking up their role as parents, preventive intervention that targets the relationship between parents as its main focus has been much slower gaining traction and establishing an evidence base.

An early attempt to address this problem from Tavistock Relationships was an action research project offering preventive help to first-time parents through groups supporting them as a couple during the last trimester of pregnancy and the first six months of their baby's life (Clulow, 1982). The project included providing training for health visitors (key health practitioners available to families at this time of change) to widen the support they offered to young families beyond the mother–infant dyad to take account of the potential significance of what was happening between parents in the services they provided. The design of this small scale project allowed little to be said about outcomes. Yet the experience provided valuable information about what kind of recruitment and retention processes yielded the best results, the difficulty of attracting vulnerable families in poor socio-economic circumstances, the pros and cons of providing unstructured support groups, the relative homogeneity of groups held during pregnancy as compared with greater fragmentation of those held after birth, and about timings – the crisis for the couple relationship did not necessarily coincide with the birth of their baby. Indeed, the question of timing effective preventive interventions became a major question for the project when the boundary between preventive and remedial work was far from clear-cut: some (but perhaps not too much) recognition of there being a potential problem was likely to motivate attendance. A broad conclusion was that intervening preventively had value in bringing people going through similar changes together before (*pre-venio*) their experiences turned into problems, preparing the ground for those relationships to be used in the future should the need arise.

More recently Tavistock Relationships ran a co-parenting intervention with a national mental health charity addressing the needs of a vulnerable group of young parents (Clulow & Donaghy, 2010); a part of this was aimed at those going through the change of becoming parents for the first time. The aim of the project was to raise awareness of the significance of the co-parenting relationship by providing a workforce development programme for its key service providers, and with them committing to develop, deliver and evaluate post-natal support groups, parenting workshops and a new relationship counselling service. The project demonstrated that it was possible to incorporate a co-parenting focus in providing front-line services for young parents with mental health problems, and that statistically significant improvements in mental health and relationship satisfaction were achievable comparing pre and post intervention time periods for the services provided. This was not primarily a research project, so caution must be exercised in claiming that the interventions were the change agents. However, the results from this relatively small group of service users were sufficiently striking to indicate a strong likelihood that they played an important part.

One of the serendipitous outcomes of the first of these projects was to link the work of Tavistock Relationships with substantial longitudinal research and intervention studies carried out at the University of California, Berkeley. This started with a random controlled trial of the efficacy of a semi-structured preventive intervention programme for couples expecting their first baby (Cowan & Pape Cowan, 2000). The results demonstrated the efficacy of intervening preventively with a community sample of first-time parents and challenged the existing orthodoxy that the best way to support new parents was to focus on improving parenting skills. These intervention studies, now extended to vulnerable families and spanning over four decades, have arrived at an important and consistent conclusion: programmes targeting co-parenting relationships have better results than those restricted to improving parenting skills. The influence of this work will be apparent in subsequent chapters of this book, and especially in Chapter 4 where, under their supervision, the Cowans intervention groups have been rolled out by Tavistock Relationships in England.

I have asserted that children are born into a pre-existing psychosocial ecology, an important part of which is their parents' relationship with each other. They are not passive agents: children make parents out of partners and they change couple relationships. Moreover, they come into the world with their own heritage, which impacts on and is capable of evoking different and multiple responses from their parents, as we shall see in Chapter 3 in connection with adoption. But they will be keenly affected by the state of the relationship between their parents, and this provides the justification for making that relationship a central part of any intervention programme. Families can be thought of as constellations of subjectivity that define relationships between their members in cycles of reciprocal influence, gradually shaping the people they become. Supporting family relationships, especially those between parents, at critical times of change, through addressing the affective experiences of its members, is a worthy and effective investment in the well-being of families and the mental health of communities as a whole.

References

Ammanti, M., Baumgartner, E., Candelori, C., Perrucchini, P., Pola, M., Tambelli, R., & Zampino, F. (1992). Representations and narratives during pregnancy. *Infant Mental Health Journal*, *13*(2): 167–82.

Belsky, J., & Kelly, J. (1994). *The Transition to Parenthood*. New York: Dell.

Britton, R. (1989). The missing link: parental sexuality in the Oedipus complex. In: J. Steiner (Ed.), *The Oedipus Complex Today: Clinical Implications* (pp. 83–101). London: Karnac.

Clulow, C. (1982). *To Have and To Hold: Marriage, the First Baby and Preparing Couples for Parenthood*. Aberdeen: Aberdeen University Press.

Clulow, C. (2009). *Becoming Parents Together*. London: Tavistock Relationships.

Clulow, C., & Donaghy, M. (2010). Developing the couple perspective in parenting support: evaluation of a service initiative for vulnerable families. *Journal of Family Therapy, 32*: 142–68.

Cowan, P., & Pape Cowan, C. (2000). *When Partners Become Parents: The Big Life Change for Couples* (2nd edn). New Jersey/London: Erlbaum.

Cowan, P., & Pape Cowan, C. (2005). Two central roles for couple relationships: breaking negative intergenerational patterns and enhancing children's adaptation. *Sexual and Relationship Therapy, 20*(3): 275–88.

Cowan, P., & Pape Cowan, C. (2009). Couple relationships: a missing link between adult attachment and children's outcomes. *Attachment and Human Development, 11*(1): 1–4.

Diamond, D., & Yeoman, F. (2007). Oedipal love and conflict in the transference/countertransference matrix. Its impact on attachment security and mentalization. In: D. Diamond, S. Blatt, & J. Lichtenberg (Eds.), *Attachment and Sexuality*. New York/London: Analytic Press.

Freud, S. (1915). The unconscious. *S. E., 14*: 159–215. London: Hogarth.

Harold, G., & Leve, L. (2012). Parents as partners: how the parental relationship affects children's psychological development. In: A. Balfour, M. Morgan, & C. Vincent (Eds.), *How Couple Relationships Shape Our World: Clinical Practice, Research and Policy Perspectives*. London: Karnac.

Lawrence, D.H. (1915). *The Rainbow*. London: Martin Secker, 1928.

McHale, J., Fivaz-Depeursinge, E., Dickstein, S., Robertson, J., & Daley, M. (2008). New evidence for the social embeddedness of infants' early triangular capacities. *Family Process, 47*(4): 445–63.

Murch, M. (2018). *Supporting Children when Parents Separate: Embedding a Crisis Intervention Approach Within Family Justice, Education and Mental Health Policy*. Bristol: Policy Press.

Von Klitzing, K., Simoni, H., & Bürgin, D. (1999). Child development and early triadic relationships. *International Journal of Psycho-Analysis, 80*: 71–89.

Reynolds, J. (Ed.) (2001). *Not in Front of the Children: How Conflict Between Parents Affects Children*. London: One Plus One.

Rodgers, B., & Pryor, J. (1998). *Divorce and Separation: The Outcomes for Children*. York: Joseph Rowntree Foundation.

Schulz, M., Kline Pruett, M., Kerig, P., & Parke, R. (Eds.) (2010). *Strengthening Couple Relationships for Optimal Child Development: Lessons from Research and Intervention*. Washington, DC: American Psychological Association.

Twenge, J., Campbell, W., & Foster, C. (2003). Parenthood and marital satisfaction: a meta-analytic review. *Journal of Marriage and the Family, 65*: 574–83.

Commentary on Chapter 2

Marguerite Reid

The conception and birth of an infant brings about change in the couple relationship. They become parents and even during pregnancy they are 'parents in waiting'. Although for some couples this brings joy and satisfaction, for others it puts their relationship under considerable strain. It can be hard for them to hold on to warm and loving feelings as they make space for a third in their relationship. There is a sense of timelessness as the past, the present and the future are brought together in the minds of the pregnant couple (Reid, 2012). Where there is healthy development these tasks involve reorganisation of the pregnant woman's psychic equilibrium as she struggles with the emotional changes of pregnancy and begins to develop a relationship with her foetus. There needs to be an acknowledgement of her sexual partner, both in her inner and external world, and a working through of ambivalent feelings about childhood and her own mother, leading to a lessening of old conflicts. Although her partner is not pregnant, similar developments and changes should take place in his or her inner world. Just as the emotional significance of the woman's mother is important at this time, so, too, is the male parental figure in the father's life.

In my response to Dr Christopher Clulow's chapter I intend to focus on three areas: perinatal mental health, the breakdown of a marriage, and a child with special needs. I am writing from the perspective of a child and adolescent psychotherapist who has specialised in the area of perinatal mental health and as a couple psychoanalytic psychotherapist whose work is mainly with couples who are struggling with relationship difficulties exacerbated by pregnancy or the birth of their baby. Prior to moving into the field of psychoanalysis I practised as a speech and language therapist for a number of years, working primarily with children with language difficulties often associated with special needs, and this experience informs my thinking.

Perinatal mental health

Pregnancy and the postnatal period can be a time when the woman's mental health is most put at risk. From a psychiatric perspective Brockington (1998) acknowledged that pregnancy and child birth involved major changes for pregnant and postpartum women that included biological, social and emotional transitions.

Attention has been paid to postnatal depression, a conservative estimate of its incidence (excluding the 'blues' immediately after birth and post puerperal psychosis) being 10% (Gavin et al., 2005), although practitioners in the field would often see this as being closer to 20% or higher. Less attention has been paid to antenatal depression, but a longitudinal study in Avon identified antenatal depression in 13.5% of the sample's population between 18–32 weeks gestation (Evans et al., 2001). It is also important to note the multi-generational nature of postnatal depression (Halberstadt-Freud, 2013).

When working with pregnant women and couples, I always hold in mind the developmental tasks of pregnancy that involve both somatic and psychological changes as the three trimesters of pregnancy are negotiated (Caplan, 1959; Raphael-Leff, 1991). For some couples this emotional development does not take place, and the difficulties of the first trimester continue throughout pregnancy, often leading to antenatal and/or postnatal depression in either member of the couple, or difficulty in bonding with the foetus or live baby.

During the first trimester (spanning conception to an awareness of foetal movements), there are significant hormonal changes and these, together with the knowledge that a conception has taken place, can result in the woman feeling overwhelmed and emotionally vulnerable. This can put strain on the woman's partner as he or she attempts to support the pregnant woman and manage his or her own feelings about the nature of their changing world. During the second trimester (covering the period between awareness of foetal movements until the mother has a sense that the baby could be viable in the outside world), the couple should settle into the pregnancy and this can be a time when couples play with ideas about their role as parents and fantasise about the identity of their new baby. During the third trimester (marked by awareness that preparation needs to be made for the birth), there should be a developing sense of a readiness to be born, as the couple make psychological space in their minds and geographical space within the environment in which they live.

All couples hope for a well-managed delivery leading to a physically and emotionally healthy mother and baby. When there have been complex issues during pregnancy a successful delivery can bring a sense of reparation to the parental couple. Difficulties can often be put behind them. But when there is a traumatic delivery resulting in damage to the mother, infant or both, the emotional turmoil that results can have a devastating effect on all those involved. This can include not only family members and the new baby, but medical and midwifery teams as well. All those who work psycho-therapeutically with couples who have suffered a traumatic delivery know that the rawness of their experience is immediately apparent, as is evidenced in the case study of Dan and Caroline in Novakovic and Reid (2018).

The breakdown of a marriage

Clulow's chapter does not give information about this couple's individual histories or the details of their relationship. We do not know how they met, fell in love or decided to conceive a child. We know nothing of their cultural backgrounds or whether they had been a 'creative couple' (Morgan, 2005). We simply know that the birth of their first child was traumatic, leaving a damaged baby, and that their relationship eventually floundered leading to acrimonious court proceedings. The woman 'fell out of love' with her husband. My immediate response to their plight was a feeling of sadness that it was many years later, when the child was in latency, that the couple eventually sought a consultation to help with the difficulties in their relationship.

Many women complain that following the birth, all interest in the mother is lost and the baby's needs take precedence. When there has been a traumatic delivery, the woman and her partner need an opportunity to think about their experience with senior professionals. They need explanations. The way the post birth period is managed usually makes a considerable difference to the couple's experience at this traumatic time (Reid, 2011).

It is understandable that when there has been an obstetric catastrophe, feelings of blame and anger take centre stage, often leading to a couple projecting their anger outwards. They join together in an atmosphere of blame and rage, remaining in a 'paranoid schizoid' state of mind instead of moving into something more 'depressive' following the birth of their child (Klein 1946). When there is litigation against a hospital, couples often lose sight of the emotional needs of their relationship, and it is only when a settlement has been reached that the parlous state of their relationship is recognised. For Tom and Tessa litigation, and the anger it contained, was focused on the relationship between them over contact arrangements.

The tragedy here is that the importance of the couple's relationship appears not to have been acknowledged by the many professionals involved in the care of this damaged child. Clulow mentioned that the father felt blamed for leaving his partner and child, whereas it was his wife who fell out of love. The distress and acrimony in their relationship was observed by many and it is possible to imagine the sense of persecution that this stirred for both members of the couple. One sensitive couple who have a child with special needs commented recently 'Of course all couple relationships need to be nurtured, but there is something about the birth of a child with special needs that makes this nurturing even more important.'

Tavistock Relationships is keenly aware of the importance of the couple relationship, not only in terms of the role of the parental couple but in terms of sustaining a loving and intimate relationship between the couple following childbirth. In his chapter Clulow mentioned two of the many projects run by Tavistock Relationships. The first, an action research project offering preventative help to first-time parents through groups, gave couples an opportunity to be supported during the last trimester of pregnancy and the first six months of the baby's life. The second, a co-parenting intervention with a national mental health charity, addressed the needs of a vulnerable group of young parents who are often hard to reach. Such initiatives provide ways forward in preventing relationship breakdown after partners become parents.

A child with special needs

Primary maternal pre-occupation was the term Winnicott (1956/1958) used to describe the state of mind that emotionally healthy mothers enter during the latter part of the third trimester of pregnancy and the earliest weeks of their infant's life. When there is a loving couple relationship the father welcomes this and supports the mother–infant relationship at this time. It is perhaps important to note that for some fathers this can lead to feelings of exclusion from the mother–infant dyad. When there has been a traumatic delivery this can impact on the mother's ability to feel this sense of maternal pre-occupation. Both parents become aware that they are not bonding with their infant in the way they imagined and their level of anxiety can be heightened. When the baby is damaged, parents may lose confidence that they can care for their infant, and if the baby remains on the Neonatal Intensive Care Unit (NICU), parents may feel that their baby belongs to the medical profession and not to them. This can lead to further difficulties in attachment.

Following a traumatic delivery parents can feel shocked, frightened and angry. Their baby can feel equally traumatised. Clulow mentioned that this child developed language and behavioural problems. From a psychoanalytic perspective Bion (1962) described how the infant projects unwanted frightened feelings into the mother, who, if her state of mind is calm and receptive, will receive these projections, detoxify them and return them to her baby. When both mother and infant are traumatised this state of 'maternal reverie' can be impaired.

Maternal reverie may be seen as the first dialogue between mother and child, and where there is a break-down in this initial form of communication it would seem that this may play a part in subsequent language difficulties. Meltzer (2000) described how he thought that the child has to have internalised the parental couple speaking to one another in order for language to develop in a healthy way. When acrimony becomes the key issue in the couple relationship their communication is one of the first areas to be affected. I was left questioning what sort of experience the child described in this chapter had when his parent's relationship deteriorated and they then separated, and what impact their subsequent acrimonious legal battle over contact might have had.

Children with severe language difficulties will have both comprehension and expressive language problems. Developing language will have been a struggle, perhaps even a battle. When parents argue in front of these children it is hard for them to understand and therefore make sense of what is being said. They can be left feeling they are living in a fog of misunderstanding. It is possible to imagine that whatever neurological damage contributed to the language difficulties of the child described by Clulow, psychological states of mind would also have played a part. As Abse (2012) wrote

> Whilst it is now universally agreed that childhood experiences of parenting impact on psychological development, psychoanalytic methodology has

been interested in detailing these impacts through exploring, historically, the relational field *between* parent and child.

(Abse, 2012, p. 59)

Abse goes on to write, acknowledging the research outlined in Harold and Leve's 2012 paper that 'it is not only the parent's capacity to parent effectively in the midst of marital unhappiness that is the problem but the child's experience of witnessing this which impacts on development' (Abse, 2012, p. 59).

References

Abse, S. (2012). Commentary on Chapter Two. In: A. Balfour, M. Morgan & C. Vincent (Eds.), *How Couple Relationships Shape Our World* (pp. 57–70). London: Karnac.

Bion, W.R. (1962). *Learning from Experience*. London: Heinemann.

Brockington, I. (1998). Puerperal disorders. *Advances in Psychiatric Treatment, 4*: 312–19.

Caplan, G. (1959). *Concepts of Mental Health and Consultation*. Washington, DC: US Children's Bureau.

Evan's, J., Heron. J., Francomb, H., Oke, S., & Golding, J. (2001). Cohort study of depressed mood during pregnancy and after childbirth. *British Medical Journal, 323*: 257–60.

Gavin, N.I., Gaynes, B.N., Lohr, K.N., Meltzer-Brody, S., Gartlehner, G., & Swinson, T. (2005). Perinatal depression: a systematic review of prevalence and incidence. *Obstetrics and Gynaecology, 106*(5): 1071–83.

Harold, G.T., & Leve, L.D. (2012). Parents as partners: how the parental relationship affects children's psychological development. In: A. Balfour, M. Morgan & C. Vincent (Eds.), *How Couple Relationships Shape Our World* (pp. 25–55). London: Karnac.

Halberstadt-Freud, H.C. (2013). Emotional turmoil around birth. In: E. Quagliata (Ed.), *Becoming Parents and Overcoming Obstacles* (pp. 41–60). London: Karnac.

Klein, M. (1946). Notes on some schizoid mechanisms. *International Journal of Psychoanalysis, 27*: 99–110.

Meltzer, D. (2000). Personal communication.

Morgan, M. (2005). On being able to be a couple: the importance of a 'creative couple' in psychic life. In: F. Grier (Ed.), *Oedipus and the Couple* (pp. 9–30). London: Karnac.

Novakovic, A., & Reid, M. (2018). *Couple Stories: Application of Psychoanalytic Ideas in Thinking About Couple Interaction*. London: Karnac.

Raphael-Leff, J. (1991). *The Psychological Processes of Childbearing*. London: Chapman & Hall.

Reid, M. (2011). The impact of traumatic delivery on the mother–infant relationship. *The International Journal of Infant Observation, 14*(2): 117–28.

Reid, M. (2012). 'For now we see through a glass, darkly': the timelessness of emotional difficulties during the perinatal period. *The International Journal of Infant Observation, 15*(3): 263–79.

Winnicot, D.W. (1958). Primary maternal preoccupation. In: *Collected papers* (pp. 300–306). London: Tavistock. (Original work published 1956).

Chapter 3

Adopting together

Julie Humphries and Krisztina Glausius

This chapter introduces the theoretical underpinnings of the Adopting Together Service, and describes the clinical work and experiences gathered from this specialist service for adoptive couples. In this chapter we will start with a case study to illustrate a typical problem of a couple presenting for treatment. We will then briefly outline the ideas and clinical services we have designed and offered for adoptive couples, reflect on the particular complexities for the transition to parenthood for adoptive parents, consider some of the particular issues associated with embarking on parenthood in the context of loss, and, finally, explore how the difference between parents in how they deal with complexities such as loss can create conflict. The above strands of thought will be brought together through a selection of composite and anonymised clinical cases.

> Maria and Paolo came to the initial meeting at the Adopting Together Service in a state of angry resistance. They did not want to be there and were cross with their nine-year-old son's therapist for making the referral. It was Jack who was the problem and who needed urgent help – he was recently in trouble at school when he was found to be carrying a small but sharp knife, hidden under his uniform. The assessing clinician was immediately curious why his therapist colleague had thought that couple therapy was the treatment of choice for Jack's behaviour. He listened to the story unfold:
>
> Maria and Paolo adopted Jack six years ago. Things had been going well, so much so that Paolo began to think that they were ready to adopt another child. Maria was not so sure as she had just re-established her career. But, she reasoned with herself, she did not want Jack to grow up an only child, so put her misgivings aside and joined Paolo in applying to adopt. The couple were seen as successful adopters and were quickly accepted and another little boy, Martin, then 14 months, was rapidly placed with them with a view to adoption. Paolo volunteered to take a year of adoption leave as he was supportive of Maria's career and she was also earning considerably more than him.
>
> Unfortunately, soon after Martin's arrival Maria was made redundant and Paolo had to return to work as a teacher. Things were going rapidly downhill for the couple. Martin was a difficult and needy toddler with a much stormier

temperament than Jack. Maria, never deeply committed to enlarging the family, found herself stuck at home, depressed, struggling, and inwardly furious with Paolo. Paolo returned to work but felt he was failing on all fronts. He worked long hours but was nowhere near able to match their previous level of income. He felt guilty for suggesting the second adoption, guilty for how Maria struggled with their difficult toddler and guilty for how Martin didnot have the parents he deserved and needed after a traumatic start. Full of unspoken hurt and resentment Paolo and Maria withdrew from each other and soon were sleeping in separate bedrooms, exchanging only the most cursory communications.

Initially, in couple therapy, Maria and Paolo were resistant when links were made between their 'knife-edge situation' and Jack's acting out at school. They maintained that there was no conflict between them – how could there be, since they hardly spoke to each other. No raised voices, no shouting, no tears. But after a while they revealed that they often used Jack to convey messages between them – seemingly innocent or incongruous comments but with a sharp edge and unmistakably designed to convey and inflict hurt. These were communications carried back and forth by Jack, who instinctively understood that in the frozen standoff between his parents he himself became the messenger and thus the knife. A part of him was describing this painful and dangerous situation by carrying a disguised weapon on his person, even to school.

Maria and Paolo, supported by their therapist, gradually found a way to begin talking directly to each other, expressing their anger, their hurt and fear. As they became less anxious about hurting the other or getting hurt themselves, they began to feel less scared of exploring difficult feelings. Their need to rely on their older son for communicating these underlying and unbearable feelings diminished, and they felt better able to help both their children adjust to their new situation.

This couple's situation was similar to many of those parents who were seen at the Adopting Together Service at Tavistock Relationships. They were near breakdown and were in urgent need of support. Opening up these areas for exploration in couple therapy clearly signalled the therapist's capacity to hear and process the emerging material and created a reflective space for the couple where the full range of their thoughts and issues could be thought about.

The adopting together service

The connection between parental relationship quality and children's mental health has been documented in a report by the Early Intervention Foundation (Harold et al., 2016). Research clearly shows that conflict between partners which is frequent, intense and poorly resolved is very harmful to children's mental and physical health (Meier, 2016). Of course, one of the common factors that couples in this service shared was that they all had children, and all were engaged in some form of unresolved conflict. By working with and helping adoptive parents we are therefore, albeit in an indirect way, helping children too.

As unresolved conflict between parents affect the adopted child, so does the adopted child impact on the parental couple. A recent report for the University of Bristol indicated that the challenging behaviour and needs of the adopted child places such an enormous strain on the parental couple that it can leave many feeling powerless and that they need to make a stark choice between saving their relationship or keeping the adopted child in their home (Selwyn et al., 2014).

Adopting Together, a government funded service, was developed as a response to the need for parental support, and is a recognition that parents often require help, not just with the relationship with their adopted child but also with their couple relationship. The Adopting Together service offered time-limited therapeutic support to parents who have either adopted or had children placed with them with a view to adoption. Parents either self-referred or were referred to us by their social workers because they needed help to manage their couple relationship. We welcomed both heterosexual and same-sex couples, and indeed many gay and lesbian parents have taken up the offer of relationship support.

Becoming adoptive parents

The problem of disclosure

The initial encounters between social workers and potential adoptive parents can be enormously stressful. Many children waiting for adoption suffer from foetal alcohol/narcotic syndrome, violent aggression, attachment issues, sexualised behaviour, learning difficulties and other developmental challenges. Social workers, in their desire to place these children, might experience an inevitable tension in how much to reveal about the child to prospective adopters. As Tollemache (2006) points out, the social workers carry a heavy responsibility for the outcome of the adoption. In clinical sessions, couples have expressed to us that they can feel that the reality of the disturbance of the child was hidden from them. In some cases, they thought they had been deliberately misled fearing, presumably, that the child would be rejected by prospective parents if the 'truth' were known.

In addition to the children's difficulties being concealed by social workers, couples also, either consciously or unconsciously, hid relationship difficulties from their social workers. They, too, had been faced with the dilemma of how much to reveal about their relationship, particularly the more challenging and less happy aspects of it. In their desire to be accepted as good prospective adoptive parents there is inevitable pressure to present as a couple without problems or tensions, for fear that they might otherwise be rejected as unsuitable adopters. Potentially everyone involved in the adoption process is then in a situation where things might be hidden for fear of rejection.

In this context, it can be challenging to create a reflective space for adoptive couples where they can talk about anxieties, conflicts or other difficulties in their relationships. As Tollemache (2006) puts it: 'If something as challenging as building a family through adoption is to have any chance of success, families and those who work with them must be open to feelings that are often hidden and emerge in unexpected ways' (pp. 129–30). Not only are couples used to hiding or concealing some of the realities of their relationship, they also often mistrust institutions and professionals by whom they feel let down.

In addition, there are likely to be significant problems that the couple might be concealing from their own conscious awareness, and are likely to find challenging to explore. The defences put in place to 'protect' themselves from facing what are often sad and painful issues have to be carefully worked with. Very complex feelings emerge, and skilled interventions to help process these are required. Psychodynamic couple therapy, which is concerned with a deep exploration of the parental couple's individual and shared unconscious worlds, can be extremely helpful. The therapeutic setting contributes to the creation of a thoughtful, containing atmosphere where such concerns can safely emerge.

What the child stirs up in parents

As we have seen in Chapter 2, the transition to parenthood can be difficult for all couples, but for adoptive couples there might be particular challenges. Earlier, and often unresolved, difficulties the couple might have had with their own parents can readily resurface when couples go from being 'two to three'. For example, the adoptive father who had an absent father growing up can not only struggle to know how to be a father himself but also have to experience once again the painful feelings of rejection from his father that he might have long since 'buried'. Whilst a resurfacing of painful feelings is a common issue for many parents, it can be exacerbated when they are taking on children who bring their own particular complex sets of challenges. As Cregeen (2017) points out, adoptive couples need particular capacities over and above those of other parents. The adopted child enters into their new family from often disturbed and traumatised backgrounds, and in addition will often carry with them a sense of unconscious guilt for the poor parenting they received in their birth families. They then look to their adoptive parents to have the necessary 'capacity to receive and tolerate these projected negative aspects of themselves' (p. 160). Couples who have experienced difficult, and in some cases traumatic, personal histories can be particularly stirred up by the arrival of a child with an equally disturbed history:

> Gemma and Hassan came to the Adopting Together Service in despair. They had struggled together for the chance of creating a family; years of failed fertility treatments left them exhausted and hurt, but with a shared determination to succeed in becoming parents. They felt sure that their

relationship was strong and united; were both agreed on adoption and were overjoyed when Susie became their daughter. They had adopted her two years previously, when she was one. Although Susie was thriving, the couple was on the verge of splitting up. Hassan was deeply distressed, alternating between angry outbursts and long periods of depression when he withdrew from the family. Both parents felt the dream of the longed-for family unit was beginning to crumble.

The couple explained that Susie and Gemma had made an immediate bond and Hassan had felt terribly left out. He had become resentful and isolated, suffering not only the loss of his idea of becoming an involved father but also the previous closeness he had enjoyed with his partner. Both Hassan and Gemma had planned to be hands-on parents, taking an equal share of caring for Susie. While knowing Susie's history and being intellectually prepared for her initial difficulties in adjusting to and bonding with them as a parental couple, nothing had prepared them for the emotionally devastating fall-out of living with a child only used to relating to one parent. Susie made a beeline for Gemma and often protested when Hassan tried to look after her.

As the therapeutic work with the couple unfolded, it became clear how the lopsided configuration of their small family unit stirred up deeply painful memories for both parents from their own history. Hassan explained that he was the fourth son of his parents and the youngest of a string of boys. As he grew, it seemed that his parents had accepted that they would not have the little girl they – and Hassan's mother in particular – had always longed for. However, when Hassan was seven and the apple of his parents' eyes, a surprise late pregnancy resulted in a little sister. Hassan lost his special place as the baby of the family and became 'one of the boys'. He felt that his sister was spoiled, cherished and 'could do no wrong'. When he saw Gemma and Susie together, it often felt like an unbearable repetition of his own childhood situation where he had been ousted from his special place. Before adopting Susie, he was 'the one'. Now he was, at best, 'mother's little helper again', a role with which he was familiar and which he hated.

Hassan and Gemma made a number of emotional discoveries together in their therapy, which enabled Hassan to say that sometimes he resented his daughter for stealing Gemma and was jealous of her. He was also able to acknowledge that a secret part of him would have preferred to have a son rather than a daughter. He admitted that at times he was responsible for excluding himself from the family; experiencing Susie as being spoilt by Gemma. Hassan felt ashamed about these feelings, but Gemma listened with warmth and was relieved. She explained that she was certain Hassan withdrew because he no longer found her attractive. She realised that in her state of suppressed fury, and fearing abandonment by Hassan, she had drawn Susie closer to herself. She became the expert mother, a gatekeeper, subtly undermining Hassan's attempts at bonding with their daughter. She now became aware of how her own childhood experiences were also playing a part in how she was behaving. She spoke about being the only child of divorced parents who had engaged in a long-running, bitter custody battle over her, and how her mother had filled her head with the dangers of contact with her father.

As both parents were able to talk and listen to each other, and to parts of their lives that had been unexpectedly stirred up by adopting Susie, they gradually re-established their closeness and trust in each other. They became more united in dealing with Susie's continuing attempts to split them apart and this, in turn, gradually gave Susie a secure foundation of a parental couple where parents were no longer at war with each other.

Children as containers

Working with parental couples whose children present with a complex set of symptoms has been an historically important part of Tavistock Relationship's theoretical and clinical tradition. Mainprice (1974) published an important paper outlining links between children's psychological or physical symptomatology and the particular disturbance in the adult couple relationship of their parents. She pointed in particular to difficulties that might occur in children whose parents were not able to sufficiently work through significant earlier traumas affecting either or both partner or the couple's relationship prior to the arrival of children:

> It seems that in cases where the marriage relationship has not been able to create for the individuals the necessary container or climate for a backwards-and-forwards bridging and integrating process between healthy regression to the sensitive area and regrowth, the problem remains unconscious and intractable between them. When this occurs, it is often a child of the marriage who becomes ill in such a manner that his symptom points up his parents' emotional problem. He appears to be at the same time the scapegoat for, and the betrayer of, his parents' unacknowledged disorder. This is not to say that he may not be disturbed or ill in his own right.
>
> (Mainprice, 1974, p. 14)

Her thoughts clearly signpost the terrain for therapeutic intervention of adoptive couples, that is the unconscious anxieties of the parental couple and the defences they employ to ward off such anxieties. Children are sometimes adopted by parents who unconsciously collude to keep their couple relationship safe from troubling internal conflicts or differences, and this can result in such difficulties being projected outside. Although the relationship might be protected in this way and experienced as good and solid, the object of such projections can became a preoccupation and focus of the parental couple's anxieties.

Reasons for adoption are complex; consciously the couple desire to give a child a home, but unconsciously there also might be a desire to keep the relationship safe, and for any conflict or difficult feelings to be projected out.

Risks arise when the adoptive child 'becomes the container of "badness" so that the marriage can remain "good"'.

Becoming parents in the context of loss

The vast majority of couples come to adoption wounded either by repeated miscarriages or by the diagnosis of infertility, scarred by several failed cycles of assisted conception. For these couples the transition to parenthood takes place in a climate of complex losses. Exploring the couples' preceding losses is widely understood by professionals to be an indispensable part of the assessment process for adoption. Nevertheless, it is our experience that many parents feel that they have not been fully able to understand or process what has happened to them.

The reasons for this are manifold. Adoptive parents do not usually have either the wish or opportunity to open up about one of the most painful areas of their lives. When they declare their desire to become parents but need professional help to achieve this aspiration, they open one of their most private areas of their shared and individual lives to public scrutiny. For the scrutineers it might feel cruel or unkind to encourage couples to revisit past areas of pain and loss. This, coupled with the parents' own internal efforts to pull themselves together, can create a powerful set of unspoken prohibitive factors that encourage parents and those working with them to avoid discussing the context of loss in which their application to adopt is being made. Consequently, parents can feel isolated with their feelings of loss, which can continue to affect their relationship and family life and impede the mourning process.

In the case of adoption the couple might often need to mourn their much hoped for biological child. Sometimes this may be children who have been conceived but lost during pregnancy, in other cases the conceived child might only have existed in fantasy. As Freud (1917) noted: 'Mourning is regularly the reaction to the loss of a loved person, or to the loss of some abstraction' (p. 242).

In her study of the impact on couples of not being able to conceive their own child, (Cudmore, 2005) draws attention to the particular complexities of mourning an intangible loss: the baby that may never have been conceived. She refers to 'the loss of an imagined, fantasized baby and a fantasized image of becoming a parent, fantasies which have been loaded with projections, often of an idealised nature' (p. 8). Where adoptive parents have not fully been able to mourn the loss of a child of their own biological creation there may be particular difficulties in taking in an adopted child as that involves replacing the fantasised but unmourned biological child. Cudmore reminds us that mourning is not linear, and can often be complicated by feelings of anger, shame and envy attached to earlier losses.

In order for mourning to take place, couples have to be able to face the reality of what they have lost. Without mourning the ability to create their own biological child the couple is likely to struggle to make room for an adopted child. The couple needs to be able to 'accept this child not the fantasised birth child' (Creegen, 2017, p. 170). Closing the gap between the couple's expectations of adoption and the reality – one of the most significant psychological tasks for adoptive parents – is likely to be more difficult if the work of mourning is incomplete.

Loss in the couple is by no means limited to the concrete biological loss of pregnancy or infertility. We have seen a number of cases where parents chose adoption without attempting to create biological children between them. Adoption in these cases was a first and deliberate choice, rather than a last resort, and may reflect the state of their relationship For example, a number of couples using the adoption service spoke about an on-going loss of sexual or emotional intimacy. Parents might hope that through adoption, they can solve some of these dilemmas, only to find that other, more hidden issues in the couple relationship emerge. Lack of intimacy makes achieving pregnancy difficult, and becoming parents brings no relief from the emotional distance in the couple. Issues that troubled the couple before the adoption are bound to resurface when parenthood not only fails to cover up some of the unhappiness but also introduces different stresses.

When difference causes conflict

It is not just the re-surfacing of problems that is difficult, but this can be further compounded by the couple dealing with it in very different ways. It can end up, as in the cases demonstrated below, causing distressing conflict within the couple. Such conflict was often reminiscent of situations observed by Grier (2011) when working with narcissistically relating couples who cannot know about the reality of the differences between them. In the therapy, as well as in their relationship, the presence of a different mind can feel very threatening. In the Adopting Together Service we have seen many couples where the partners seemed to differ drastically in the way they managed their painful history of infertility and loss.

> Patrick and Nadia adopted after a number of miscarriages. In an early session Nadia was distressed and tearful, recalling in painful detail each traumatic loss. Patrick was trying his best to hold steady and console Nadia, and insisted that now that their dream of becoming parents had finally come true there was no more reason to be tearful. Nadia was enraged each time Patrick put forward these thoughts as she felt that Patrick did not understand her pain nor was interested in really finding out what it was like to be her. At the same time she was so overwhelmed by her own experience that she had very little space really to be curious about Patrick's own thoughts and feelings. Both partners ended up feeling alone and cut off from each other and instinctively understood that this atmosphere was unsettling to their adopted daughter. This was what had brought them to couple therapy.
>
> This couple initially appeared very split and appeared to show a 'psychological division of labour' whereby Nadia experienced the emotional pain of the couple's predicament whilst Patrick, not being able to bear these feelings, projected a lot of his into Nadia. He was more in touch with their resilience,

and provided the necessary resources they both needed to help them get through the hurdles of the adoption process. This unconscious arrangement between them functioned sufficiently well until the arrival of their adopted child, but broke down when their transition to parenthood called for more resources and new ways of bearing the strain their challenging daughter brought into the relationship. In other words, the couple dynamics functioned to hold the couple together through the adoption process but subsequently were in danger of collapsing.

When, in the course of their therapy, the couple found some shared space to think, Patrick was able to explain his own internal dilemma. He was trying his utmost to remain positive as he was worried that if he were to show his distress about the loss of several pregnancies, Nadia might feel blamed. He kept up a stoic façade because he was terrified that by showing his pain he would only add to Nadia's distress. To Patrick's surprise Nadia was able to hear about her partner's pain and felt much less alone with her own struggles when she realised how much of her feelings of loss were shared between them. Over the course of the therapy the partners were encouraged to explore the real and imagined losses that were inherent in their choice to adopt. As the couple showed a growing capacity to be able to reflect together about their losses, they also emerged as a much more robust adoptive parental couple who showed a good capacity to allow space for their adopted child's losses to be thought about.

Sally and Bianca had different feelings about the biological impossibility of creating children between them. We, as therapists, often start our thinking with such seemingly divided couples wondering about their own personal and relationship histories. As with Sally and Bianca, it is frequently discovered that what attracted them to each other in the first place – their difference – is linked to what is causing them difficulties now.

Sally and Bianca had both been keen to adopt following a series of unsuccessful IVF attempts. Sally, although supportive of Bianca and the idea of starting a family, had never wanted to try for biological children and was keen to adopt. They were thoughtful, well-prepared and delighted when a group of three young siblings were placed with them. The children had had a challenging start in life, particularly the oldest, who, at seven, had spent the majority of his life with his neglectfully abusive birth family and had considerable needs. The partners agreed that they would share childcare, and both of them arranged to work part-time to cover the week between them.

Soon after the arrival of the children, Sally became withdrawn and began to suffer from debilitating migraines. She had been trying to talk to Bianca about her growing dread that they had made a terrible mistake, and that she was not able to manage the three siblings. However, this had been extremely difficult, as Bianca seemed to be thriving, and insisted that she was enjoying motherhood tremendously. Bianca became resentful about Sally's growing misery and withdrawal. Things came to a crunch point when somebody reported Sally screaming at the baby and striking the oldest child when out at the playground. The adoption order was put on hold and the placement threatened to break down. At that point Bianca had to take over full time childcare and it was decided that Sally's contact with the children should be supervised. The couple were then referred to the Adopting Together Service.

In therapy, the couple explained that they feared that if the adoption was to proceed it would lead either to a breakdown in Sally or her exclusion from the couple and family. Alternatively, if the adoption did break down, Sally would be consumed by guilt, feeling solely responsible for the disaster. This would leave Bianca, who had made a warm and loving attachment to the children, utterly devastated.

Working with Sally and Bianca we discovered that Bianca was always attracted to Sally's capacity to be in touch with her feelings, including those that were painful, confusing or troubling. This felt so different from the family in which Bianca grew up, where no one raised their voice and losses were swept under the carpet. Bianca might have hoped that in her relationship with Sally she could get in touch with these feelings. At the same time Sally had hoped that Bianca could bring some much longed for order into her life after a chaotic childhood where her 'hippy' parents failed to create a safe and containing environment.

As it turned out, both Sally and Bianca secretly longed for a different experience when they dreamed of creating their own family. Sally was hoping for a safe, orderly experience but the chaotic needs of their new children stirred up terrible unconscious memories of her own childhood, memories and experiences she hoped to have left behind. Whilst Bianca embraced the 'free-flowing mess' that the children brought with them, Sally's withdrawal panicked her as it brought up memories of her own withdrawn but controlling parents. She did not want her own children to experience such parenting, and this was why she began to take over more and more of the childcare, leaving Sally out.

During the therapy, Sally and Bianca were interested to notice that they both held hopes and fears about their situation in fairly equal measure. The initial split began to recede and the couple rediscovered their capacity to hear each other out and to provide support in areas of their emotional fragility.

As an integral part of working with couples and parents it is usual for a therapist's sense of where the problem lies to move around, taking in different points of view whilst simultaneously holding the couple's relationship in mind (Morgan, 2001). As Abse (2013a, 2013b) points out, these different points of view, which present themselves to us over and over again, are only manageable because of the fundamental stance that we take when working with co-parents. This stance is based on an underlying assumption that problems are generally shared and that the distress and disturbance of one almost certainly pertains to the other as well. This important position allows us to ask questions and assimilate information so that we can synthesise our experiences into an understanding of the shared aspects of the difficulties. We can then encounter not two separate partners, where one is for and the other is against the adoption, but instead a couple who are carrying a lot of shared ambivalence, as in the case of Bianca and Sally.

Pre-existing conflicts around intimacy

As pointed out earlier, we saw a surprising number of couples who reported no sexual connection or any form of physical or emotional closeness between them. This was sometimes linked to apparently organic, psychosomatic or psychosexual conditions, such as debilitating skin conditions, rheumatic joint or muscular pain, erectile dysfunction or pain on, or fear of, intercourse. These difficulties sometimes appeared following the adoption but more often had been present from the onset of the couple relationship, suggesting that we were working with long standing, deep seated and ingrained difficulties and anxieties.

When a couple is not able to be physically and emotionally close and intimate, it is likely that the partners struggle with knowing about or achieving what Morgan (2014) has termed as a creative couple state of mind: In a creative couple, the relationship itself is continually being created by the couple's intercourse of every kind, at every level, as the different, or sometimes opposing, perspective of the other can be taken in to one's psyche and allowed to reside there where it mates with one's own experience to create something new... 'It is the outcome of the couple's intercourse that becomes a symbolic third' (p. 117). In an adoptive couple who struggle with intimacy this might be linked to a couple's repeated failure to conceive, carry a pregnancy or indeed create a live healthy baby between them. We saw a number of couples who managed to achieve pregnancy but not a healthy baby, or whose babies or children died, severely challenging their confidence in their intercourse having a creative outcome.

As we have demonstrated, this difficulty in coupling can be linked with the partners' struggles to know about and bear their differences. It can also be linked to their struggle to know about the possibility or even desirability of psychic intercourse, and to tolerate the feelings that have been generated by this struggle. What can result is a rather airtight defensive psychic organisation where difficulties are projected outside of the couple into children, as pointed out earlier in the chapter. The children, of course, arrive with their own difficult and complex histories, which gives them a propensity to identify with such projections, carry them, and, in turn, project violently into their adoptive parents, putting the fragile couple under further strain, as the case of Fred and Anna illustrates:

> Fred and Anna, a professional, thoughtful and attractive couple in their late 40s have been together for over 20 years. They had, nine years prior to the start of their therapy, adopted twin boys, who were five years old at the time.

The assessing therapist was immediately struck by both partners' exhaustion. She was unsure if Fred and Anna could even manage to climb the stairs to the consulting room, so burdened by bags and various cups of hot and cold beverages they appeared to be. What they communicated through their physical appearance was very much in contrast to the description of their marriage, which suggested the highest possible level of relationship satisfaction. When they began to talk about their teenage sons they showed a markedly different picture. The children were described as extremely unwell, suffering from a wide range of emotional and physical difficulties and giving tremendous concern to both parents.

As a consequence the couple was deeply depressed. During the early stages the therapy was similarly depressed, seemingly devoid of life and movement. The only lively interruption was the frequent intrusion into the room by the boys. Both parents kept their mobile phones on and their children invariably texted and called with various emergencies that needed immediate attention and made it impossible for the couple to think about their relationship. When Fred and Anna did speak it was often about their sons, whom they experienced as monstrously destructive; both parents were clearly terrified of their teenagers.

Initially the couple dismissed anything offered by the therapist that suggested the presence of a different mind. They said that they felt attacked, misunderstood, and even judged by various interpretations that aimed to bring a fresh perspective to the situation. However, eventually and gradually their therapist was able to create a more containing therapeutic frame by bringing a strikingly different thought: that mobile phones can be switched off for the duration of the therapy and that it will be helpful for the boys to know that there are brief periods of time when their parents are not immediately accessible to them as they are attending to each other. Once the therapist found a voice to clearly speak up for the therapy, things began to change and the couple began to explore their differences.

Improving outcomes for adoptive parents

At Tavistock Relationships the therapeutic help we offer to adoptive parents supports not just the parental couple but fundamentally contributes to the stability of the adoptive family, preventing adoption breakdown and ultimately – and most importantly – supporting children's well-being and development. In this chapter we have discussed a therapeutic intervention that supports the adoptive parental couple in mourning their previous losses and bearing the challenging realities of adoption. We have argued that couple therapy can create a containing environment for the couple's often unprocessed feelings around intimacy, conflict, difference and trauma. We believe that this better equips them to take in and contain the complex feelings of their adopted children.

These assertions are supported by evidence. Data collected from parents at the end of their twenty couple therapy sessions indicated improvement on a number of indices as compared with when they commenced therapy. For example, of the parents displaying clinical levels of distress prior to the start of therapy 42.9% were no longer 'clinical cases' when the therapy ended. Of those displaying clinical levels of depression, 40% were no longer depressed when the therapy ended. Partners reported statistically significant improvement with regard to the quality of their relationship with one another after attending the programme, and, importantly, there was significant improvement with regard to their perception of their children's adjustment as well. This builds on the evidence discussed earlier, that improvement in the parental relationship has a positive impact on the child's health and well-being. This improvement was largely accounted for by a reduction in emotional problems, which is likely to have occurred because parents had a better capacity to contain the emotional distress of their children after their therapy as compared with before.

Ultimately, however, the therapy helped partners to understand each other better. Many adoptive couples who came to us for help reported a lack of deeper connection between them, and exploring their relationship often uncovered a history of pre-existing difficulties. Helping these couples to think more freely about the losses inherent in their difficulty in achieving intimate connection often proved helpful and brought considerable relief. As one couple wrote:

> our therapist somehow enabled us both to fully communicate where we felt let down by the other, and yet managed to ensure we both felt safe; ... it enabled us to listen to each other and actually hear the other person's views instead of always shouting. It helped us to think more about working as a team rather than pulling each other apart.

Scant resources often result in prioritising support for parenting adopted children. While vital and beneficial, this overlooks the enormous strain that adoption puts on the parental couple's relationship. As we hope to have demonstrated in this chapter investing in supporting the couple relationships of adoptive parents can pay huge dividends. It can lead not only to better couple relationships but also contribute to preventing the breakdown of adoption, thereby significantly increasing the life chances of the children joining these families.

References

Abse, S. (2013a). When a problem shared is a problem ... Whose illness is it anyway? Questions of technique when working with a borderline couple. *Couple and Family Psychoanalysis*, *3*(2): 163–77.

Abse, S. (2013b). Further thoughts on when a problem shared is a problem ... Whose illness is it anyway? *Couple and Family Psychoanalysis*, *3*(2): 178–87.

Cregeen, S. (2017). A place within the heart: finding a home with parental objects. *Journal of Child Psychotherapy*, *43*(2): 159–74.

Cudmore, L. (2005). Becoming parents in the context of loss. *Sexual and Relationship Therapy*, *20*(3): 299–308.

Freud, S. (1917). Mourning and melancholia. *S. E.*, *14*: 237–258. London: Hogarth.

Grier, F. (2011). Psychotic and depressive processes in couple functioning. *Fort da*, *XVII* (1): Spring 2011.

Harold, G.H., Acquah, D., Sellers, R., & Chowdry, H. (2016). *What Works to Enhance Inter-parental Relationships and Improve Outcomes for Children*. London: Early Intervention Foundation.

Mainprice, J. (1974). *Marital Interaction and Some Illnesses in Children*. London: Institute of Marital Studies.

Morgan, M. (2001). First contacts – the therapist's 'couple state of mind' as a factor in the containment of couples seen for consultation. In: F. Grier (Ed.), *Brief Encounters With Couples – Some Analytic Perspectives*. London: Karnac.

Morgan, M. (2014) Why can being a creative couple be so difficult to achieve? The impact of early anxieties on relating. In: D.E. Scharff & J. Savege Scharff (Eds.), *Psychoanalytic Couple Therapy: Foundations of Theory and Practice*. London: Karnac, pp. 116–22.

Meier, R. (2016). *What works in relationship support – an evidence review*. London: Tavistock.

Selwyn, J., Wijedasa, D. N., & Meakings, S. J. (2014). *Beyond the Adoption Order: Challenges, Interventions and Disruptions*. London: Department for Education.

Tollemache, L. (2006). Minding the gap: reconciling the gaps between expectation and reality in work with adoptive families. In: J. Kendrick, C. Lindsey & L. Tollemache (Eds.), *Creating New Families: Therapeutic Approaches to Fostering, Adoption, and Kinship Care*. London: Karnac.

Commentary on Chapter 3

John Simmonds

Humphries and Glausius have outlined a crucial set of issues for the adoption sector resulting from the Adopting Together Service. What is difficult to reconcile is the contribution of and challenge to the couple relationship in adoption, as discussed in their chapter, with what feels like a broader silence about couples when it comes to the operation of and discussion within the adoption sector itself. The focus of the sector has largely been a combination of:

- the number of children with adoption as their permanence plan (subject to a considerable fall over recent years);
- the recruitment of sufficient numbers of adopters with the 'right' qualities to place those children with and;
- the 'matching' of children with adopters, particularly for 'hard to place' groups such as older children, children in sibling groups, children with complex health needs or disabilities, and children from minority ethnic backgrounds.

There has also been a surge in the recognition of the challenges that adopted children bring with them resulting from early experience of abuse and neglect. The view that adoption was in itself the solution, and that the 'ordinariness' of family life was sufficient to facilitate a child's development – a view strongly associated with relinquished infants – is outdated and does not reflect the reality of adoption today. But many of the new developments have focused explicitly on the child and the developmental challenges they face in recovering from adverse early experiences. The adoptive parents are expected to facilitate that recovery through appropriate and sensitive parenting, but there can be a view that they remain neutral as they rise to the challenge. Even where the idea of 'therapeutic parenting' has entered the vocabulary of adoption, the focus can be on developing more effective skills and knowledge. That may indeed be appropriate and helpful, and there is evidence to support this, but the material explored in this chapter opens up a whole new perspective on the dynamics of the relational world and particularly that of the couple. Although I am familiar with the issues identified in the case studies, I was shocked by the intensity, depth and consequences of what was identified for these couples through their therapeutic engagement with the service.

The couple relationship is largely defined as a private, intimate and almost secret arrangement. The detail is for the couple alone, although there are continuous public and community debates what this might mean, what is 'normal' or what is satisfying. Sex is one significant part of this, but this extends through to daily routine, common interests, purpose, beliefs and values, and the part they play in the couple relationship. For anybody considering adoption, one of the critical issues is opening up this private and intimate space to the inspection by the State through the actions of an adoption agency charged with the responsibility to determine 'suitability to adopt'. And what determines this suitability? In law there are three exclusion criteria –you must be over 21, have not been convicted of a defined set of serious offences and be habitually resident in the UK. But if you are not excluded, then the range of factors that might be considered as relevant are far ranging – your motivation to adopt, your understanding of adoption as it is today, your child centeredness, the stability, security and resources that enable this, your physical and mental health, your life history that has led to you becoming the person you are today, your hopes and wishes for the future. While there may be facts and evidence to support any of this, these issues are probably best thought of as a range of qualities that together mark out your suitability. Relationships will play a part in this, and your relationship as a couple[1] a significant part of this. But what does that mean?

Again, Humphries and Glausius identify that this is a hugely significant question. Arriving at the decision to apply to adopt is likely to indicate a powerful and painful journey where the 'normality' and 'simplicity' of bringing a baby into the world has failed.[2] In some respects, this might indicate something of a powerful failure in the couple relationship, although that is likely to originate in fertility issues on one or both sides, the medical investigations into this and possibly (failed) IVF interventions. The sense of personal failure, the potential for blame and recriminations and the sense of loss and grief for both individuals and between the couple are powerful. How this becomes expressed, the degree to which emotions are expressed and talked about and the way that this helps and heals or creates anger and blame in the immediate and over the longer term is very important. But how does any of this become something that can be safely and fully explored, with a sense of confidence, robustness and openness, when the over-arching objective for the applicants is to establish their suitability to adopt? Being open is a risk for the applicants, and the last thing that they need to introduce are further levels of risk into their lives by discussing any of this with their assessing social worker when they are trying to emerge from their experience of the multiple risks associated with infertility. The long-term consequences of this can be seen in the chapter, with levels of defensiveness and anxiety in the adoptive couple centring on the question 'What have we as a couple got to do with this?'

These are challenging issues. How do you create a context and process within which irreconcilable objectives are reconciled? How do you as prospective adopters explore, reflect on and enable a process where you present, and are required to present, the best of yourself or yourselves when what has happened to you as an individual or a couple seems to be the worst of who you are? Adoption should be centred on the best of care seeking and care giving – sensitive, responsive, reflective and insightful. That is certainly the case when it comes to parenting children placed for adoption, and to some degree that has been helped through the attention paid to the concept of attachment. But Humphries and Glausius' chapter highlights the challenge in enabling both the process and the dynamic of care seeking and care giving that can impact on the couple, between the assessing social worker and the applicant(s), and finally between the couple and the therapist. When the going gets tough, the common human response of blame, avoidance, threat and defensiveness are quite the opposite of what anybody needs. Care seeking at its best means reaching out to somebody you trust, who listens, responds appropriately and is warm and empathetic in that response. But the drivers in many human encounters seem to create quite the opposite dynamic: reaching out, but then feeling ignored, blamed, misunderstood and rejected. Creating a therapeutic space within which 'reaching out' enables a sense of being cared for or cared about is at the heart of the chapter. Enabling the couple to reach out has to be the first objective when so much of the couple's experience from the past has created a belief or anticipation that this is a highly risky thing to do.

There is a second strong and core issue identified in the chapter, and that is the primary focus in many referrals appearing to centre on the adopted child or children: their behaviour is reported by the adoptive parents to have become difficult if not impossible to manage, there has been an escalation in the issues, and what may have worked in the past no longer seems to work in the present. This has then pushed the family into a crisis. These issues have become increasingly familiar in the adoption sector with high levels of concern being commonly expressed – child to parent violence emerging as one common but previously unnamed experience. Humphries and Glausius identify the importance and challenge of connecting the couple in their relationship with each other and the couple in their relationship with the child(ren). The dynamic interplay from the dyadic relationship to the triadic relationship, and particularly who is at risk of becoming or has become excluded, is powerfully identified in the case examples. The other question identified in the chapter linked to this is the typical set of issues that have come to explain the range of challenges adopted children might face in their development. They are multi-factorial and include genetic and epigenetic factors, poor ante-natal care – including exposure to toxic substances, and then post birth abuse and neglect, including the significant uncertainty of what is going to happen to the child in the longer term. Predicting any of this with certainty is not possible, and while that is true for any parent with any child, the high degree of uncertainty about development for adopted children is a significant part of the process. But there are also key issues that inform this as they do for born to children: learning to trust, reaching out to parents, anticipating and expecting a responsiveness to need – physical and emotional. Care seeking with an expectation of care giving is a primary driver, although the child has no control over the responsiveness of others and will make adjustments in their own expectations depending on that responsiveness or lack of it. These are the dynamics of relationship making and the basis upon which children engage with, respond to and make sense of the relational and wider world around them. But, as discussed earlier, the care seeking and care giving dynamic can become infected by distrust, the heightened anticipation of threat, and the fear of blame or withdrawal into a safer space. This is the challenge for adoptive parents – re-working the child's experiences and expectations of the relational world where care seeking and care giving create a safe sense of connection that enables, reassures and promotes the child's sense of who they are, what they are connected to and what they might anticipate.

Humphries and Glausius identify the challenge for the couple in this re-building task in both its dyadic and triadic versions. The intensity and complexity of the challenge is all too apparent – for couples, children and therapists. What comes first, whose needs are the priority and how to articulate this throughout the therapeutic process to enable a more positive, responsive and sensitive way of thinking and feeling, are key. The couple needs to be able to move towards a dynamic where partners feel they are being listened to, understood, and supported, with the therapist acting as intermediary. The parents and child also need to be able to move toward a dynamic where the child feels that, above all, the parents are on their side as caregivers – as much as the child might distrust, doubt or have anxieties about this. And the triadic dynamics of this part of the process must be able to address the fear that when two come together this is not with the intention of excluding the third.

The chapter is a major challenge to the adoption sector in its current ways of thinking and practising. While the relational world has become embedded in the concept of attachment – and attachment is a much-used concept in adoption – the dynamics of relationships is a sadly missed part of this. The Adopting Together Service provides a significant opportunity to directly re-introduce some of this into ways of thinking, planning and delivering services. It could not be more important.

Notes

1 Single people can apply to adopt and should be treated no differently to those in couple relationships.
2 Same sex couples are also entitled to apply to adopt and they should be treated no differently to others. The issues raised here will typically not be the same as those discussed in relation to heterosexual couples. For some other applicants, altruism may play a more significant part than infertility.

Chapter 4

Working with couples in groups

Lucy Draper

What happens when couples meet other couples in everyday life – at family events, school parents' evenings, on holiday with groups of friends or in hospital waiting rooms? One couple might look at another and see two people who share a sense of humour, are tender or supportive with each other, enjoy their children together, or seem to appreciate the other's physical qualities. This may make the observing couple suddenly aware of the lack of these qualities in their own relationship. Or they might see two people who cannot bear to be near each other, who look bored, seem irritated, or undermine the others' parenting. The original couple might draw closer together, thankful that though they have their differences, they are not *that* bad.

Or a woman, watching another pair, might notice that the man seems to interrupt jokily every time the woman speaks, and thinks to herself, 'I'd never put up with that in my relationship' while her partner is thinking, 'I really like the way they seem to be able to banter with each other and no-one gets upset.' Almost all of us have probably also witnessed serious, sometimes violent confrontations between partners in public, possibly with a toddler in a pushchair watching intently, or an older child urgently tugging at their parent's arm.

What happens above all is that everyone is noticing the *relationship* between the pairs and reflecting on their own.

This chapter describes the work we have been doing at Tavistock Relationships with parental couples in groups, and is concerned with the specific benefits and challenges of the group setting. The thought of working in a group is what potential participants find most frightening and shame-provoking in anticipation. By the end of the groups at Tavistock Relationships it is what they cite consistently as having been the biggest source of support and learning.

Over the last five years, more than three hundred parental couples (and some separated co-parents) have participated in a group programme known as Parents as Partners. We have run a large number of general groups, drawing their members from any co-parenting pair with a child under the age of 11, but have also developed some specialist interventions – for separated co-parents, for adoptive couples, for same sex parental couples and for parents of children with autism. This chapter will explore the differences between the heterogeneous and homogeneous groups, with case examples from a general group and from a group attended by six gay and lesbian parental couples.

To illustrate this, I have followed the journey of one couple through a Parents as Partners group programme and will refer to them throughout the chapter.

> Siobhan and Graziella are a lesbian couple, who have been together for seven years, and have one child, a son, Luka, now eighteen months old. The couple enjoyed a mostly very happy relationship before the baby was born. It was Graziella's first relationship with a woman, and she had fallen 'madly in love'. They had many shared interests, and Siobhan, older and with much more experience of the lesbian community, had enjoyed introducing Graziella to her world. Though the decision to have a child was a shared one, since Luka's birth, Siobhan had felt increasingly that she was losing Graziella, who was busy and preoccupied with their son. Siobhan worked long hours, and when she came home, she felt awkward with Luka, who often rebuffed her attempts to play with him, choosing instead to be with Graziella. Siobhan felt she had lost her lover. She really missed the salsa classes they used to go to together and the friends they saw there. She also feared she was failing as a mother.
>
> Graziella meanwhile was juggling work and motherhood, and feeling exhausted and unsupported. She had imagined a close family in which she and Siobhan would enjoy their child together, instead Siobhan seemed barely present, and when she was, she was irritable and sometimes angry with Luka, making Graziella feel protective of him, which Siobhan saw and resented. Graziella continued to have difficult phone calls with her mother back home who found it hard to accept her daughter's sexuality and was worried about her grandson.

Parents as partners: an evidence-based parenting programme for couples and co-parents

Having children is probably the single biggest challenge to the resilience of a couple, rewarding though it may also be, and the Parents as Partners programme acknowledges this. The programme's design was intended deliberately to address some of the gaps in existing parenting group programmes, which traditionally promote positive parenting practices and parent–child relationships, but often are attended by mothers and pay little attention to fathers, the couple or co-parenting relationships.

Harold and Leve (2012) argue that the most 'substantial dividends' can be gained by targeting investment at the level of the inter-parental relationship because of the centrality of this relationship in the family system, and the potential for wide-reaching short- and long-term benefits for parents and children. There is now a large body of international research, gathered over several decades, to support this connection between the quality of the couple relationship and other aspects of family functioning (see for example Casey et al., 2017; Cummings & Schatz, 2012, Grych et al., 2000, Zemp et al., 2016).

While the persuasiveness of the research is beginning to convince policy makers, children already knew this from lived experience: in a large survey conducted by the Children's Society, 70% of children said that parents getting on well is one of the most important factors in their happiness.

The Parents as Partners programme offered at Tavistock Relationships is based on the work of Professors Phil and Carolyn Cowan and Marsha and Kyle Pruett (in the US it is known as Supporting Father Involvement). This intervention has been shown over many decades to bring positive change for couples and for their children (Cowan et al., 2009). As an intervention, it lies somewhere between psycho-education and group psychotherapy, with an assessment phase for each couple, sixteen two-hour group sessions, and additional support outside the group from a family case worker. Each group is co-facilitated by clinically trained male and female group workers.

It is a manualised programme, and has a carefully constructed curriculum, which introduces ideas and invites discussion and reflection across five domains of family life – individual, couple, parenting, three-generational and the wider world. The different domains have their origins in research evidence about risk and protective factors, which are known to have an impact on outcomes for children, both positive and negative. Each of the sixteen sessions focuses on one of these domains, and they are then recapitulated several times over the sixteen weeks, allowing couples to reflect on each aspect of the programme, try out new ideas and conversations, and develop their understanding of themselves, each other and their children.

The first domain concerns each individual adult's unique life story, their social and cultural origins and their psychological strengths and vulnerabilities, including their personal history of attachment and loss, and where that has brought them to now, in the world, and in relationships with their partners and their children.

The next domain engages them as parents and as co-parents in thinking about their individual and shared ideas about bringing up children (in relation to discipline, for example), and the reality of how they share the co-parenting tasks. There is a particular emphasis on the importance of fathers– or second parents – in children's lives, and a consideration of how mothers might hinder or support fathers' involvement.

The third domain concerns the couple relationship, with attention paid to the difficulties between each pair. Some ideas are offered about developing more constructive ways of communicating. The fourth domain importantly invites participants to consider the impact of previous generations in the family, from whom couples have inherited powerful ideas – for better or worse – of how to have relationships and bring up children. Finally, we consider the wider community, including the world of work, and the support and stressors there.

Linked to the five domains are exercises for participants in small groups and pairs. There are also brief presentations from the two group facilitators on the impact of stress on the couple or the effects of different parenting styles, often illustrated with film clips. The scripted exercises are not didactic, but rather serve as prompts for discussion, both between partners and with the whole group. For two of the sixteen sessions, the partners divide into two sub-groups according to gender, and the content is linked to the theme of increasing father involvement with their children and the impact of that for the mothers and children. (With same sex couples, how they divide at this point is decided by the group, in one of many conversations about how same sex parents do and do not fit in with hetero normative constructs of parenting.)

The domain-linked structure provides a framework for the programme, but in fact much of each group is always given to open-ended discussion, as couples bring important material from their lives and respond to each other's contributions. This makes for a rich, sometimes unruly environment. Considerable skill is required of the group facilitators, as they hold in mind each individual, each couple and the group as a whole, and make decisions almost second-by-second about which themes are the most helpful to pick up and develop.

Sometimes couples will bring what feel like urgent dilemmas to the sessions, in relation to an argument they have had, or a crisis with one of their children, and there can be a strong push felt by everyone in the group for it to be attended to right then, right there. If this seems potentially helpful to the group as a whole – and links to the topic of the session – then the facilitators might indeed pick it up. The group leaders may, for example, re-wind the argument, encouraging some perspective taking, looking for the feelings underpinning any defensive blaming and accusation. Other group members are encouraged to comment and reflect on what it might mean for them too. At other times – particularly with rambling, repetitive contributions, or long anecdotes that seem to block fresh insight – the facilitators' role may be to intervene in order to keep the group on task. The decision, to stay in the moment or to move on, is a common source of difference between the two group leaders, mirroring a common difference for couples, sometimes characterised as a preference for reflection versus action. This is valuable material for the group leaders to reflect on in supervision, but, in the present, in the group, how they negotiate and resolve these frequent clinical decision-making moments will certainly be registered by group members.

An important element in the safety of the group experience for vulnerable couples is provided by the group leaders, whose thoughtful presence enables it to operate as a container or social and emotional 'skin' in Bick's terms (1968). The use of a group leading pair means that the group are also 'subliminally offered the internalization of a couple relationship that is confronting, fair and containing in a flexible way that echoes what may have been left to be desired in the families in which group members have grown up' (Morgan-Jones, 2016, p. 176).

To give the reader a picture of how the manualised exercises are brought to life in practice, I shall describe an exercise introduced in an early session, known as

'Confide, Avoid, Attack'. This is a way of looking at couple disagreements; it contains the simple but helpful idea that when two people disagree, each person may do one of three things – s/he may attack, turning her partner into an enemy, s/he may avoid, turning her partner into a stranger, or s/he may confide, making her partner an ally. Within a pair, very often one is attacking as the other avoids and vice versa.

The group leaders illustrate this idea by standing up and throwing a bean bag to each other in silence. The bean bag represents the message being communicated. For a while, it passes gently and smoothly between the two and is caught easily. Then it goes suddenly way over the other's head and falls to the ground. Bean bag retrieved, the easy to-and-fro resumes. But the second time it is thrown a little out of reach, and returned with some force. One of the two facilitators gives up and stops trying to throw or catch at all ...

Visual symbols seem sometimes to enable a greater richness of discussion than simple words. The group joins in with associations to their own style of communication. They suggest what either thrower or catcher might be feeling, and how they might respond. Later in the session, they bring examples of arguments they have had as couples, then coach the group leaders who enact these using the bean bag, while other group members make suggestions of what they might do or say differently, trying to 'confide' i.e. to name their feelings. Some group members may say nothing at all, but watch and listen intently.

Two things are understood here. There is the message about 'confiding' as a better way to have a disagreement than avoiding or attacking. The group leader pair are also offering themselves as a couple who can demonstrate good and bad communication, have an argument and recover from it, and who can think about what just happened. What's more, they look like they are enjoying it and each other.

Couples in groups

Working on this project, we have been struck time and again by the value of the group setting. The presence of ten or twelve others often has a containing effect. Facilitators were initially worried that the group topics could be too emotionally stirring or enraging for couples in difficulty. However, on the whole, participating couples have tended to experience the group as a safe place to talk about their differences and are markedly more contained than when they are alone. The group setting has a normalising effect that brings a release of stress; participants often express relief that 'others have the same troubles as we do'. There are also more challenging moments of recognition, where someone sees a difficult aspect of themselves or their relationship in another group member, or pair, and this can enable both insight and change. So one group member might look at another and think 'maybe that's what I sound like when I'm criticizing my partner' or 'I hadn't realized that's what we look like when we're arguing'. This is a common idea in group analytic psychotherapy. Zinkin (1983) wrote about both benign and 'malignant' mirroring in groups; what is interesting to us here is the way that both individuals and couple *relationships* can be subject to mirroring in a group context.

Assessment and group composition

In assembling the group we look for potential commonalities and helpful differences, both in individual characteristics (race, class, sexuality, age), and in presenting relationship difficulties (disagreeing about the children, lack of intimacy, struggles with in-laws, managing mental or physical illness).

We are also trying to determine whether this would be a helpful intervention for each particular couple. We are looking to see whether they are both interested in the possibility of change. Can they tolerate being in a room together and talking about their relationship? Are they willing to commit to attend, so that neither feels coerced by their partner to come (though it will not be unusual for one to be more actively interested and the other to express ambivalence).

> Siobhan read about Parents as Partners on social media and made cautious inquiries. She was particularly interested in the possibility of a group specifically for same sex parents, but in an initial phone conversation discovered that they might have to wait several months longer for this, whereas a mixed group was due to begin soon.
>
> The group leaders, John and Mary, were in the last stages of assessing couples for a general group when they met with Siobhan and Graziella. They were immediately presented with a dilemma: should this couple wait for the same sex group to begin? They could picture the couples already assessed for the general group and wondered how Siobhan and Graziella would fit in, and whether they would be welcomed by the other group members. In the assessment, Siobhan spoke tearfully about having 'lost' her lover to motherhood, and John found himself thinking that this was something she might have in common with many new fathers. As if she had read his mind, Siobhan said quite sharply 'I don't want anyone to go thinking of me as the "man" in this relationship – I can't bear that stuff'.
>
> Graziella was curious about the other couples in the group. Mary responded with a thought about the potential value of difference in a group and how the most surprising and diverse people had come to make connections with each other in past groups. Siobhan said sadly that she was not very interested in difference – that what she missed was having a community of people who understood her.
>
> The couple were encouraged to go away and think together about how they would like to proceed. John and Mary then discussed their assessment in supervision. They felt that a connection had been made in this first meeting and that Siobhan and Graziella had felt understood. John and Mary mentioned that they had both expressed curiosity about the couple's baby and

how he had been conceived prior to the assessment, but that this had not come up. The supervisor thought that might directly relate to the choice the couple were making about which group to join. Our experience has been that for same sex couples 'how we got our baby' is usually a very early topic of shared conversation. With a same sex couple working in a mixed group, it is almost certainly a question in the minds of many group members, but will probably remain unvoiced. John and Mary, heterosexual group leaders, had wondered but not liked to ask, leaving the onus on Siobhan and Graziella to assess whether this was safe territory to share. This then led to a helpful supervision discussion about how group leaders needed to enable thinking about different group members' life experiences more widely, especially when they do not share those specific life experiences with other group members.

Group psychotherapy, as Dalal (1998, p. 177) says – and he might as easily have been talking about couple relationships – 'has the possibility of freeing one from being stuck in one discourse, one experience of self and world, and opens up the possibility of connecting with other discourses, other ways of being and experiencing that one did not have previous access to'. Yet opening up to a range of other perspectives – and the internal change that entails – can also be a challenge. A couple interviewed recently for their first assessment said anxiously: 'the others won't all be clever will they?'

Yalom (1995) argued for heterogeneity in groups (of psychological difficulties, as well as of race, gender etc.), but also thought it important that there should be 'at least two of everyone', while S.H. Foulkes, pioneer of group analysis, stipulated that when assembling a group, nobody should be isolated in any particular respect (Foulkes, 1975). In Parents as Partners we have not managed always to avoid this, but have aimed for the group not to be an isolating experience for anyone. Intentionally, our group leaders are diverse in background and life experience and this increases the collective knowledge of the team. On a very simple level, it gives an early opportunity for a wider range of group members to identify with, and increases the hope that they might be understood. The man-woman facilitator pairing is a powerful symbol of the possibility of cross-gender compatibility, while a culturally similar or culturally different pairing will both represent different kinds of possible understanding. From experience we have learnt that where there has been one person, or couple, who are clearly very different to the others, there is a much greater likelihood that they will drop out in the early weeks.

> Siobhan and Graziella described to their case worker the discussion they had about which group they would like to join. Graziella had been keen on the one starting sooner; she felt desperate that they were quite close to splitting up and that their relationship might not last long enough to wait for the other one. Privately, she also thought that Siobhan needed quite urgently to be 'told' how to be less harsh in her parenting. As a foreigner in

London, she was also interested in the possibility of meeting other parents. Siobhan, like Graziella, knew that things were pretty bad between them, but had felt it would be supportive for both of them to meet other lesbian parents. On balance, though, she agreed they should give the mixed group a try.

The 'Tuesday group'

Graziella and Siobhan were the final couple to agree to join John and Mary's group, which met on a Tuesday early evening in a children's centre in West London. A crèche was available for all the children who needed it, though some parents made other arrangements for babysitters.

On an early evening in spring, the six couples (Siobhan and Graziella, Katryn and Adrian, James and Shelley, Ade and Grace, Tye and Jamilla, Sophie and Lek) arrived for the first group meeting. John and Mary had conducted all the pre-group assessments, but this was the first time the couples had seen each other. The chairs were in a circle; all chose to sit next to their partners; Katryn and Adrian, the only separated co-parents in the group, moved their chairs a little distance away, and did not look at each other. The group confessed to feeling apprehensive.

The group members mostly lived locally and their ages ranged from 24 (Jamilla) to 46 (Siobhan and Adrian). They were from a wide range of cultural backgrounds and, interestingly, all but one pair – Ade and Grace – had cultural differences between the partners. One of the themes (and possible connections) that had emerged at the assessment stage had been that four of the women (including Siobhan) had been diagnosed with depression, and with each of them there was a sense that their partners were presenting them as the problem to be fixed. Three of the men, however, had scored very highly on their intake CORE questionnaire, a measure of psychological distress, but none had either asked for, or received, any help with their emotional difficulties.

> In this group, all the couples had children under five and, in the first session, some of the children found it hard to settle in the crèche and could be heard crying. Immediately, there was an opportunity to think about which parent responds first to their child's voice and whether they have the same view as each other on whether they should be responded to immediately. A semi-joking conversation, initiated by Tye, ensued about the question of whether men's biology means that they cannot distinguish their own child's cry from another's. The conversation ended slightly awkwardly as the group noticed Siobhan withdrawing slightly and Graziella meeting her eye.
>
> As part of this first session, the group leaders invite the participants to think about the different priorities in their lives and how much each aspect preoccupies them (parent, wage earner, friend, partner, lover, football player etc.).
>
> In this group, several of the women expressed a wish that their partners were more available to share household tasks. Sophie said that she did not care so

much about the tasks, her husband Lek was a good father, but she missed him as a partner and was dismayed that he had not even thought to mention her as one of his priorities. Siobhan looked interested in this, but said nothing. Suddenly it seemed that everyone was complaining about their partners, good-humouredly, but with some edge. The group leaders registered this, but spoke fairly simply at this first session of the possibility for change that was perhaps being expressed across the group.

On the whole, John and Mary were pleased with this start the group had made. There were two couples they wanted to give further thought to – Katryn and Adrian, the separated co-parents, and Siobhan and Graziella. They felt there was some risk they could lose either pair.

They decided to begin the next session with a summary of some of the dilemmas which couples had brought to the group; 'it sounds like for all of you, things have really changed since you've had children, and that often that's brought up differences in perspective on how you want to live your lives, to be parents, to be a couple.' They referred to differences both within the couples and between group members, and referenced themselves as a black-white co-facilitating pair.

Encouraged by this, Jamilla made a link with Graziella as to their common South American background, and was helpfully curious about her sexuality in the context of her family. This warmth of connection was received as an invitation to Siobhan and Graziella to join in and they said a little about what it had been like for them as lesbian parents deciding to join the group. Other group members appeared to be listening, but did not respond directly.

Adrian, however, one of the pair of separated co-parents, did not attend the group session. His ex-partner Katryn said she did not know where he was, that it was typical of his non-communication that he not only did not come, but had not let her know. She used some of the group time to tell a series of critical anecdotes about his behaviour. At one level, she was trying to link with the previous week's more light-hearted discussion of partner 'uselessness'. However, something of the venom in her tone led to others choosing not to respond to her – perhaps seeing something of themselves in her and not liking it – and she was left more isolated. (She was subsequently absent at the following session, which Adrian attended, using the time to be similarly critical of her.) They continued to attend rather erratically until the midway review session where Adrian said he felt the group was not very relevant to them as separated parents. Threatened, the group tried to rally them. Sophie said she thought it was brilliant what they were trying to do, to work together as parents, even though separated, and that her parents had never spoken to each other again from the day her father left. In spite of this offering, Adrian did decide to leave, and Katryn could not helpfully continue without him, so the group was reduced to five couples.

In supervision, John and Mary, wondered if Katryn and Adrian would have done better in a group specifically for separated co-parents, where the focus was more on managing respectful co-parenting communication. The evident growing intimacy between the other couples over the weeks of the group had been too painful a reminder for them of what they had lost.

The remaining group settled and now attended regularly.

> A collective theme emerged around early parental bereavement, and this linked with important discussions about keeping family traditions alive. While Graziella, connecting very emotionally with these ideas, threw herself into the life of the group, Siobhan continued to keep herself at some distance from the closest interactions. Their relationship appeared to become more strained. Siobhan described their son's bedtime routine, where she sat downstairs, feeling more and more upset, while Graziella put Luka to bed and stayed with him for so long that she fell asleep. They had often argued about this, but only in terms of how long the 'right' amount of time was for a parent to stay with a child at bedtime. John and Mary commented that something seemed to be happening for them in the group that mirrored their relationship at home, where Siobhan, feeling excluded from intimacy shared between Graziella and others withdrew, and ended up even more hurt and angry. With the support of other group members, many of whom shared similar dilemmas, Siobhan was able to share how much she envied Luka's closeness with Graziella, which Siobhan missed and also grieved for, never having experienced it herself as a child. Other group members offered them recognition and sympathy, and also shared some simple observations about the different ways they each managed their children's bedtimes.
>
> At the following session, Jamilla and Tye fortuitously told them of a gay colleague of theirs who attended a social drop-in for same sex parents, and passed on the details. Siobhan started to go to this weekly with their little boy, and something in this seemed to free her up to participate more fully in the group. She became very interested in the group discussions. She said she was having much more fun with their son and wanted to be at home more. On top of this, she reported that the family, as a three-some, was having some enjoyable times together. There was still much for them to resolve, but overall they felt the group had been a helpful experience.

The same sex group

Some months later, Tavistock Relationships was finally able to offer a specific group for same sex couples, the group that Siobhan and Graziella might have waited for, but did not. This turned out to be an exciting and challenging group from the start. Diverse in gender, age, class and ethnicity, the group seemed relieved and excited in their commonality as gay and lesbian parents. Humorous and active from the outset, some of the couples appeared determinedly upbeat and defensively positive, defiantly united in a common understanding of how the world doubted their ability to be adequate parental couples. It was hard at first for them to acknowledge any struggle at all as there was such a risk of their being misunderstood. This posed special challenges for the group facilitators, who had to follow the lead of the group sensitively, allowing for couples to be in difficulty, but not wanting to push for it and seem to reinforce their 'pathologising' world view. In a parallel process of how these parents experienced life, 'becoming a gay or lesbian parent attracts especial hostility and anxiety both inside and outside the psychoanalytic community' (O'Connor & Ryan, 1993, p. 254), the group leaders felt within a hairs-breadth of being attacked for getting it wrong all the time.

Specific themes for same sex parents were very alive in the first few weeks of the group, and anecdotes were shared about coming out, talking to teachers and developing a new language for describing their families. Linked to the 'coming out' process, unarticulated fears about loss, rejection and separation, which felt in some cases barely survivable, were present. One couple told a story of the difference between them over whether or not to tell their son's schoolteachers that they were a gay couple. One father, who acted as the main carer, felt it was too risky, that their child could be punished because of staff homophobic attitudes, while his partner felt that not coming out meant that he was rendered completely invisible as the other parent. It was a painful dilemma, deeply understood by other group members.

Another couple, Sharin and Angelina, from different religious backgrounds, had been hurtfully cut off from one partner's family after the birth of their baby. Every day, Angelina (the non-birth mother) would speak to her mother on the phone, but would ask her partner and child to go to another room so they could not be heard, as her mother found the sound of them too unbearable.

What was striking about this group was the way in which the couple dilemmas felt both universal and very specific. One difficult theme was around the splits between biological and non-biological parent. O'Connor and Ryan suggest that 'the intensity of envy towards the one who gives birth can be especially great (for lesbians), since this is a capacity that both partners may feel they have'. This was palpable among the women in the room, and yet there were many instances where feelings were voiced which could have been spoken by any heterosexual couple. For instance, one woman described feeling shut out of the closeness between her partner and the baby 'I came home from work and they were asleep together on our bed – *my* bed – and he was hanging off her breast. I felt alone and heartbroken, that had been *my* breast'. Specifically gay themes, such as the need for asserting the value of same sex parenting, seemed to be much stronger in the early weeks, but the group leaders felt that by the seventh or eighth session 'it could have been any Parents as Partners group'. The group appeared more at ease in owning their relationship difficulties, and the discussions became much more like those of a generic couples group.

Compared to all other Parents as Partners groups, there was very little discussion of the parenting role being seen as a source of stress or difficulty and the children of the group, all attending the crèche, were strikingly bright, lively and co-operative, a source of curiosity for the group facilitators. 'The isolated couple' of the group appeared to be left out not by virtue of gender, class or race, but were different in the way they had got their child, who was adopted. As neither of them was the birth parent, they were saved that split within their relationship. Their particular experience of raising an adopted daughter, however, was not shared by anyone else, nor were the very real challenges they were facing in co-parenting a troubled and oppositional child. This was not much spoken about, but they were noticeably quieter than other group members, and brought less of the stress in their relationship.

Interestingly, in a different group offered for parents of adopted children, the group members bonded around a shared experience of raising traumatised children, and endless struggles to get the additional help which they felt their children deserved. This group contained two gay couples, who did not talk about their sexuality at all, but were thoroughly engaged in the adoption discussions.

Conclusions

Where groups have been formed of couples with clear characteristics in common, it has enabled an initial bonding and some important shared understandings, but we are now beginning to be able to see the commonalities as well as the differences between the many different couples groups we have run. At the heart of all the work is the story of each couple's unique relationship and the way in which they start to talk to each other differently within a supportive group context.

Couples are often reluctant at first to commit to a group. For 'different' couples, whose specific circumstances mean that they live in a society that at best fails to understand and, at worst, stigmatises and pathologises them or their children, these worries can be significantly ameliorated by being offered the opportunity to meet with others who share similar life experiences. Wherever we have offered specialist groups – to separated parents, same sex parents, adoptive couples, parents of children with disabilities – for some participants, there has been a palpable and understandable relief in the first meetings.

But *all* relationships are about negotiating both similarity and difference; people may look for partners with whom they seem to share everything in common, and discover that after all they are very different, or they seek out somebody who is refreshingly and excitingly different, and after a while find them disappointingly familiar. So too with groups, which for some can be daunting at first, and for others found to be more challenging as they go on and differences emerge. Couples joining groups may fear the shame of exposing their most private selves in front of others, and they may also struggle with having to share the time and attention of the group as a couple. These are two essential aspects of the group setting; showing vulnerability to others on the one hand and having to share the 'emotional space' – on the other. This is a fundamental struggle in all human relationships which can be worked with *in vivo* as it emerges within the group. As our research into this work with couples and groups demonstrates (Casey et al., 2017), wherever there is fear, anxiety and challenge, there is also learning to be had and gains to be made – leading to positive outcomes not only for the adult couples involved, but for their children as well.

References

Bick, E. (1968). The experience of the skin in early object relations. *International Journal of Psychoanalysis*, *49*: 484–86.

Casey, P., Cowan, P.A., Cowan, C.P., Draper, L., Mwamba, N., & Hewison, D. (2017). Parents as Partners: a UK Trial of a US couples-based parenting intervention for at-risk low-income families. *Family Process*, doi:10.1111/famp.12289

Cowan, P.A., Cowan, C.P., Pruett, M.K., Pruett, K., & Wong, J.J. (2009). Promoting fathers engagement with children: preventive interventions for low-income families. *Journal of Marriage and Family*, *71*(3): 663–79.

Cummings, E., & Schatz, J. N. (2012). Family onflict, emotional security, and child development: translating research findings into a prevention program for Community Families. *Clinical Child and Family Psychology Review*, *15*: 14–27. doi:10.1007/s10567-012-0112-0

Dalal, F. (1998). *Taking the Group Seriously*. London: Jessica Kingsley, p. 177.

Foulkes, S.H. (1975). *Group Analytic Psychotherapy Methods and Principles*. London: Karnac.

Grych, J. H., Fincham, F. D., Jouriles, E. N., & McDonald, R. (2000). Interparental conflict and child adjustment: testing the mediational role of appraisals in the cognitive-contextual framework. *Child Development*, *71*(6): 1648–61.

Harold, G.T., & Leve, L. (2012). Parents and partners: how the parental relationship affects children's psychological development. In: A. Balfour, M. Morgan & C. Vincent (Eds.), *How Couple Relationships Shape Our World: Clinical Practice, Research and Policy Perspectives*. London: Karnac.

Morgan-Jones, R. (2016). Belonging to a body larger than one's own: the pair in the group, the organization, and society. In: A. Novakovic (Ed.), *Couple Dynamics* (pp. 165–92). London: Karnac.

O'Connor, N., & Ryan, J. (1993). *Wild Desires and Mistaken Identities*. London: Virago.

Yalom, I. (1995). *The Theory and Practice of Group Psychotherapy*. New York: Basic Books.

Zemp, M., Milek, A., Cummings, E. M., Cina, A., & Bodenmann, G. (2016). How couple- and parenting-focused programs affect child behavioral problems: a randomized controlled trial. *Journal of Child and Family Studies*, *25*(3): 798–810.

Zinkin, L. (1983). Malignant mirroring. *Group Analysis*, *16*(2): 113–26.

Commentary on Chapter 4

Philip A. Cowan and Carolyn Pape Cowan

Lucy Draper's description of the Parents as Partners (PasP) group intervention provides a vivid, dynamic picture of what can happen when couples meet together weekly in a semi-structured programme over 16 weeks. As two of the four co-creators of this programme first trialled in California in the 1970s and joined by colleagues Marsha Kline Pruett and Kyle Pruett in 2002, we hope to provide a little historical and developmental context of this intervention.

Considerations surrounding the birth

Parents as Partners had its origins in our own lives as we made the transition from being partners to becoming parents (Cowan & Cowan, 2000). Sometime after emigrating from Canada to the US in 1963 with one toddler and a second baby about to be born (and a third two years later) to take up Phil Cowan's post in the Psychology Department at the University of California, Berkeley, we began to experience what we now know are fairly typical strains of young couples raising young children. Our stressful experiences were exacerbated by the spike in divorce rates and the chaos of the 1960s surrounding shifting definitions and family politics of what it meant to be a couple juggling family, work and our own personal needs.

After some time to get our bearings in managing our personal challenges, we began to search for what could be helpful to young families to lessen the strain that so many were clearly experiencing. What was available for families who had not found their way into the mental health system were parenting classes offered in most US communities. In our view, there were three problems with these classes. First, they were focused on parenting as if that was the key family problem. Second, the vast majority appealed to mothers, which gave the message that fathers were unimportant in children's development, an idea now sharply contradicted by hundreds of studies over the last 30 years (Lamb & Lewis, 2013). Third, parenting classes focused only on the relationship between parent and child, ignoring the family systems dictum that the relationship *between* the parents is a driving force in creating the environment in which children are raised, whether the parents are married, cohabiting, separated or divorced (Pruett & Johnston, 2004). Of course, there were couples therapy approaches for couples in enough pain to seek help but none focused specifically on the couple as co-parents.

Our choice of couples groups as an intervention modality was influenced by several factors. The 1960s saw an increase in the general trends for individuals to move far from their families of origin, leaving them without the support of family or friends going through similar life changes. We were also hearing from couples who attended 'prepared childbirth' groups about the reassurance of preparing for labour and delivery along with other expectant couples, but once their babies were born, the groups ended and they were on their own for the next 18 years! The transition to parenthood seemed an ideal time to bring couples together in small groups to share the inevitable challenges for partners becoming parents.

A research-based determination of programme content

We spent a year planning what to include in a couples group intervention. Guided by a review of the literature available at the time and conversations with a group of new parents, we created a curriculum focused on five domains that function as risk or protective factors affecting individual family members and the quality of their key relationships:

1. The transmission of positive and negative patterns across the generations.
2. The hopes, expectations, anxieties and mental health of each parent.
3. Couple communication challenges and healthy problem-solving strategies.
4. Parent–child relationships and the effects of different parenting styles.
5. Life stresses and social supports outside the nuclear family.

Research available in the 1970s and continuing to the present day suggests that without any intervention, negative patterns from our families of origin tend to be repeated in the next generation. This often produces discrepant expectations or mental health problems in the parents that can lead to unresolved overt conflict or silent withdrawn tendencies as a couple, which, in turn, can lead to harsh, permissive or neglectful parenting. Many studies since the 1970s have shown that without intervention, marital satisfaction declines for couples over time (Twenge et al., 2003) and results of other studies reveal clearly that this decline has negative implications for children's development and well-being (Zemp et al., 2016). These negative cycles can be exacerbated by stressful conditions outside the immediate family (neighbourhood, work-related, financial) if they are not buffered by supports from friends, services or institutions.

The evidence base

From the beginning, we insisted that the design of a new intervention programme be accompanied by systematic evaluation. Two early incarnations of

Parents as Partners convinced us that we were on the right track. Our Becoming a Family Project groups (Cowan & Cowan, 2000) were able to help first-time parents maintain their satisfaction with their relationship as a couple over a period of six years from pregnancy to their first child's completion of kindergarten, whereas comparable couples randomly assigned to a no-treatment control condition reported declines in satisfaction with their relationship over the same period of time. In the Schoolchildren and their Families Project, we followed 100 new families from their first child's transition to elementary school through their transition to high school (Cowan et al., 2005) and again found positive benefits of the early couples group intervention from prekindergarten to ten years later. An added feature of this study was that some couples were randomly assigned to groups in which the leaders emphasised couple relationship issues in the open-ended discussion at the beginning of each week's meeting, while leaders of other couples groups focused more on parenting issues. Otherwise the group curricula were identical. Both variations provided benefits – enhanced parenting quality and positive child outcomes – but only the groups that focused on couples' issues helped the parents buck the typical declines and maintain relationship satisfaction over time.

The Supporting Father Involvement intervention (SFI), was developed in collaboration with Marsha Kline Pruett and Kyle Pruett. The direct forerunner of Parents as Partners, this version of the intervention, targeted to primarily low-income families, has completed five published clinical trials of interventions like those described by Draper in her chapter. The first SFI study in the US, a Randomised Control Trial (RCT) with 289 Mexican American and European American low-income families in four California counties, compared a 16-session fathers-only group with a 16-session couples group and a one-session, three-hour couples group that served as a low-dose information control condition (Cowan et al., 2009). Fathers and mothers in the control group showed no positive and some negative changes. In the 16-week fathers-only groups, fathers' involvement in care of the children increased, but both fathers and mothers declined in marital satisfaction over the 18-month study. Parents from the 16-week couples groups showed reductions in parenting stress and, as in our earlier trials, no decline in marital satisfaction.

The next SFI study (Cowan et al., 2014) included 234 new Mexican American, European American, and African American families enrolled in couples groups in five California counties using the same curriculum. A pre-post assessment found statistically significant declines in parents' reports of violent problem-solving, parenting stress, and children's aggressive behaviours, and increases in father involvement and household income. As in the first SFI trial of the couples groups, mothers' and fathers' satisfaction as a couple remained stable.

A third study of the SFI intervention with 106 couples in four sites in Alberta, Canada (Kline Pruett et al., 2016) also used a pre-post quasi-experimental design and enlisted primarily Caucasian couples in middle- and working-class families. Twelve months after entering the Canadian study, SFI-Alberta participants changed significantly and positively on nine of 11 measures used in prior US SFI studies, including fathers' involvement in care of the children, parenting stress and the quality of the co-parenting and parent–child relationships.

A fourth study, with 239 low-income participants in California, recruited community couples as above and couples who had been referred by the Child Welfare System in California (Pruett et al., in press). Some couples were enrolled in groups right away, while others were placed on a waitlist and offered a chance to participate in groups six months later. The immediate intervention produced a significant reduction in couple conflict which, in turn, was related to reductions in harsh parenting and in both aggressive behaviours and depressed symptoms in the children 18 months after parents entered the study. Positive outcomes for Child Welfare-referred couples were not different from the outcomes for community couples.

These four studies provided the evidence base for the UK Parents as Partners programme. The first research evaluation of the UK programme (Casey et al., 2017) found very similar positive results for low-income, often troubled parents from varied ethnic backgrounds. A pre-post design to evaluate changes in the first 100 participating couples – many referred for recognised relationship and/or adjustment problems in the parents or children – revealed statistically significant reductions in the parents' reports of anxiety and depression, parenting stress, violent problem-solving, and children's acting out, shy and depressed behaviours.

We have been asked frequently what changes were required as the project moved from the US to the UK. Our quick answer has been 'the spelling of colour, neighbour, and programme!' Our more serious, reflective answer from regular consultation with the British staff is 'very little'. Except for participants' accents, the challenging issues, hopes, and dreams discussed by parents in the UK sound almost identical to those discussed in both farming and suburban communities in California and Alberta, Canada.

In brief, then, as background to Parents as Partners, we have shown that our model of a couples group intervention that focuses on exploring five aspects of family life weekly over a four-month period has consistent, positive effects on fathers' involvement with their children, couple relationship quality, parenting and co-parenting quality, and children's behaviour and well-being.

Starting up and bringing the intervention to scale

Published accounts of interventions usually sound as if they emerged fully functioning from the start, ready to receive the first participants and enter their information as data. In this case, the Parents as Partners intervention that Draper has described was preceded by almost 40 years of gradual, systematic trials in the US and Canada, testing several variations of the programme. Nor did PasP begin immediately after the initial four-day training in London in 2012. The dedicated staff of group leaders hired by Tavistock Relationships, along with case managers hired by Family Action, a social service agency serving UK families for more than a century, were ready to begin immediately, but it took months of devoted work – first to establish collaborative relationships between Tavistock Relationships and Family Action staff, and second, to establish referral sources in each borough.

An ongoing issue in the adaptation of SFI to the UK has not been the curriculum or the general format, but finding common ground between our theoretical approaches as guidelines for group leaders' intervention strategies. From the perspective of couples work in the US, our SFI approach could be described as at a mid-point between open-ended psychodynamic and attachment approaches and more didactic, behavioural psychoeducation. From the UK Tavistock perspective, our strategies were viewed as more behavioural, less psychodynamic. Where these perspectives converged was in the power of the group in which learning could proceed at multiple levels. Group leaders worked with individuals to examine intrapsychic conflicts, with the couple to improve their communication and problem-solving strategies, and at the group level to provide a safe haven in which individuals and couples could learn from others facing similar dilemmas and discover that they are not the only ones struggling. In the process of developing Parents as Partners, we now have a greater appreciation of what can happen when we allow space for couples to explore a strongly held idea or feeling, and the PasP leaders say that they have a greater appreciation of what can happen when they encourage parents to go beyond understanding the roots of their current predicaments to actually try out new strategies to create more satisfying and productive relationships – with one another and with their children and parents.

Another issue in dissemination of this intervention approach, as it moves away from its original creators, is a new teams' ambition to adapt the intervention for new target populations as Tavistock Relationships has done – offering a similar curriculum in groups for couples who are gay, separated, divorced, or adoptive parents, or for parents of children with specific disorders. Our view is that each of these adaptations represents an exciting opportunity to help vulnerable families, although they cannot claim that they are 'evidence-based' programmes until the evaluation work has been done.

Conclusions

While most fatherhood programs have involved men in groups led by male staff, Parents as Partners/Supporting Father Involvement shows that including both partners in an intervention designed to include fathers has positive benefits for men's involvement with the mothers of their children, for parenting their children, and for the fathers themselves. As we look with pleasure at Parents as Partners, we see that our 'baby' has come a long way to its current early adult stage – both conceptually and geographically. We look forward with anticipation to the next paths Parents as Partners will take as it finds its way to maturity.

References

Casey, P., Cowan, P.A., Cowan, C.P., Draper, L., Mwamba, N., & Hewison, D. (2017). Parents as partners: a U.K. trial of a U.S. couples-based parenting intervention for at-risk low-income families. *Family Process*, 56(3): 589–606.

Cowan, C.P., & Cowan, P.A. (2000). *When Partners Become Parents: The Big Life Change for Couples*. Mahwah, NJ: Lawrence Erlbaum.

Cowan, P.A., Cowan, C.P., Ablow, J.C., Johnson, V.K., & Measelle, J.R. (2005). *The Family Context of Parenting in Children's Adaptation to Elementary School. Monographs in Parenting Series*. Mahwah, NJ: Lawrence Erlbaum Associates.

Cowan, P.A., Cowan, C.P., Pruett, M.K., Pruett, K., & Gillette, P. (2014). Evaluating a couples group to enhance father Involvement in low-Income families using a benchmark comparison. *Family Relations*, 63(3): 356–70. doi:10.1111/fare.12072

Cowan, P.A., Cowan, C.P., Pruett, M.K., Pruett, K., & Wong, J.J. (2009). Promoting fathers' engagement with children: preventive interventions for low-Income families. *Journal of Marriage and Family*, 71(3): 663–79.

Lamb, M.E., & Lewis, C. (2013). Father–child relationships. In: N.J. Cabrera & C.S. Tamis-LeMonda (Eds.), *Handbook of Father Involvement* (pp. 119–34). New York: Routledge/Taylor & Francis Group.

Pruett, M.K., & Johnston, J.R. (2004). *Therapeutic mediation with high-conflict parents: effective models and strategies.* New York: Guilford Publications.

Pruett, M.K., Gillette, P., & Pruett, K.D. (2016). Supporting father involvement to promote co-parent, parent and child outcomes in a Canadian context. *Psychology & Psychological Research International Journal*, 1(1): 1–14.

Pruett, M.K., Pruett, K.P., Cowan, P.A., Cowan, C.P., & Gillette, P. (in press). Supporting Father Involvement: a group intervention for low-income community and child welfare referred couples. *Family Relations*.

Twenge, J.M., Campbell, W.K., & Foster, C.A. (2003). Parenthood and marital satisfaction: a meta-analytic review. *Journal of Marriage and Family*, 65(3): 574–83. doi:DOI 10.1111/j.1741-3737.2003.00574.x

Zemp, M., Milek, A., Cummings, E.M., Cina, A., & Bodenmann, G. (2016). How couple- and parenting-focused programs affect child behavioral problems: a randomized controlled trial. *Journal of Child and Family Studies*, 25(3): 798–810.

Chapter 5

Let's talk about sex …

Marian O'Connor

An intimate couple relationship is usually founded on sex. Erotic pleasure can provide a strong, hidden bond between a couple, eliciting feelings of exclusivity and closeness, both physically and emotionally. These subjective feelings have been backed up by science: during lovemaking dopamine, a pleasure hormone (also associated with addiction), is released, as is oxytocin, sometimes known as the 'love hormone' because of its role in bonding between mother and infant and between sexual partners.

Nearly two decades ago, the World Health Organization (WHO, 2002) described sexual health as an important and integral aspect of human development and maturation throughout life, but sex is not always straightforward, particularly when it involves another person.

Sex can go wrong in a number of ways: a mismatch of libidos, painful intercourse, impotence, too quick, too slow or too boring. There are unconscious barriers that might cause difficulties with sex: anger, resentment, shame, anxiety, fear of losing control, of getting too close, of being overwhelmed, of penetration or of penetrating. One common factor in sexual problems is that sex is difficult to talk about, not only for the partners involved but also for the psychotherapists and health professionals from whom they seek help.

This chapter will explore why sex is hard to talk about whilst arguing its centrality in the work of couple psychotherapists. It will outline how couple therapists can explore safely and assess successfully a couple's sexual relationship and describe what is really meant by a 'psychosexual assessment'. Woven throughout the chapter are composite clinical vignettes of work with couples, using an integrated model that combines psychodynamic psychotherapy, psychoeducation and cognitive behavioural techniques such as sensate focus.

> Soraya and Anna were a lesbian couple in their late 30s who had been together for five years. They sought couple therapy because of arguments, especially about money and household tasks. Soraya worked full time in finance and was the main provider. She felt that Anna had become lazy and now was taking advantage of her hard work. Anna was an artist and was

increasingly convinced that Soraya was obsessed with material possessions and no fun anymore.

Despite these difficulties, the couple were planning to get married the following year. At the initial consultation they were asked about sex. They said it was 'fine' and did not refer to it as a problem between them.

Should therapists actively pursue details about a couple's sexual relationship?

What does the description 'fine' mean for Anna and Soraya? Does it point to a happy, mutually satisfying sex-life? Or could it obscure wider anxieties such as 'we have sexual problems but I don't know how to talk about them without getting embarrassed,' or 'I'm afraid if we bring up sex, it will cause a row, make me cry or cause further damage to the relationship'?

Therapists who nod at the word 'fine' and do not enquire further may have various reasons for this. Psychoanalytically trained couple psychotherapists may choose to stay with material the couple brings, rather than imposing their own agenda on the therapy. They may maintain that, in the safe, facilitating environment of the consulting room, the couple will feel free to bring up sex when and if they need to. However, therapists have little problem probing into other areas that couples or individuals dismiss as 'fine'. If Anna had described her family life growing up as 'fine' few therapists would consider that there was nothing more to be said. They would be alert to potential links with the past in the manner in which she talked about a recent encounter or event. Or they might use their countertransference or sensitivity to pick up unexpressed emotions and start to explore these in the room. So a reluctance to talk about sex may have it origins in a more complex picture, especially as it seems unlikely that sex is never on the minds of clients: a 2012 study suggests that, on average, men think about sex 19 times a day and women ten times a day (Fisher, 2012).

Why are psychotherapists not alert to unexpressed emotions or thoughts about sex?

There is a popular misconception that Freud and his followers were obsessed with sex, that no patient with a bandaged finger could ever enter a therapist's room without some allusion to castration anxiety (Freud,1905). However, a review of 30 years of studies on sexual communication showed that therapists as well as health care professionals find it hard to address their patient's sexuality (Byers, 2011). The study also showed that most romantic partners, even in long term relationships, have difficulty telling each other what pleases and displeases them sexually.

Critics have said that psychoanalytically informed therapy may not address the current sexual problem a couple or individual present with, only what might have caused it in their pasts. This criticism is echoed by many practitioners in the field (Colman, 2009; Fonagy, 2001).

Kahr (2009) observes the reluctance of psychoanalysts to talk about sex and recommends that every psychoanalyst develops 'sexpertise' to facilitate discussion of sexual material with patients. Couple psychotherapists do not fare any better than individual therapists. 'While it is true to say that a sexual difficulty can have a corrosive effect on the entire relationship it is also a notoriously difficult topic to discuss for both patient and therapist' (Seymour, 2014, p. 228). It may be that many, if not most, psychotherapists would rather avoid any conversation about sex.

There is no doubt that sex can be hard to talk about. The pleasure infants discover in exploring their own bodies is preverbal, and their delight in genital pleasure does not get mirrored or named by their parents. Stein (2008) writes that the child's experience of genital pleasure has to remain secret, even shameful, until later when he or she finds a 'resonating desirous other who validates the transgression and joins it and who is excited by one's own excitement' (p. 66). The difficulty is that by the time adult intimate partners are chosen, sensual delight or discomfort may be hard to name or talk about.

Moreover, what goes on behind the parental bedroom door is a taboo subject in most families, and this taboo may accompany therapists into the consulting room when they work with a sexual couple. The sex lives of others, including clients, may elicit fear or shame in therapists, as if they are peeping through the door of their parent's bedroom. Envy, too, can be evoked; any glimpsed sexual rapture may stir-up oedipal anxieties of being left out and inadequate. Therapists may worry, too, about being intrusive, even abusive, if they bring up sex, like parents intruding on the genitalia of their children. Or they may be following in the footsteps of their own therapists and clinical supervisors, their quasi professional parents, who also overlooked sexual material in their work, for similar complex and unconscious reasons. With no internalised parental model for talking about sex, therapists may feel ashamed of their ignorance: although well-versed in intricate, theoretical jargon, they may not feel confident enough to use words like 'labia' and 'scrotum', or to explore further a client's complaint about painful sex. Feelings of shame and inadequacy may be exacerbated in the therapist if clients have a different sexual orientation; concerns about voyeurism may pervade if, for example, a heterosexual therapist asks for specific detail about a gay couple's sex life. It is also important to consider that clients may fear, correctly in some cases, that their therapist will disapprove of or pathologise non-heteronormative sexuality. Weber (2002)), writing about people in polyamorous relationships, describes how 38% of those in therapy chose not to mention this to their therapist, and, of those who did, many experienced negative responses.

> Anna and Soraya brought up so many problems in the first weeks of therapy that it was hard to imagine that their sex life was the one area that

brought satisfaction. The therapist, who had training in psychosexual assessment, decided to explore further. Soraya revealed that she was dissatisfied as she would like to have sex more frequently. Anna had little interest in sex and would be happy to live in a non-sexual relationship. As it stood, the couple reported having sex every few months, always initiated by Soraya.

The therapist noticed that the sexual relationship mirrored their couple relationship, with Anna accusing Soraya of being tense and dissatisfied and wanting control, and Soraya complaining that Anna was selfish and made no effort in the relationship.

In their first few months as a couple, Anna and Soraya had enjoyed a satisfactory sexual relationship, but Anna had quickly lost interest in sex leaving Soraya rejected and angry about the situation. The couple were asked to describe a recent sexual encounter in some detail, from who initiated the contact and how this was done, to the end of the sexual encounter. Asking clients to recount in precise detail a recent or typical sexual encounter is common in psychosexual assessments in order to help identify exactly where the difficulties lie.

The couple described the last time they had sex. Soraya, as always, made the first move, by suggesting they 'fool around for a while'. Anna agreed because she was aware that they had not had sex for some months and she did not want an argument. Anna asked Soraya to give her oral sex and then reciprocated. They both had orgasms, but Soraya said the sex was ultimately disappointing because she would like more kissing, touching and cuddling. Anna said she had sensitive skin and did not like being touched, especially on her breasts. She also commented that Soraya's touch was either too hard or too soft, never in between. She said that Soraya had an orgasm, so what was the problem? She accused Soraya of always being critical.

Sex was a battlefield, like the rest of their relationship. The therapist wondered why they were considering getting married? Areas of kindness or pleasure had seemingly disappeared and the couple shared few interests, including sex. In the countertransference, the therapist experienced feelings of shock, helplessness and bewilderment. Was this a clue to the couple's experience of relationships?

As therapy progressed, the fact they both had lived alongside depressed mothers seemed important to think about. In Soraya's case, her mother was bedbound with clinical depression. Her father made up for this by being very active in Soraya's life, involving her in his interest in sport, helping with her homework and driving her to school events. Soraya openly despised her mother, not wanting children in case she ended up like her. There was no positive model of an adult relationship: a couple meant one half active while the other was passive and despised. When she was seven years old, her mother gave birth to a second child, a boy, which Soraya described as 'a shocking thing to do', especially as she thought her mother could not even manage one child. The therapist wondered whether the idea that her parents had a sexual life together, which excluded her, was particularly shocking.

Anna's father left when she was an infant. She described her mother as loving and cautious – she kept Anna off school whenever Anna complained of an ailment. More exploration revealed that the mother suffered from anxiety and phobias, and needed Anna at home to look after her. Again, there was no model of a creative couple in Anna's childhood, only that of a depressed mother and a child who had to sacrifice her childhood to become her mother's carer.

Soraya found it hard to show vulnerability. She said she did need and want Anna as a companion and a lover, but her fierce independence and anger seemed impregnable. Anna held all the weakness and incompetence for the couple, and Soraya despised these attributes in Anna, as she did in her mother, rather than knowing about and caring for these aspects of herself.

Anna became the child who could finally play and be looked after. She was unconsciously terrified of the loss of self that being in a couple might involve. It turned out that she did experience sexual desire and masturbated daily, but she firmly locked Soraya out of her sex life as she did in all areas. Perhaps she was afraid that, as in childhood, her needs for play and pleasure would be subordinated to another's needs.

Soraya was shocked to discover that Anna masturbated so often. Her shock was rather like when her mother gave birth to her brother, a blow to her narcissism and sense of omnipotence. There was a gradual acknowledgement of Anna as a separate person with her own strength and power and Anna was also able to start to see Soraya as someone multi-dimensional, with needs and weaknesses as well as power and strength.

As they let down their emotional barriers to intimacy, the couple started to talk more about their sexual difficulties. It was not just Anna who had difficulties around sex. Soraya found it difficult to let go and trust Anna to care for her; she only ever initiated sex when time was short, so avoiding the caressing and kissing she claimed she wanted. In this case, the therapist had felt confident to probe deeper into the couple's sexual relationship. The discussion not only allowed the couple to find a way of talking about difficulties there but also opened up the discussion about giving and receiving in other areas of their lives.

Who will talk about sex?

Much research around the difficulties about talking about sex focuses on the patient–doctor relationship. There is evidence that most patients would like to have an opportunity to discuss their sexual concerns but embarrassment to do so, reluctance to initiate the conversation, or anxiety that their doctor will dismiss or judge them prevents their doing so (Verhoeven et al., 2003). Doctors themselves are reluctant to talk about sex, citing a lack of time, fear of intrusion or embarrassing the patient, cultural difference, and general discomfort with the subject (Lindau et al., 2007a).

Roxanne Nelson writes that only about 15% of patients reported getting counselling for sexual activity after an acute myocardial attack (Nelson, 2015). Even when the patient's problem is clearly related to sexual functioning, doctors are reluctant to talk about sex: a study among very long-term survivors of vaginal and cervical cancer showed that 62% had never had a discussion with their doctors about the effect of genital tract cancer on sexuality, but wished that the doctors had brought up the subject (Lindau et al., 2007b). Both doctors and nurses say that it is a good thing to discuss sex with patients, but repeated surveys suggest that each professional group regards this topic as 'not my job', and that it is rare for patients to find someone who does regard it as their job.

Why psychotherapists are well placed to discuss sex

From Freud onwards, the mind has been closely associated with sexuality, and there has long been a truism that the brain is the largest sex organ. Colman (2009) writes, 'We might be able to describe the physiological processes of sex in great detail, but this says nothing about the experience of feeling turned on – or turned off' (p. 13). For example, the physical feeling of being stroked will be impacted by our emotional connection with whoever is doing the stroking. We may find the touch pleasurable, sensual or sexual when we are in a loving and erotic relationship with the person stroking us. If our arm or backside is stroked by an unwelcome stranger or someone we dislike we will find the same touch unpleasant, even disgusting.

Leiblum (2007) points out that the advent of oral medication such as Viagra for erectile dysfunction has shown that long-term success is unlikely to be achieved by treating the genitals alone. Even when the cause of sexual difficulties is organic and medical treatment is indicated, the quality of the sexual relationship may not improve unless attention is paid to unconscious and conscious beliefs and fears, and the personal histories and expectations (conscious or otherwise) of both partners of the couple (McCarthy & McDonald, 2009). Sexuality is not simply about biology, but incorporates psychological and interpersonal processes.

Why couple psychotherapists are particularly well placed to discuss sex

One of the goals of couple therapy is to help clients find a language to express their fears and concerns to one another in a safe, facilitating environment. This involves relinquishing some of the familiar but avoidant and defensive patterns of communication that they might have learnt from childhood. Expressing sexual desire can cause anxiety and, if the therapist avoids the subject, may reinforce the clients' belief that their thoughts are unspeakable.

The therapist who is comfortable about talking about sex in an open, inclusive way can provide a model for the couple to internalise. The therapist can model making mistakes and recovering, mirroring an aspect of resilience in talking about sex that the couple may lack.

Also, their knowledge of couple dynamics means that they look at sexual issues in the context of the relationship as a whole, rather than seeing the problem as being 'the fault' of one or other member of the couple. This sense of being 'at fault' or to blame can increase feelings of inadequacy and lead to further avoidance or denial.

> Isaak was referred by his GP to seek therapeutic help because he lost his erection whenever he attempted sexual intercourse with Bella, his first ever girlfriend, whom he had met online. Medical tests had revealed no organic cause for this dysfunction. Isaak attended the first few sessions of therapy on his own. His therapist suggested that the work would be more productive if the couple were seen together and, after some weeks, Bella arrived, very reluctantly. Both partners explained that Bella had no problems. Unlike Isaak, who was still a virgin at 32 years of age, she, aged 29, had a history of successful sexual relationships.
>
> An exploration of both their family backgrounds revealed that Isaak had a powerful, dominant father and a depressed, shadowy mother. The therapist hypothesised that Isaak's anxieties about getting close to his partner in intercourse related to his negative image of an internal couple, where only one person had life and presence, and a fear of identifying with his potent but destructive father. He had no access to any rage towards his father or towards his mother who had failed to stand up for him.
>
> It was difficult to elicit a coherent account of Bella's history. She was angry about being 'forced' to come to couple therapy and insisted that her life was fine, her parents fine, her only frustration was that Isaak was impotent. Her parents had both been heavily involved in competitive dog shows and as a child she had to attend events with them all over the country. In her teenage years she was often left home alone and she started a sexual relationship with an older man when she was fourteen years old. She initially said this was not abuse as she made the choice to have sex with him. She came across as defended and closed off, and the therapist wondered whether just as Isaak was unable to penetrate her sexually she too had a history of needing to protect and defend herself against emotional penetration.
>
> Therapy was difficult at first. Isaak tried everything the therapist suggested but nothing seemed to work or make any difference to his erectile difficulties. Everything suggested to Bella was dismissed as irrelevant. Grosz (2013) writes that patients tell their stories by unconsciously making the therapist feel like them. Isaak made the therapist feel what it was like to be him, helpless and resentful at never being good enough. Bella made the therapist feel shut out, unwanted. These countertransference feelings reflected the

couple's internal worlds, and this information helped the therapist bear the assaults on the therapy.

Eventually, through exploring their unconscious fears and the couple dynamics, and through asking them to complete some homework exercises related to the dysfunction, Isaak was able to achieve satisfactory penetration and intercourse. They were able to give a more coherent narrative about their lives, with Isaak able to see his father and mother's relationship in more realistic terms and Bella to talk about the loneliness she suffered in her childhood. She also revealed, both to Isaak and to the therapist, that she suffered from bulimia and at times felt depressed and vulnerable. When she spoke about her depression, Isaak was able to get in touch with his strong, potent side and she was able to get in touch with her neediness.

Berne (1966) describes people as adopting parent, adult or child roles in intimate relationships. The problem occurs when each member of the couple gets rigidly stuck in one role. In this relationship, Isaak was stuck in the helpless child role and Bella the dismissive parent. As their emotional and sexual relationship changed and developed, the couple were able to feel safe to play a little and to try out different and more creative roles.

What is a psychosexual assessment

Learning to make a psychosexual assessment is not the same as learning to be a psychosexual therapist. Instead, it enables the clinician to talk more easily and confidently about sex, to explore in more detail sexual difficulties a couple might bring, and to know about sexual functioning and dysfunctions and when to refer to medical or psychosexual specialists.

Some couples argue openly about sex. For others, embarrassment about talking about sex, or shame about being judged as inadequate, might mean that they have not even discussed the sexual difficulty between themselves, never mind with a third party. In such cases, complaints that one of them spends too much time watching TV or out with friends may stem from a feeling of being ignored or undesired sexually. 'A gentle exploration of the sexual relationship is an important part of any assessment process even if only to rule it out as a part of the problem' (Seymour, 2014, p. 228).

In order to conduct even a gentle exploration, therapists need not only to question their reluctance to talk about sex but also the confidence to start the conversation. Knowledge of sexual anatomy and sexual functioning and dysfunctions gives them the language and information to pursue lines of enquiry. For example, if one partner complains that his or her male partner is no longer interested in sex, therapists need to know that this could be for a variety of reasons. These might be relational: he might be angry with his partner, and lack of sex could be an unconscious way of communicating this; he may be having an affair and preoccupied with the new lover; perhaps the couple have agreed to try for a baby and this has brought up anxieties and withdrawal; it might be that he is addicted to online pornography and ordinary sex with his partner is no longer stimulating; he may be suffering from depression or taking certain antidepressant medications, both of which can affect libido.

For some men, sex can work in a new relationship, but as the relationship becomes more committed, anxieties stemming from childhood may surface, leading to sexual withdrawal. This may because of childhood sexual abuse or an experience of claustrophobia or abandonment in early intimate relationships with parental figures. On the other hand, he could be suffering from erectile dysfunction and too embarrassed to reveal this – it can be less shameful to say he is just not interested. The erectile dysfunction may be caused by relational or emotional factors as described above, or medical factors such as diabetes, cardiovascular problems, aging or drug and alcohol abuse.

A psychosexual assessment will explore early childhood relationships, and experiences through later childhood, adolescence and early adulthood that might have an impact on the client's psychosexual development. It is important to enquire about the history of the current relationship, including the sexual history, and any current or historical personal/relational/medical factors that might have influenced the presenting problem.

When to make a psychosexual assessment

Individuals and couples in therapy may not bring up their sexual problems directly for many of the reasons already discussed. Nevertheless, it is important that the therapist invites talk about sexual issues early on in the therapy. Mattinson and Sinclair (1979) write that couples in trouble exhibit the same attachment behaviours as infants under stress. In the consulting room, as we become aware of clients' vulnerability and defences, many of which may have stemmed from childhood, therapists can be in danger of falling into a maternal transference relationship, which could make it difficult to talk about sex. It can feel intrusive and shocking for both therapist and patient if the therapist–mother figure suddenly starts knocking on the bedroom door and asking for intimate details about sex.

The 'integrated model' in the treatment of psychosexual disorders

Tavistock Relationships' integrated model of psycho-sexual therapy is based on a psychodynamic framework, which explores the dynamics of the current relationship, individual histories, and countertransference and transference relationships in the here and now of the therapy room between partners and between them and their therapist. It also involves information giving, psychosexual education, challenging cognitive distortions and setting behavioural exercises as homework (Green & Seymour, 2009; O'Connor & Hiller, 2014).

These exercises will be tailored to the specific problem clients bring, but will include self-focus and sensate focus exercises first introduced by Masters and Johnson (1970).

> Sylvia and John are a heterosexual couple in their mid thirties who have been together for eight years and married for three. They came for help two years after the birth of their first child because they wanted another baby but had attempted sex only twice since their daughter was born. Sylvia found sex painful and John hated the idea of inflicting pain on his wife and did not want to put pressure on her to try.
>
> The couple's sex life was good before the birth; they were committed to the relationship and both wanted another child. They had a good life together, with successful careers and many friends; none of their friends would suspect that they had not had sex for nearly two years.

This is not an uncommon story, but why? Recovering from a difficult birth, mothers are often exhausted and preoccupied with getting to know and settling down with a baby. They find themselves occupying a new position in relation to their partner, perhaps more separate than before. Partners, whether male or female, may feel excluded from the close physical and emotional bond between mother and baby. But what if this situation continues for several months, even years? Is the problem psychological, perhaps stemming from early unconscious messages or phantasies about sex and the parental couple? Is saying no to sex an expression of anger, a way of creating distance or asserting control? Or is there an unconscious block about managing three people in the relationship, with one person always having to feel left out – an echo of their own experience of infancy with the family being mum coupled to child and dad on the outside, or the child feeling neglected, abandoned and not thought about by the parents?

Perhaps problems around penetrative intercourse are medical, concerning physical damage from pregnancy or birth: traumatic, life-threatening births can affect not only the woman physically but also the partner who witnessed it. Or perhaps a lack of sexual intercourse between a couple is because of poor sexual education: changes in the woman's body after childbirth might mean she needs more foreplay or a different position in order to find sexual intercourse comfortable and enjoyable. As already stated, training in psychosexual assessment, which integrates a psychodynamic relational perspective with a physiological, specialist knowledge of medical symptomology of sexual difficulties, gives the therapist a varied toolkit, beyond the purely psychological.

> An exploration of Sylvia's and John's personal histories and their sexual relationship showed that the couple had had a very satisfactory relationship right up to the birth of their daughter, and they felt that their sexual intimacy not only gave them physical pleasure but also brought them closer emotionally. Conception and pregnancy were straightforward but

the birth involved a serious third to fourth degree tear (extending to the anus) in her perineum. This was repaired after the birth, but Sylvia continued to experience pain and discomfort in the area, accompanied in the first year by mild faecal incontinence which led to occasional staining of her underwear.

Interestingly, this couple said they had been able to talk openly about sex before their baby was born, but Sylvia had found herself unable to discuss the faecal incontinence. Rather than talk about it, she avoided sex, saying she was not ready, it did not feel right and was still painful. Sylvia revealed this for the first time when the therapist asked her directly about it on learning about her perineal tear.

Sylvia had been in the care of an obstetrician, midwife, health visitor, and GP who all knew about and had treated the tear, but none of them spoke to her or to the couple about the possible effect on sexual functioning. Sylvia had also had individual therapy because of concerns about returning to full time work after her maternity leave, and again her sexual anxieties had not been discussed nor had her worries about faecal incontinence, which she found too shaming and 'dirty' to talk about. She admitted that part of her concern about resuming her professional career was connected to feelings of incompetence about her bodily functions.

Lack of control in the bowel can cause primitive anxieties about helplessness and shame. Although this chapter is about encouraging more openness to talking about sex and sexual difficulties, it is worth noting that, according to many specialists in the field, one taboo persists in the UK–that of bowel function (Kaplan 2012; MacKenzie & Clubb, 2007; Yarde, 2013). This is despite the fact that injury to the anal sphincter during childbirth is the major cause of faecal incontinence in women each year in the UK and in 2002 was estimated to affect 5% of women who had a vaginal delivery (Fernando et al., 2002). This number has continued to rise in the UK and other industrialised countries (Ekeus et al., 2008; Ismail et al., 2014).

Sometimes a recent physical or emotional trauma will reawaken anxieties related to previous traumatic events in a client's history, and these will need to be explored and worked with before a psychosexual programme can be undertaken. The homework exercises, which involve an exploration or one's own and one's partner's body, may bring up unmanageable feelings, particularly where there is unprocessed childhood sexual or physical abuse. Sylvia had not reported any history of trauma. John had been sent away to boarding school at the age of seven, which he did not describe as traumatic, only difficult at first but then fun, once he got used to it. This information did not preclude starting a behavioural programme but alerted the therapist to the fact that there might be some shared anxiety about resuming sexual activity after the birth of their child: perhaps John felt left out by the baby's arrival, as he once might have felt left out when he returned home from boarding school.

Another important consideration in starting a couple on a behavioural programme is the quality of the relationship. Abuse, coercive control, violent arguments are all contra-indications. There has to be some mutual kindness and trust so that each partner feels safe enough to open themselves up physically to the other.

> With John and Sylvia, the behavioural programme started off with a self-focus exercise, each exploring their own bodies in private before discussing the associations and feelings this bought up with their therapist in the next session. The exercise was repeated a number of times as Sylvia initially found it hard to think of her body as anything other than disgusting and damaged. John, perhaps due to his early experiences of boarding school and the abrupt separation from maternal touch and care this entailed, found it hard to think about his body at all: it was just there, he had no emotion about it. It was as if his body did not exist, all the focus was on Sylvia's, which added to her shame of not being perfect. As their cognitions started to change and they began to reclaim positive feelings about their bodies, the couple started mutual stroking (sensate focus) exercises. Although soiling was rare, Sylvia ordered online a special mat for the bed to alleviate her anxiety, and as she became more confident she started to enjoy the pleasuring touch John gave her.
>
> The couple were diligent and enthusiastic about their homework exercises. The block came when John was asked to insert his penis into her vagina and stay still, without thrusting. The couple were asked to notice the physical and emotional feelings of being together. John lost his erection on the first attempts at penetration. The therapist wondered if this might link both to John's fear of being rejected now that Sylvia was a mother and also to his trauma at witnessing the birth and a fear of damaging her further through penetration. The couple went back to mutual pleasuring while John's anxieties were discussed in therapy. Eventually the couple achieved penetration and gradually resumed a very satisfactory sexual relationship. They decided to put on hold for some time their plans for having a second child in order to enjoy being a sexual couple again.

In our thinking-dominant culture, focusing on bodily experience can seem unimportant, shameful or even alien to many people, even though from infancy onwards everything we experience is channelled through the body. An integrated approach was important here to allow the couple to be curious about both their physical and emotional response to resuming a sexual life together. It would not have been sufficient only to have talked about the couple's anxieties and fears – or, indeed, only to have given them behavioural exercises to complete. The graded homework exercises, combined with a careful psychosexual assessment and opportunities to explore their anxieties, enabled Sylvia and John to get back in touch with the pleasure their own bodies could bring and to enjoy once again the intimacy of sexual play and intercourse.

In conclusion, this chapter has explored how sexual problems may cause a great deal of distress for couples and individuals, about which neither they nor those they turn to for help may find it easy to talk about. Individual therapists, couple psychotherapists and health professionals all need specialised training to enable them to explore the psychological and educational blocks they may have in addressing sexual concerns with their clients and patients. Tavistock Relationships has taken a significant step by putting this on the curriculum of all in-house clinical trainings and is developing new courses that will extend this training to a wide range of therapists and health professionals throughout the UK. Whether the problem is a physical one, an emotional one, or a symptom of other problems in the relationship, attending to this important dimension in our clients and patients' lives has the potential to increase the happiness and well-being of the individuals and couples we see.

References

Berne, E. (1966). *Games People Play–The Psychology of Human Relationships*. London: Andre Deutsch.

Byers, S. (2011). Beyond the birds and the bees and was it good for you? Thirty years of research on sexual communication. *Canadian Psychology*, *52*(1): 20–8.

Colman, W. (2009). What do we mean by sex? In: C. Clulow (Ed.), *Sex, Attachment and Couple Psychotherapy* (pp. 25–44). London: Karnac.

Ekeus, C., Nilsson, E., & Gottvall, K. (2008). Increasing incidence of anal sphincter tears among primiparas in Sweden: a population-based register study. *Acta Obstetricia et Gynecologica Scandinavica*, *87*(5): 564–73.

Fernando, R.J., Sultan, A.H., Radley, S., Jones, P.E., & Johamson, R.B. (2002). Management of obstetric anal sphincter injury: a systematic review & national practice survey. *BMC Health Services Research*, *2*: 9. doi.org/10.1186/1472-6963-2-9

Fisher, T. (2012). Sex on the brain? An examination of frequency of sexual cognitions as a function of gender, erotophilia, and social desirability. *Journal of Sex Research*, *49*(1): 69–77.

Fonagy, P. (2001). *Attachment Theory and Psychoanalysis*. New York: Other Press.

Freud, S. (1905). *Three Essays on the Theory of Sexuality. S. E.*, 7: 123–246. London: Hogarth.

Green, L. & Seymour, J. (2009). Loss of desire, a psycho-sexual case study. In: C. Clulow (Ed.), *Sex, Attachment and Couple Psychotherapy* (pp. 141–64). London: Karnac.

Grosz, S. (2013). *The Examined Life*. London: Chatto & Windus.

Ismail, S., & Puyk, B. (2014). The rise of obstetric anal sphincter injuries: 11-year trend analysis using Patient Episode Database for Wales (PEDW) data. *Journal of Obstetrics and Gynaecology*, *34*(6): 495–98.

Kahr, B. (2009). Psychoanalysis and sexpertise. In: C. Clulow (Ed.), *Sex, Attachment and Couple Psychotherapy* (pp. 1–24). London: Karnac.

Kaplan, R. (2012). Book review: does James Bond go to the toilet? Psychology in the bathroom. *Australasia Psychiatry*, *20*(6): 529–30.

Leiblum, S. (Ed.) (2007). *Principles and Practices of Sex Therapy* (4th edn). New York: Guildford Press.

Lindau, S., Sobecki, J., Curlin, F., & Rasinski, K. (2007a). A study of sexuality and health among older adults in the United States. *New England Journal of Medicine, 357*(8): 762–74.

Lindau, S., Gavrilova, N., & Anderson, D. (2007b). Sexual morbidity in very long term survivors of vaginal and cervical cancer: a comparison to national norms. *Gynecologic Oncology, 106*: 413–18.

McCarthy, B., & McDonald, D. (2009). Sex therapy failures: a crucial, yet ignored, issue. *Journal of Sex & Marital Therapy, 35*(4): 320–9.

MacKenzie, R., & Clubb, A. (2007). Faecal incontinence following childbirth. *Nursing Times, 103*(14): 40–1.

Masters, W., & Johnson, V. (1970). *Human Sexual Inadequacy*. New York: Bantam Books.

Mattinson, J., & Sinclair, I. (1979). *Mate and Stalemate: Working with Marital Problems in a Social Services Department*. Oxford: Blackwell.

Nelson, R. (2015). How to talk to your patients about sex. *Medscape-Oct15, 2015*. Available at: www.medscape.com/viewarticle/849345 (accessed January 23 2018).

O'Connor, M., & Hiller, J. (2014). Psychodynamic aspects of psychosexual therapy. In: P.S. Kirani, F. Tripodi, Y. Reisman, & H. Porst (Eds.), *The EFS and ESSM syllabus of Clinical Psychology* (pp. 446–63). Amsterdam: Medix.

Seymour, J. (2014). Assessing the sexual relationship. In: D. Scharff & J. Savege Scharff, (Eds.), *Psychoanalytic Couple Therapy: Foundations of Theory and Practice* (pp. 228–36). London: Karnac.

Stein, R. (2008). The otherness of sexuality: excess. *Journal of American Psychoanalytic Association, 56* (1): 43–71.

Verhoeven, V., Bovijn, K., Helder, A., Peremans, L., Hermann, I., Van Royen, P., Denekens, J., & Avonts, D. (2003). Discussing STIs: doctors are from Mars, patients from Venus. *Family Practice, 20*(1): 11–5.

Weber, A. (2002). Who are we? And other interesting impressions. *Loving More Magazine, 30*: 4–6.

World Health Organization (2002). *Defining Sexual Health. Report of a Technical Consultation on Sexual Health*. Geneva: WHO. Available at: www.who.int/reproductive health/publications/sexual_health/defining_sexual_health.pdf (accessed January 2018)

Yarde, D. (2013). Common bladder and bowel problems. *Practice Nursing, 24*(1): 43–6.

Commentary on Chapter 5

Janice Hiller

Psychosexual therapy has come a long way since directive exercises were first described in the 1970s, and O'Connor's chapter exemplifies the current approach to working with complex sexual and relationship issues, based on a biopsychosocial model of sexual responsiveness. For psychosexual therapy to be effective, sensate focus exercises are introduced in the context of a formulation including the couple fit, unconscious factors, countertransference to the relationship and the couple communications seen in the room. This can be achieved with an integrated model, using psychodynamic understanding but also keeping a focus on the behaviour patterns. The aim here is to connect cognitions, emotions and sexual behaviour. Psychoeducational methods are part of this model too, so that patients may be shown diagrams and pictures, with prior permission, to help with a lack of knowledge of arousal patterns or genital structures. This approach can be adapted for individuals as a way of helping them become aware of bodily and cognitive responses to anxiety-provoking situations.

Sex needs to be talked about because for many people it is a major driving and motivating force. I am referring here to the ability of sexual urges to organise thinking, and to mobilise and determine action, and behaviour, in different ways over the life course. Sexual activity is a central feature of most intimate relationships, but we know too that not everyone is driven at phases in their life by sexual urges. As a biological drive it differs from other essential needs like hunger and thirst in that some people can avoid sexual contact throughout the life course, embracing a non-sexual lifestyle, without a threat to their own survival or health, despite the well documented health benefits. At the same time, I think we have a responsibility as couple therapists to find out how central sexual expression is to our patients, in an open-minded non-judgmental way, just as we are interested in their inner worlds, conflicts and conscious thought processes.

During the many years when I was head of an NHS relationship and psychosexual service in East London I was always struck by how ready and keen our patients were to talk about their distressing sexual problems from the initial session. Yet in some areas of clinical work, as O'Connor suggests, sex remains an uncomfortable topic for discussion. Perhaps the readiness of people who were referred to our service could be explained by the referral process via the GP, psychiatrist or other health care professional: patients knew why they were attending and were no doubt relieved to be taken off the waiting list. They were in many ways prepared for the specific questions in the assessment procedure. A major factor though, is no doubt the degree of comfort demonstrated by practitioners when working with intimate sexual issues, which allows patients to feel at ease with the therapeutic environment. O'Connor rightly points out that an open discussion about sex in a non-blaming atmosphere can set the scene for deeper explorations of developmental processes and couple dynamics, and how they precipitate and maintain the difficulties. On another level the atmosphere around sex in the home, sex education in schools, and cultural factors around relationships in general, will all have a part to play in maintaining or removing inhibitions. Social media might appear to expand the acceptance of varieties of sexual experiences, but many young people absorb unhelpful messages that lead to increased anxiety. I had hoped that knowledge about sexual behaviour, genital changes and anatomy would increase over the years, but my impressions from tutoring students, and the anecdotal evidence from my own practice, indicates that sadly, an inadequate understanding about how our bodies function is just as prevalent as when I started to work in this area. Even more important then, that as relationship therapists we are sufficiently trained.

Of the many noteworthy changes in society in the last few decades, attitudes to same-sex relationships, understanding the impact of mental and physical illness, and developments in pharmacology, have all broadened our methods and techniques. We adapt interventions for each person to facilitate positive sexual behaviour. Whatever the sexual orientation or proclivities the physical relationship is seen as linked to more general aspects of the couple's interactions and placed in their socio-cultural context. Sexuality is multi-determined and serves many functions; what people think and feel about themselves and the other is as central to sexual behaviour as the circulating hormones and genital changes that underpin arousal. In her cases O'Connor shows how an integrated psychosexual approach can be formulated for a range of presenting issues, and that psychodynamic exploration can be interwoven with behavioural exercises to restructure sexual responsiveness. Treatment models integrating psychoanalytic theory with psychosexual therapy techniques have been described for male erectile difficulties (Hiller, 1993) and female arousal problems (Hiller, 1996). In all cases the goal is determined by the couple, and it may not be penetrative sex, but we would always aim for pain-free, rewarding and mutually enjoyable sex for each partnership.

Outcome studies to validate therapy techniques are as difficult to carry out in psychosexual work as in other treatment options, but psychosexual therapy progresses through taking account of practice-based evidence and evidence-based practice. One example from pharmacology is the introduction of oral medication to enhance erectile capacity; an additional aid but also a challenge. Although PDE5 (phosphodiesterase type 5) inhibitors have enabled and enhanced male arousal it is well-recognised now that such medications require a context for successful sexual interactions. As therapists we may incorporate the use of Cialis and Viagra as part of the regimen but be clear that pharmacology on its own rarely solves erectile difficulties long term. Many young men are reluctant to become dependent on taking tablets and seek therapy to help them find psychological solutions. For women the efforts to find a pharmacological product have not been successful, due to the way female genital structures are connected to brain responses. An increase in physiological/genital arousal in women will not automatically be experienced subjectively to enable the women to feel aroused. Whereas male arousal tends to produce rapid cognitive awareness, women, by contrast, are generally more responsive to context and relationship factors than men (Chivers et al., 2010). These gender differences are generalisations, albeit based on validated studies, and there will always be some individual differences.

Reluctance to engage in sex with a partner or complete avoidance is one of the most common presenting issues. Research in this area has highlighted further typical gender differences, with evidence indicating that women in long term partnerships often have sexual contact for reasons other than experiencing desire; instead they initiate or agree to sex for reasons such as alleviating a partner's tension, avoiding arguments, keeping the peace and general couple harmony. Basson (2003) described a model of women's arousal that showed how they might be emotionally and physiologically neutral when physical contact begins, and then access feelings of desire once becoming aroused. My own clinical work has included many cases of women who were not motivated to initiate sex because they lacked the urge, but who were able to respond when their partner showed emotional connectedness and interest and hugged or stroked them. Men tend to be far more driven by conscious awareness of the desire for sex, while women are more responsive to feeling desired. By describing female desire as following arousal rather than preceding it, Basson helpfully clarified women's sexual response needs. These differing sexual interest patterns are a common topic for complaint and explaining this model can be useful as part of psycho-education with couples presenting with discrepant desire. Both women and men, however, will lose sexual interest when feeling resentful, hostile and angry. Sexual withdrawal in the context of negative emotional states is viewed as an adaptive and psychologically understandable phenomenon rather than an indication of individual psychopathology (Bancroft, 2002, Hiller, 2006). Sensate focus methods can still be interwoven with an object relations perspective once tension and hostility have been reduced.

For both genders of course, sexual activity exists within an interpersonal framework. Additionally, the intrapersonal framework has recently been studied via research on the impact of body image – feelings, thoughts and perceptions about one's body – which has linked a negative body image to avoidance of sex or decreased pleasure. Enzlin (2014) suggests that anxious self-consciousness during sexual behaviour leads to distraction from sexual stimuli. Anxiety from any source is known to cause blood to drain from genital areas, triggering brain chemistry to revert from arousal to survival mode, so that pleasure is absent.

Eventually if anxiety persists, desire is likely to plummet, and avoidance of sex becomes the norm, as illustrated well in O'Connor's case vignette of the woman struggling with disgust and shame about her body.

Looking beyond our usual literature base, neuroscientific research has burgeoned in the last decade due to new brain imaging techniques and equipment to measure hormones circulating in the blood stream. Evidence giving neurobiology a prime role in underpinning sexual responses is growing, yet as a topic it appears antithetical to most psychotherapy practice. To what extent can current neuroscience data have a role in the therapy world, and how much of it is useful for us?

A brief overview of the more relevant findings would include information from studies using fMRI (functional magnetic resonance imaging) machines to indicate which parts of the brain become activated when we experience certain emotional states. fMRI scans allow scientists to identify functions associated with brain areas, and which neurochemicals are released from those sites when people engage in sexual activity along with the subjective concomitants. Brain–body connections have been studied by measuring the levels of certain hormones, released from specific neural pathways, which underpin strong emotions. For example, the neurotransmitter oxytocin, which promotes trust, attachment and emotional bonding, increases in the blood when we feel safe and secure with people. Oxytocin also reduces the stress hormone cortisol, which creates tension and prepares the body for action. Of significance from a psychosexual perspective, oxytocin is released by both women and men with orgasm, thereby linking sex, bonding and anxiety reduction. Vasopressin is a similar neurotransmitter but with certain gender differences, and more associated with protective behaviour, vigilance and persistence. Another vital neurochemical is dopamine, associated with anticipation, motivation and response to novelty. Dopamine regulates the release of oxytocin and vasopressin, explaining how increased excitement leads to greater pleasure. Insights such as these help us to see why sex can be so much more rewarding at the start of a relationship, when excitement is high, compared to years later when novelty has gone and familiarity sets in (Hiller, 2004).

The challenge then is to decide whether and how neurobiology can inform our clinical work. My view is that knowledge of how brain, mind and body are synchronised in intimate connections can only deepen our understanding of troubled relationships and enhance our skills. Just as our hypotheses about unconscious couple fit, projection and the impact of family-of-origin experiences may or may not be shared in a therapy session, but nevertheless inform our techniques, so too explaining the neural correlates of sex and emotion may or may not be considered helpful to our clients. Here we use clinical judgement and sensitivity to the people in the room. From the standpoint of a couple therapist who has studied neurobiology in depth, Fishbane (2013) is convinced that 'neuroeducation' with her clients is highly beneficial for self-regulation and promoting real change, describing neuroscience as enriching her work. I have found that too; connecting brain function, neurochemicals and sexual behaviour has been informative and illuminating for my own understanding. But interpersonal neurobiology is not a subject for everyone. As an occasional adjunct to the skill-set it might be possible to include knowledge derived from neurobiology if it can be incorporated flexibly and suits our personal style. However, neuro-education is not essential and should never replace the core approach. Faced with highly complex issues we could nevertheless keep an open mind to the inclusion of another treatment dimension with potential benefits. Meanwhile, the evidence to date certainly confirms the use of current integrated methods, and those are firmly grounded in psychodynamic concepts.

References

Bancroft, J. (2002). The medicalization of female sexual dysfunction: the need for caution. *Archives of Sexual Behaviour, 31* (5):451–5.

Basson, R. (2003). Biopsychosocial models of women's sexual response: applications to management of 'desire disorders'. *Sexual and Relationship Therapy, 18*(1): 107–15.

Chivers, M.L., Seto, M.C., Lalumière, M.L., Laan, E., & Grimbos, T. (2010). Agreement of genital and subjective measures of sexual arousal in men and women: a meta-analysis. *Archives of Sexual Behaviour, 39*: 5–56.

Enzlin, P. (2014). Sexuality in the context of chronic illness. In: Y.M. Binik & K.S.K. Hall (Eds.), *Principles and Practices of Sex Therapy*. New York: Guildford Press.

Fishbane, M.D. (2013). *Loving With the Brain in Mind: Neurobiology and Couple Therapy*. New York: W W. Norton.

Hiller, J. (1993). Psychoanalytic concepts and psychosexual therapy: a suggested integration. *Sexual and Marital Therapy, 8*: 9–26.

Hiller, J. (1996). Female sexual arousal and its impairment: the psychodynamics of non-organic coital pain. *Sexual and Marital Therapy, 11*(1): 55–76.

Hiller, J. (2004). Speculations on the links between feelings, emotions and sexual behaviour: are vasopressin and oxytocin involved? *Sexual and Relationship Therapy, 19*(4): 393–412.

Hiller, J. (2006). Loss of sexual interest and negative states of mind. In: J. Hiller, H. Wood, & W. Bolton (Eds.), *Sex, Mind and Emotion*. London: Karnac.

Chapter 6

Couple Therapy for Depression

Kate Thompson

A disabling condition, depression affects a large swathe of British society. The 2014 Adult Psychiatric Morbidity Survey (APMS) highlights that, every week, one in six adults experience symptoms of a common mental health problem, such as anxiety or depression, and one in five adults have considered taking their own life at some point.

Despite feelings of isolation being a symptom of depression, those suffering are likely to be in relationships with partners and children, who are also affected. A Tavistock Relationships' study that included interviews with depressed unemployed men and women, graphically describes the alienating aspect of this mental illness:

> ... it feels like being mildly drunk, or concussed. There is a sort of invisible blanket between the world and me. I find it hard to take in what anyone says. Or perhaps, hard to want to take it in. It is so uninteresting.
> (Mattinson, 1988, p. 98)

If we translate this description of depression into a relationship, what damage can this state of mind engender? If a husband becomes depressed, how easy is it for his wife to feel blamed or resent that she in herself is not enough to jolt him out of it? How does it affect the intricate union of the hopes of two individuals, joined in the common endeavour to love and be loved by each other? Put like this, it would seem impossible for one half of a couple to be depressed without affecting the relationship, and thus the partner.

In exploring the relational aspect of depression, this chapter will open with a composite case study illustrating, in some detail, the application of couple therapy in the treatment of depression. The case study, which takes us inside a couple's experience of depression and therapy, is followed by a description of the context, evolution and specific content of this integrated couple treatment. The chapter concludes with reflections on mental ill-health, its impact on intimate relationships and discusses the spread of couple therapy within the NHS.

> On entering the consulting room, David's manner was furtive and anxious-to-please, and he frequently looked towards his partner before speaking. A

property developer, David had been employed by the same building firm for the past 12 years. Self-made and driven, David spoke about his adolescence being lost in drugs and alcohol, both of which he turned to as an escape from his chaotic upbringing and said that he had nearly 'gone bad ways'.

David's job meant he was often on call and therefore unable to spend much time with his family. His wife, Denise, aged thirty-one, took chief responsibility for raising the couples' two young sons. Denise had the hangdog air of someone who has given up any ambitions for herself, weighed down physically by what she frequently referred to as her 'poor figure', and more generally a sense of mental bleakness which she appeared to voice on behalf of them both.

Denise and David left school with few qualifications but had achieved a good quality of life with some degree of security, thanks to David's salary. A year previously, however, government cuts had led to David's redundancy, a blow which was swiftly compounded by the unexpected death of Denise's father. Denise wondered if she had properly mourned the death of her dad, speaking as if 'grief' were too defined and neat a description for the nothingness she felt. As she spoke in their initial session, David looked towards her as if to gauge how he should react to the therapist's assessment questions.

Their couple relationship had suffered from these two life-changing events. Denise, in particular, seemed unable to cope, retreating from the world, withdrawing even from her two sons. After nine months of increasingly bitter rows, followed by David's long, resentful silences, a desperate Denise went to her GP. She maintained she had only sought help because their eldest son's teacher had contacted them to complain about his deteriorating behaviour in class. This 'shameful' commentary on her parenting abilities finally jolted Denise out of her lethargy into seeking help. Alongside a prescription for anti-depressants, Denise's GP referred her to the local IAPT service. It was here that the psychological well-being practitioner (PWP) who assessed her identified a relational aspect to her depression and the couple were referred for couple therapy for depression.

In talking to the PWP, Denise had tried to describe her sense of hopelessness and entrapment. She described being in a relationship littered with potential mistakes, lying in wait like trip-wires, over which she invariably fell. Reluctant to accept any kind of couple treatment at first, convinced that David would not agree to joint therapy for 'her problem', Denise bravely consented to the couple trying one or two sessions together and, to her surprise, David also agreed.

Denise and David's relationship was assessed by their therapist, Anna, a former individual CBT practitioner, who had undertaken eight months training in couple therapy for depression. In an initial joint session, Anna attempted to understand their presenting problem with particular emphasis on what they wanted to change in their relationship. She explored depression in some depth, for both halves of the couple. What was it like to experience and what was it like to witness? How bad did it get? What were the symptoms? What doctor's treatment plan was Denise on and had they noticed any change because of it? Did David ever feel depressed? Throughout the assessment process, the therapist used her countertransference, what it felt like to be with the couple, to inform her growing picture of their relationship. Anna's registering of a particular emotional deadness between the couple and a feeling of mutual dread infusing the consulting room, gave her a sense of the couple's unconscious, shared dynamic (see Chapter 1).

Denise said that David had stopped talking to her completely. She accused him, since losing his job, of intruding on her role as mother, leaving her feeling utterly redundant. David, in turn, said he had lost respect for Denise, sofa-bound and steeped in self-pity, oblivious to his distress. He had tried to support her around the death of her father but her helplessness overwhelmed him; he needed to stay positive to find work and support the family. As money dwindled, their feelings of blame towards each other mounted.

Their therapist identified a mutual relational trap and pattern in their interpersonal dynamic which, rather than emotionally protecting the couple, as unconsciously intended, exacerbated their difficulties. It began with David being unable to articulate his grief over losing his job; instead he sought refuge from his feelings by finding fault in Denise and criticising her parenting, thus projecting his self-blame and persecutory guilt into his wife. This affected them both, drawing them into rowing about their domestic life to avoid thinking about their fears for the future and their anger at an unfair world that had made David redundant. David's loss of status and role was subsequently eclipsed by the death of Denise's father, which pitched the couple into a strange, rivalrous world of 'who had got it worse'. A mutual lack of empathy left both feeling isolated, unheard, misunderstood, and increasingly despairing.

As well as providing the couple with some psycho-education around the symptoms of depression, their therapist went on to identify a malign interpersonal cycle that might be maintaining it: the more Denise appealed to David and described her grief in the hope he might comfort her, the more he withdrew and refused to engage, except to denigrate her. Anna wondered if his emotional departure from their intimate relationship was a symptom of his unconscious desire to protect them both from overwhelming grief and his own fear of breakdown. The couple had stopped having a sexual relationship, and all gestures of affection between them had ceased seven months previously. Anna reflected on how rejected each might be feeling, adding to their shared experience of loss and bewilderment.

In the fourth session, Anna bought a formulation of her ideas of their relationship difficulties, inviting the couple to pool these thoughts with their own wishes for change. Anna described Denise and David as being caught up in a distance–closeness dilemma. This stuck, polarised stance created a mutual trap that was distressing to them both. The couple were able to hear this and feel understood, for the first time in along while. The therapist also identified the strengths in their relationship and their commitment to getting it back on track, which instilled a sense of hope that had been absent.

Contained within a secure therapeutic alliance, the couple were able by session six to experiment with some of the communication exercises suggested by Anna and then practised them at home. The 'communication wheel' exercise, consisting of a set of prompts such as 'I regret …' and 'I wish …' designed to broaden entrenched shut-down responses between a couple and expand their understanding of each other's perspectives, was revelatory. David heard some of the history behind Denise's close relationship to her father, intensified by the death of her mother when she was fifteen. For her part, Denise understood for the first time how David's trust in the world had been shaken by being made redundant, along with his sense of masculinity, and that this crisis was reflected in his lack of libido.

Through learning to listen to his wife, creating space for her in his own mind separate from his own worries, David began to understand how the normally resourceful Denise had felt suffused with her own uselessness. Her sense of agency had evaporated as she felt unable to help with his joblessness, a passivity that was, ironically, reinforced when he superseded her as main carer of the children. Anna was again assisted in recognising and guiding the couple to uncover these more hidden feelings by using her countertransference to reflect on her own sense of uselessness as a therapist, a thought that tended to preoccupy her before the sessions.

Midway through the therapy, Anna was surprised to find that David's Patient Health Questionnaire (PHQ9)[1] score, which he had filled out as '0' for the first five sessions (communicating to his therapist that he had no symptoms of depression), had begun to creep up. By session ten, David was scoring 12, indicating he was in the range of 'moderate depression'. Denise's score on the PHQ9 had fallen from 15, classed as 'moderately severe depression', to 12, 'moderate depression', which communicated to the therapist that the treatment was helping her. David's rising score seemed to suggest something else. Alarmed, the therapist took the case to her supervisor and together they thought about David's silence at the start of therapy and how he had begun to open up and talk about more vulnerable feelings for the first time in a long while. They also linked this development to some genogram exploration that the couple had worked on some weeks earlier. David had described his grandmother as being bed-ridden with depression for most of his childhood and said that his mother feared a similar fate. This helped Anna to understand why Denise's depression was so frightening for David and why, as a result, he defensively pushed her away.

Session 12 saw the couple embark on some behavioural and problem-solving exercises. With a growing warmth and new understanding of each other's perspectives and fears, Anna felt the time was right to think about changing some ingrained behaviours. Their patterns of behaviour and broken communication had contributed to their remoteness towards each other and to Denise's depression. Both had said they no longer felt special to the other and found it difficult to identify positive things between them. Anna hoped that in encouraging them to change certain behaviours and introduce some deliberate actions, such as increasing caring gestures, Denise and David would get back in touch with the pleasure they had taken in each other when they first got together.

When these behavioural exercises occasionally broke down with a return to anger and blame, Anna reverted back to the communication exercises that had helped Denise and David slow down their interaction enough to be able to understand the fears that were prompting the defensive pattern between them. In one emotional session, David was able to say how much he missed 'the old Denise' and how he worried that she would never be happy again, that he 'just couldn't reach her'. Denise said she had no idea that he felt like that. The couple were united as they both realised that they shared an anxiety that things might never go back to what they had been before their difficulties. This enabled them to mourn what had been lost together and conveyed a new reality to the depressed feelings. They could now see that their relationship had been overloaded with stress and grief. In sharing this loss, the couple were then able to think about how they could move forward, and gradually the energy to create a new intimacy began to gather momentum.

In sessions 15 and 16, the therapist worked with Denise and David to formulate a relapse prevention plan and to focus on what it was that had particularly helped them, both during the treatment and in the time at home between sessions. This essential work allowed the couple to feel confident that they had assimilated a new toolkit to handle any return of depression differently in the future. They also thought together about the support system around them as a couple and decided that they would approach Denise's best friend to see if she would help out with the children in order to free up some time for Denise to try to find some work.

In reviewing the PHQ9 forms that they had filled out at each session over the course of treatment (which their therapist had helpfully transposed into a graph), along with a form measuring couple satisfaction (Couple Satisfaction Index) that they completed at the start and end of therapy, Denise and David could see how their levels of depression could go down, as well as up during times of stress. They were both pleased that their partner's satisfaction in the relationship was higher at the end of therapy than at the start, as was their therapist.

What is Couple Therapy for Depression?

The case of Denise and David illustrates the application of Couple Therapy for Depression, an evidence-based, integrated behavioural couple therapy available on the NHS. It is NICE's treatment of choice where the couple relationship is deemed to be a causal or maintaining factor in a diagnosis of depression. It is also suggested in cases where the relationship can act as a dynamic resource for recovery or where a partner can help the patient adhere to the treatment plan.

In their research on intimate relationship distress and mental health problems, Whisman and Uebelacker (2003) calculated that individuals in unsatisfactory couple relationships were three times more likely to have a mood disorder than individuals in partnerships that functioned well enough, and that up to 30% of severe depressive episodes could be prevented if the couple relationship was improved. Despite this clinical evidence linking depression and the quality of relationships, there is a pervasive lack of awareness amongst healthcare providers about the connection between relationship issues and depression.

The Couple Therapy for Depression model formulates a dynamic picture of the couple interaction incorporating the therapist's use of self and practice of hypothesising on the couple's unconscious, defensive 'fit' manifest in the depressive symptoms of one or both partners. Therapists are trained to move skilfully between a psychodynamic understanding and a more systemic picture of the couple's world and history, to help couples to form their new understanding of themselves, also using cognitive and behavioural techniques to promote change when hopelessness is likely to pervade.

The therapy starts with the premise that one size does not fit all; that relationships are unique and couples need different techniques at different stages of treatment to move towards recovery. In delivering this model, therapists are required to plot a path between facilitating and exploring proactive couple exercises, and stepping back to maintain an overview of the internal worlds of the couple, comprising both the individuals and their relationship.

Different therapeutic approaches are afforded equal place in this truly integrated model, including techniques that may seem contradictory. It begins with a thorough assessment of risk relating to domestic violence and substance misuse as well as to depression and its severity. This screening for suitability, which is vital in the treatment of depression, is done with the couple together and individually, and family histories are explored. The assessment culminates in a session where the couple are invited to create goals for the therapy with their therapist who feeds back a formulation of the main themes in the work. As in Denise and David's case, a mutual trap is identified as the therapist will have formed an initial 'picture' of the couple's defensive interaction, where their differences have become divisive and their communication has broken down.

Considering the function depression may play within relationships is part of the therapy. Couple defences may well be in place for protective purposes, against mutual anxiety around intimacy, for example, or fear of the contagion of depression, enacted by one half of the couple desiring a refuge in 'space' and psychic distance from their partner while the other pushes for closeness. Blocking the possibility of intimacy, in its widest sense, restricting relational and individual development and growth, closing down the possibility of communication of needs and resisting an acceptance of loss, are all examples of what the couple may unconsciously be avoiding.

Therapists work actively to reframe the couple's entrenched way of seeing each other's behaviours, opening up a different interpretation of what occurs between them. This alternative or third perspective of understanding from the therapist's point-of-view transforms the couple's concrete beliefs around the other's motivations and feelings into a more flexible way of thinking about their relationship. If successful, the therapist gradually comes to represent the couple's relationship and, in trusting the therapeutic space, so too the couple begin to shift from their defensive and non-trusting strongholds to a more open and curious state of mind.

Countering the heavy sense of hopelessness that often prevails around depression, therapists ask couples to recall, in detail, instances of past resilience in times of stress; how they coped during other times of transition, such as the arrival of children or death of a parent? Everyday stressors are also emphasised and explored. Understanding past and current coping strategies and why these might no longer be effective is important too. Enlisting the couple's commitment to the relationship and the therapeutic process are key to this early stage. The couple's passivity and helplessness to elicit change are gently challenged by the therapist, adopting an active stance and offering psycho-education around depression and its manifestations. This normalising of symptoms provides relief for the couple and reduces mutual feelings of blame, alleviating the communication 'shut down' and opening up new avenues to explore relationship difficulties.

In this early stage of the work, therapists aim to create a new understanding between the partners, a process known as 'empathic softening'. When Denise hears for the first time that David's faith in the world has been badly damaged by his redundancy, her warmer feelings of concern are triggered. This new couple awareness is aided by active communication exercises to unlock discussions in a slower, non-critical, more structured style. These tasks, set carefully by the therapist, aim to open up damaged pathways to understanding, hopefully gaining that 'eureka' moment of one partner turning to the other to say, 'I didn't realise you felt like that'. That simple phrase can be the first step to a new understanding of each other and the possibility of change between them.

Where patients feel shut out and powerless, it is helpful to work with a preordained shape to the process and a dynamic therapeutic stance. It is also crucial to addressing cognitive distortions and changing perceptions linked to depression. Untangling the couple's entrenched views and defences involves partners accepting and tolerating their differences. Therapists aim to help couples to create a safe and optimal emotional distance, at a point where they are likely to be experiencing either intolerable separation from their partner or claustrophobic psychic merger, where difference is denied. This distance–closeness readjustment creates shared psychic room within which there is the potential for creativity and intimacy to flourish, without the partners becoming disconnected.

Throughout the therapy, the couple's sexual relationship is thought about. Patterns in their physical interaction can be viewed as a microcosm of their couple dynamic and a clue to what might be problematic. For David, Denise's loss of libido fed into a sense of his masculinity diminishing through unemployment. This needed to be understood by them to counter the mutual feelings of rejection they otherwise experienced.

Problem-solving and exercises to prompt changes in behaviour are practiced in the latter half of the therapy, both during sessions and as 'homework' for the couple, along with communication exercises. The aim is to ingrain these activities in the couple's repertoire, so they continue to be used once the therapy ends. Whether these techniques are actually utilised by the couple independently is not crucial as they will have experienced the change in communication during the sessions, altering expectations. That their therapist models a different way of relating to their interactions is important. A thorough revision of the work, and ownership of the changes achieved, is made during the final sessions, along with considering how the couple can better deal with stress and create new support networks.

Couple Therapy for Depression's place in the system

How has Couple Therapy for Depression evolved and where it is delivered? This question necessitates revisiting the advent of the Improving Access to Psychological Therapies (IAPT) within the National Health Service (NHS) (DH, 2007; IAPT Programme, 2012). IAPT's requirement for evidence-based treatments placed a new demand on talking therapies and saw the proliferation of the availability of cognitive behavioural therapy (CBT), which had the largest randomised controlled trial (RCT) evidence-base. Other non-CBT modalities recommended for the treatment for depression by the National Institute for Clinical Institute for Health and Care Excellence (NICE) have been introduced on a small scale, Couple Therapy for Depression being one of them.

Couple Therapy for Depression's overarching competencies were formulated by an expert reference group who drew on RCT studies of efficacy, as well as 'best practice' in behavioural, cognitive, emotionally-focused, systemic and psychodynamic couple therapies to create an integrative model, focusing on the couple relationship as the agent of change.

A long list of competencies was then conceptualised as a coherent therapy by Tavistock Relationships, and a national training programme was established. This conceptualisation was tested and amended as the model was delivered under supervision.

The vision behind the model, and a significant reason for calling on a variety of theoretical modalities in its creation, had both a practical and an ideological basis. The vision was that a new workforce of clinicians, derived from different therapeutic backgrounds, would be encouraged to train to work with a relational focus around symptoms of depression in patients. This integration of different modalities in one model also catered for the practical constraints of NHS services containing an eclectic mix of clinicians. The skill of the therapist lies in the ability to move betwixt and between the five modalities that make up this integrated model; alternating their therapeutic stance, for example interweaving more active behavioural exercises with stepping back and thinking about their impact on the relationship through a more psychodynamic or systemic lens. Relate's national workforce of couple counsellors was identified as a potentially important source for delivering the model, an idea that has yet to fully come to fruition. An additional distinguishing factor in advancing the model was that it was subsequently captured in a syllabus for practising the therapy, (Hewison et al., 2014).

As in all IAPT-approved therapies, Couple Therapy for Depression is validated by the couple completing the IAPT minimum data set (PHQ9 and GAD7) at each of the 16–20 sessions of treatment (DH, 2007; IAPT Programme, 2012). This steady stream of data recording levels of anxiety and depression from both partners allows the therapist to track the depression as it moves around the couple's dynamic system and record it diminishing as the therapy progresses.

Across the country, practitioners feedback via Tavistock Relationship's supervisors that couples rarely disengage from treatment once it has started. Patients report that authentic negotiation around their individual needs, sufficient time to understand their distress and the introduction of new strategies to improve communication between them, all offered by their therapist, bring with it an easing of their difficulties. Couples' adherence to treatment is further aided by transparency of practice and a genuine co-creation between the partners and their therapist of a treatment plan that acknowledges the positive and negative values of the relationship and their current coping strategies. Couples grow to realise their depression scores can go up and come down during the course of treatment, a valuable learning in itself. On ending, they describe an increased sense of connection within the relationship, evidenced in their scores on the Couple Satisfaction Index that they complete at the start and end of treatment.

The inclusion of Couple Therapy for Depression within the NICE guidelines for the management of depression within adults has created ripples in routine NHS practice where the norm is to care for patients on an individual basis. The introduction of a relational approach to aspects of physical and mental ill-health could be seen as a sea-change: change being the operative word, with its inherent implication of loss that can generate resistance.

Improving access to psychological therapies

Any consideration of the efficacy of this model is best done with reference to the context in which it is currently offered in England. To do this justice, some familiarity with the ground-breaking introduction of IAPT within the NHS is required to gain an understanding of the wide variety in quality and availability of services across the country (Harris, 1948).

The IAPT programme began in 2008 with the aim of providing evidenced-based psychological therapies delivered by fully trained and accredited practitioners. These therapists and health professionals would be matched to the mental health problem, its intensity and duration, in a service designed to optimise outcomes.

The idea of IAPT was introduced by a Labour government in response to the Layard (2005) report, 'Mental health: Britain's biggest social problem', which marshalled economic arguments of a potential loss of £12 billion a year in absenteeism to demonstrate that depression and anxiety were growing threats to the British workforce. Subsequent governments have expanded IAPT's remit to include children and young people, older people and those with long-term health conditions.

The IAPT programme was set up on the basis of a stepped-care model according to NICE guidance on depression. The first step of care comprises assessment; step two offers a range of treatments including guided self-help and computerised CBT for individuals. Patients should only be 'stepped-up' to a higher intensity and more resource-intensive intervention if they do not respond to treatment at the lower step.

Digitised self-help can be stepped-up if necessary to individual CBT or a range of non-CBT talking therapies for the treatment of depression, such as dynamic interpersonal therapy, interpersonal psychodynamic therapy, eye movement desensitisation and reprocessing, mindfulness-based CBT, and counselling for depression for individuals. Couple Therapy for Depression was recommended as a treatment for mild to moderate depression by NICE; it was classified as a high-intensity therapy to be delivered at step 3 of the model. It is the only treatment whose sole aim is to look at the relational aspect of a diagnosis of depression and which works with the couple relationship as patient.

IAPT was originally given a national access target of treating 15% of the population with depression or anxiety as well as achieving a recovery target of 50%. In 2016, new waiting-time standards were introduced, requiring that 75% of people referred to the IAPT programme should begin treatment within six weeks of referral, and 95% should have begun treatment within 18 weeks of referral. In 2017, IAPT's access target was revised upward to 25% of the relevant population, and a new focus on people with long-term conditions sought to integrate IAPT services with physical health services in the NHS.

Choice of therapy for patients is acknowledged by the Department of Health as an important factor in recovery rates, but unfortunately for Couple Therapy for Depression, no specific targets for its availability have been introduced, which might have helped to increase its uptake across the country. Denise and David could consider themselves lucky as approximately half of IAPT services currently do not offer couple therapy for depression.

Outcomes, availability and barriers

Good news for couples in England who are experiencing depression was documented in Psychological Therapies Annual Report on the use of IAPT for 2015–2016. It notes that Couple Therapy for Depression achieved patient recovery rates of 61.8% for anxiety and 58.8% for depression. These rates are significantly higher than CBT and counselling, which are the standard offers in most IAPT services (NHS Digital, 2016).

Despite this practice-based success, the relational component of diagnoses of depression remains relatively hidden and it has proved difficult to extend availability of this therapy. The reasons for this dearth are myriad and complex. The following is not an exhaustive list, but it sets out some of the main barriers.

Funding for training

Since 2012, training to deliver Couple Therapy for Depression within the NHS has been funded by Health Education England (HEE), the body responsible for ensuring that there is an adequate workforce to deliver healthcare in the NHS. Accreditation comprises a combination of formal teaching and experiential learning over five days, which is then consolidated through the supervision of training cases over eight months or so of clinical practice, the submission of training tapes and written work.

Training in NICE-recommended therapies (other than CBT) is classified as 'continuous professional development' (CPD). CPD budgets for healthcare practitioners in the NHS are administered by HEE and in some areas non-CBT therapies have had to compete for funding against a wide range of other CPD trainings such as pharmacy and nursing.

Lack of awareness

Tavistock Relationships has long argued that the patient assessment process in IAPT should require referrers actively to assess whether a patient's difficulties have a relational component. Such direct action is necessary because there is little imperative for providers to assess the relational factors, particularly if their service does not currently offer Couple Therapy for Depression. Only when such relational factors are identified through assessment will the true prevalence of the link between relationship health and depression come to light.

Setting up a couple service within the NHS involves the PWPs mainly responsible for undertaking assessments in IAPT being trained to 'think couple' and 'speak couple'. In considering relevant factors and talking to patients about their couple relationship, PWPs can explore with patients whether there is a relational aspect to the symptoms of depression or if the relationship would be an effective resource and pathway to recovery. As it stands, PWPs often express dismay at being asked to add another assessment criterion to their already onerous list, particularly one that they can sometimes perceive as an intrusion into a patient's intimate life. Training to help them recognise the benefits of a couple intervention for depression is not currently available.

If services do decide to offer Couple Therapy for Depression, therapists are often required to set up couple services from scratch within IAPT. This involves practicalities such as extended hours of service to attract couples, size of rooms and the collection of couple data on complex digitised systems geared to individual patients. Perhaps it is not surprising, despite some thriving pockets of good practice, in many cases, trainees report struggling to find couple referrals (Cahill, 2006).

The dearth of provision of couple treatments for depression seems markedly at odds with Tavistock Relationships' own experience of providing couple therapy at its two central London centres: analysis of its intake data revealed that 70% of people accessing our services were suffering from mild to severe depression, which would qualify them for treatment within IAPT. This suggests that the paucity of couple cases identified within the NHS is anomalous and might indicate a problem with the assessment process (Kupfer et al., 1996; Lewinsohn et al., 1999).

A fantasy of 'cure'

A major depressive disorder is one of the most common forms of psychopathology and one that will affect approximately one in six men and one in four women during their lifetime (Kessler et al., 1993). It is also usually highly recurrent, with at least 50% of those who recover from a first episode of depression having one or more additional episodes, and approximately 80% of those with a history of two episodes having another recurrence. Once a first episode has occurred, recurrent episodes will usually begin within five years of the initial illness and, on average, individuals with a history of depression will have five to nine separate depressive episodes subsequently.

Whilst all therapies attempt to ease symptoms and distress, evidence suggests the likelihood with depression is that it will recur and that, to some extent, mild depression that passes is an understandable reaction to difficult life events and stages that afflict the majority of the population at some points in their lives. An understanding and acceptance of this might help mitigate the stigma that depression still carries within society. However, with the high percentage of recurrence for a severe depressive episode, working with relationships and depression to enable better 'couple' management and understanding of the condition is crucial.

We have noticed, as deliverers of this NHS training nationally, that the increasing pressure faced by IAPT workers to achieve access and recovery targets is connected to the proliferation of sickness absence due to stress and depression in its own workers. This problem begs the question of how depressing it is working in a service which exclusively treats depression.

The Francis Report (2013) highlighted a systemic failure to provide basic, compassionate care in the NHS. The report recommended that 'the blame culture must be eradicated and compassion must be put back at the heart of everything the NHS does'. Whilst Sir Robert Francis could not have been clearer, the pressures the NHS is faced with, including financial cuts, increased public expectation and intensive scrutiny are unlikely to lead to a return to a compassionate organisational culture any time soon (Kuehner, 2003; Kupfer & Frank, 2001).

A relational approach to treating depression

Depression is disorienting and debilitating. Its very symptoms can sabotage patients seeking the help they need. Despite recent efforts, stigma around mental illness pervades with the fear of contagion, narratives that depression cannot be recovered from, that anti-depressants are addictive, and that it signifies mental weakness, are often alive in patients' minds.

In the lifecycle of a couple there are many experiences of loss and change, life events that trigger past trauma and impact on a couple's dynamic interpersonal system. Losses affecting the couple are necessarily going to be difficult to assimilate as both partners are likely to experience these losses differently. Mourning and depression are closely linked. In his seminal paper, 'Mourning and melancholia,' Freud wrote that the

> mental features of melancholia are a profoundly painful dejection, cessation of interest in the outside world, loss of the capacity to love, inhibition of all activity, and a lowering of the self-regarding feelings to a degree that finds utterance in self-reproaches and self-revilings, and culminates in a delusional expectation of punishment.
>
> (1917, p. 243)

These traits, he maintains, are mirrored in mourning with one exception, the 'disturbance in self-regard is absent in mourning; but otherwise the features are the same' (Freud, 1917, p. 243).

Mourning, an essential component of all change, can mutate into a defensive sense of separation and rivalry if a couple's relationship becomes overloaded and no longer functions as a suitable container for their distress. The hope is that this is temporary and, given the right support, that a relationship can recover, with symptoms of depression being reduced and a couple's balance of loving and hating restored, their relationship becoming a place of creativity, mutual acceptance and refuge.

In working with depressed couples, Tavistock Relationships has come to have a greater understanding of how depression can cause damage to the intimate couple relationship, how it can move around in the couple's dynamic system, how it is defended against and what can help to alleviate its symptoms.

Couple Therapy for Depression, with its unique blend of proven couple theory and intervention can reaffirm a relationship, providing couples with skills to better negotiate the hurdles of life and reintroduce their capacity for change and development. Eroded at the outset, they will recover a sense of couple confidence in their relationship as a resource and search for new meaning in their difficulties. Fresh understanding of each other is gained through safe exploration of their relationship's defence system to unearth vulnerabilities, improve communication and promote acceptance of differences, with new behaviours introduced to enhance and repair the relationship.

Acknowledgement

Kate Thompson would like to thank Richard Meier for his contribution to this chapter and for his steadfast work in promoting Couple Therapy for Depression as a model for patients to choose when diagnosed with depression.

Note

1 The Patient Health Questionnaire (PHQ9) is part of the IAPT minimum data set that patients fill out at every session. It is a multipurpose instrument for screening, diagnosing, monitoring and measuring the severity of depression.

References

Cahill, J., Barkham, M., Stiles, W.B., Twigg, E., Hardy, G.E., Rees, A.,& Evans, C. (2006). Convergent validity of the CORE measures with measures of depression for clients in cognitive therapy for depression. *Journal of Counseling Psychology, 53*(2): 253–59.

Department of Health (2007). *Improving Access to Psychological Therapies (IAPT), a Stepped-care Model of Service Provision Which Distinguishes Between High and Low Intensity Interventions*. London: Department of Health.

Francis, R. (2013). *Report of the Mid Staffordshire NHS Foundation Trust Public Inquiry. (3 Vols)*. London: The Stationery Office.

Freud, S. (1917). Mourning and melancholia. *S. E., 14*: 237–258. London: Hogarth.

Harris, S.W. (1948). *Report of the Departmental Committee in Grants in the Development of Marriage Guidance*. London: HMSO.

Hewison, D., Clulow, C. & Drake, H. (2014). *Couple Therapy for Depression: a Clinician's Guide to Integrated Practice*. Oxford: Oxford University Press.

IAPT Programme (2012). *Improving Access to Psychological Therapies. IAPT Guidance for Commissioning*. IAPT Training 2011/12–2014/15.

Kessler, R.C., McGonagle, K.A., Swartz, M., Blazer, D.G., & Nelson, C.B. (1993). Sex and depression in the National Comorbidity Survey I: lifetime prevalence, chronicity, and recurrence. *Journal of Affective Disorders*, 29: 85–96. [PubMed]

Kuehner, C. (2003). Gender differences in unipolar depression: an update of epidemiological findings and possible explanations. *ActaPsychiatricaScandinavica, 108*: 163–74. [PubMed]

Kupfer, D.J., & Frank, E. (2001). The interaction of drug- and psycho-therapy in the long-term treatment of depression. *Journal of Affective Disorders, 62*: 131–7. [PubMed]

Kupfer, D.J., Frank, E., & Wamhoff, J. (1996). Mood disorders: update on prevention of recurrence. In: C. Mundt & M.J. Goldstein (Eds.), *Interpersonal Factors in the Origin and Course of Affective Disorders* (pp. 289–302). London: Gaskell/Royal College of Psychiatrists.

Layard, Richard (2005). Mental health: Britain's biggest social problem? Paper presented at the No.10 Strategy Unit Seminar on Mental Health, 20 January 2005, London.

Lewinsohn, P.M., Allen, N.B., Seeley, J.R., & Gotlib, I.H. (1999). First onset versus recurrence of depression: differential processes of psychosocial risk. *Journal of Abnormal Psychology, 108*(3): 483–9. [PubMed]

Mattinson, J. (1988). *Love, Work, Marriage: The Impact of Unemployment.* London: Duckworth.

Meier, R. (2013). A drop in the ocean: couple therapy for depression in IAPT. Tavistock Relationships' report from an investigation into the availability of couple therapy for depression in Improving Access to Psychological Therapies (IAPT) services. London: Tavistock.

NHS Digital (2016). *Psychological Therapies: Annual Report on the use of IAPT Services 2015–2016*, (Online) NHS Digital. Available at: www.content.digital.nhs.uk/catalogue/PUB22110

Whisman, M. A., & Uebelacker, L. A. (2003). Comorbidity of relationship distress and mental and physical health problems. In: D.K. Snyder & M.A. Whisman (Eds.), *Treating Difficult Couples: Helping Clients with Coexisting Mental and Relationship Difficulties* (pp. 3–26). New York: Guilford Press.

Bibliography

Isher, G., & Costello, C.G. (1988). Relapse after recovery from unipolar depression: a critical review. *Psychological Bulletin, 104*(1): 84–96. [PubMed]

Davila, J., Karney, B.R., Hall, T.W., & Bradbury, T.N. (2003). Depressive symptoms and marital satisfaction: within-subject associations and the moderating effects of gender and neuroticism. *Journal of Family Psychology, 17*: 557–70.

Krueger, R.F. (1999). The structure of common mental disorders. *Archives of General Psychiatry, 56*: 921–26. [PubMed]

Rao, A. S., Bhutani, G., Dosanjh, N., Clarke, J., Hacker-Hughes, J., Easton, S., Van Laar, D., & Cohen-Tovée, E. (2016), *Psychological Wellbeing and Resilience: Resetting the Balance.* London: British Psychological Society.

Whisman, M.A., Sheldon, C.T., & Goering, P. (2000). Psychiatric disorders and dissatisfaction with social relationships: does type of relationship matter? *Journal of Abnormal Psychology, 109*: 803–8.

Commentary on Chapter 6

Jeremy Holmes

Responding to this chapter is a somewhat strange experience. I find myself role-playing a Dickensian elder, huddled in the corner of the room, vaguely observing the younger generation through misted senses, bemused and exhausted by the ceaseless activity, impenetrable acronyms and insistence on whistling-to-keep-spirits-up 'evidence'. Vainly (in both senses) I cling to old-man convictions that a) the world is going to the dogs, or b) if it is not, there is nothing new under the sun.

Banishing this reverie, let us see, from an ingrained attachment perspective, if I can find a sensible gloss on this clear, humane, and optimistic paper. I will start from two rather minor-seeming points, on the principle that it is often through apparently trivial details that one gains entree into the heart of psychological problems.

Getting worse means getting better

The first is the role of the 'PHQ9 forms' (horrors!). They seem to 'work', not just in the sense that tick-box 'improvements' will satisfy the NHS managers. David's score went up in the course of therapy; this suggests a much more subtle treatment process than the 'drug metaphor' on which the dominant psychotherapy paradigm of cognitive behavioural therapy's (CBT's) success rests.[1] Psychotherapy is not like taking a 'talking therapy pill', analogous to antibiotics for an infection. It is an interactive, interpersonal process, beset by complexity, in which things often have to get worse before they can get better: *reculer pour mieux sauter*. As first steps on the road to recovery David needed to 'get depressed', to own his feelings – sadness, shame, guilt and rage – and find ways to bring them into the dialogic interpersonal field.

Affect regulation

From an attachment perspective (Holmes & Slade 2017) a crucial function of attachment relationships is *affect regulation*. This is self-evident in the case of babies and young children, where parents continuously monitor, resonate with, name and help modulate their offspring's feelings. This process continues into romantic/spousal relationships in adulthood. Couples act as 'hidden regulators' of one another's feelings, available to be activated at times of adversity. Typically, the less stressed member of the dyad bears the brunt of emotional pain on the other's behalf (Coan et al., 2006), thereby lessening their hypothalamic and other neuro-endocrine alarm systems.

For David and Denise this system was not working. David had not been able to help Denise with her bereavement, nor she with his redundancy. Neither, it seems, had supported the other with their older son's school problems. The affect-regulatory process has both contemporary and historical determinants. Denise's mother died when she was in her teens. She became 'close' – perhaps too close – to her father, and her depression started with his death. There is much to unravel here. Had there been a role reversal, where she the teenager was 'regulating' her father's grief while hers was left to one side? Did she have to hold back because of the dangers of adolescent intimacy with an opposite sex parent, especially one who would have been emotionally and sexually deprived? Did this constellation spill over into her marriage, so that she could not 'trust' David with her feelings, including feelings of anger at not being able to trust him? Did this restraint play out in their etiolated sex life?

Was David similarly frightened to reveal to Denise *his* inner world of affect, including 'depression' (whatever that tired term denotes), for fear she would further reinforce his sense of failure by consigning him to 'bed-ridden-ness'. Based on the known links between the use of language and attachment status, the latter was yet another phrase which needed to be deconstructed. Good therapy entails picking up and getting to the hidden affect that lies behind the half-baked clichés and empty phrases and sterile dialogue that avoidant clients – and managers – tend to live by.

Anna rightly homed in on the impasse in David and Denise's affect regulation system. Denise was frightened to let David know how miserable, useless and marginalised she felt, for fear of exacerbating his depression. He likewise feared that his feelings of impotence could only get worse if he were to risk fully exposing them to his wife, who might respond with ridicule and belittlement rather than acceptance and sympathy.

David and Denise, once they relinquished their deathly rigidity, were both in states of unregulated fear, which neither, wrapped up as they were in their own problems, were able to assuage for the other. There was, for both, a perverse safety in a lifeless marriage, compared with the imagined chaos and destruction that bringing vitality into their relationship might entail. They were 'attached', but their attachment was 'insecure' – rigid and constraining in the sense that it precluded exploration of both pain and pleasure. David's heightened depression score was a sign that he was ready to feel his feelings, but with the hope of a different outcome.

Couples and the system

The second seemingly minor point concerns opening moves of therapy and the role of their son in initiating help-seeking. Couple therapists need to think systemically as well as dyadically. Even without including the son himself in the therapy, it would be important to look at what his school difficulties 'represented' for the family and its functioning. Whatever its other meanings, a key function of families and their founding couples is procreation, protection and bringing up the next generation. Denise rightly sensed that if their son was in trouble, that meant that she and David were too. It is likely that as a mother, were she faced with a choice between David and their son's well-being, she would opt for the latter, especially as she felt that David had usurped her maternal role – and presumably abandoned his complementary paternal one. Their son's 'deteriorating' behaviour in school might be a manifestation of the very missing liveliness, including unfocused but necessary rage, so lacking in their marriage.

Attachment injury

Their son's plight might well have evoked Denise and David's own childhood traumata. A fearful child whose attachment dynamic is activated without assuagement cannot play or learn. A comparable attachment impasse is a common basis for marital difficulties and breakdown. Both members of the dyad are in states of attachment arousal, unable to provide the secure base the other needs. Johnson (Johnson et al., 2001) construes this as 'attachment injury', a bedrock moment in a couples' history where one member fails to be the secure base needed to withstand, mitigate and repair emotional pain and trauma. Such traumata include the illness – worse still, death – of a child; parental bereavement; life-threatening illness; or an 'affair' (a word again in need of deconstruction – slight flirtation, passionate sexual relationship, 'one-off' or prolonged clandestine relationships?). 'Kitchen sink' rows in which seemingly minor incidents end up with mayhem return again and again to seminal moments where one or other, or both, felt utterly let down, alone, unsupported and/or betrayed.

As Anne's work admirably demonstrates, in these situations the therapist has to occupy the role of secure base, affect regulator, mediator and orchestrator of couple communication. Where there is attachment injury, the 'injured' and resentful partner needs to be helped to tell his or her story in vivid detail. As mentioned, a feature of insecure attachments are discourse styles in which liveliness is diminished or extinguished, and this is especially the case where couple dysfunction leads to or emerges out of depression. The 'accused' partner has to be helped to listen attentively and non-defensively to the other. These first steps may take several sessions, together with prescribed listening/telling 'homework', with the caveat that the latter is often initially ineffective.

Next, the injury-inflictor has to be helped to take responsibility for his or her part in what happened, acknowledging the suffering the other has experienced. This can lead to genuine remorse and the wish to make reparation. None of these are easy tasks. The sufferer needs to trust that the inflictor is not just going through the motions of repentance. The 'guilty' one needs to face his or her own failings. Finally, the injured party needs to accept the partner's apologies, see that they are truly meant, and start to look at his or her own part in the debacle, including the need to let go of the past and move on.

The developmental origins of depression and their role in couple functioning

As already suggested, couple therapy for depression, especially in a CBT context, is typically seen as an adventitious 'illness' needing 'treatment', just as an infection descends on an unsuspecting and blameless victim. From my fogey-ish viewpoint this is an example of the 'supermarket' model of health in which 'customers' go to a health emporium and 'choose'[2] a treatment, hopefully resulting in a return to a disembodied state of health. 'Disembodied', because what is so egregiously missing here is the developmental process which determines a life-course – of body and mind, from cradle to grave.[3]

In psychiatry I see increasing ablation of the life-history. Psychiatric disorders are no longer seen as psycho-socio-biological process reaching back to early childhood. This de-developmentalised model has some benefits. It can help counteract depressive guilt, where psychoanalytic emphasis on the role of narcissistic rage may reinforce rather than mitigate recrimination and self-dislike.

'Assortive mating' means that like tends to pair with like. David and Denise had both underperformed at school, but had subsequently 'done well'. An interesting variant of this process is mentioned by Thompson. She refers to the idea, originally put forward by Dicks (1993), that there is often a shared childhood phantasy, problem, or trauma that unconsciously shapes the attraction, persistence *and difficulties* which couples bring for therapy, especially, perhaps, where depression is the dominant theme.

Denise and David, in different ways, had implicit psychosexual low self-esteem. Denise was dissatisfied with her 'poor figure', while David had 'lost his libido' (again the devil would be in the detail as to what exactly this meant and how it played out in their sex lives). Loss too: Denise's mother's death in her teens and then her father dying; David's hard-won job and income gone, built up to counteract a childhood sense of impoverishment and emptiness ('loss' of what one had never had is doubly difficult).

In the Dicks' picture, couples are drawn together by this shared underlying theme, together with the hope that their love will result in a different outcome or 'new beginning'. Denise and David had jointly helped one another to believe in themselves as sexual attractive beings, and to overcome their adolescent under-achievement.

When this process goes awry, as it typically does in depression, it sets the stage for marital difficulties. Denise had lost her mother and a grandmother for her boys; David was 'type-cast' as a replacement, but, having lost his job, his now maternal role in the family disequilibrated their sex life and disempowered Denise's femininity. Beware of what you wish for. David hoped that Denise would help him to overcome his emotional avoidance; but the more she tried to draw him out, the more switched-off he became, for fear of a catastrophic explosion.

From an attachment perspective, the role of the therapist is to help the couple get back on track by providing first, the reassurance of familiarity; including accessing familiar difficult feelings with which they need help – in David and Denise's case, feelings of loss, under-achievement, and physical inadequacy. Second, the role is to facilitate new outcomes, so that David can be helped to sense his potency and capacity to make good, Denise to like her body and, despite the absence of a maternal role-model, still become a good mother.

From an attachment perspective, two necessary and related therapeutic skills stand out. First is the capacity to help couples to begin to 'mentalize' – to see themselves from the outside and others from the inside (c.f., Holmes & Slade, 2017). The reciprocal balance between anxiety and mentalizing needs to be born in mind in this process: couples can be helped to lower their anxiety through recalling early happiness, mindfulness, humour, fun and play, approaches that might be especially important where there has been an attachment injury. Second is the capacity to help couples see their relationship, and the family as a whole, as entities in their own right, separate from the individuals who make them up.

'The marriage' needs to be treated as one would a child whose attachment needs are aroused by threat. Couple-dom needs comfort, reassurance and security before attempting to ventilate feelings of disappointment, rage, anger and hopelessness. This precept runs counter to much practice, where negative emotions are seen as needing to be immediately 'ventilated'. But they will be already near the surface, and premature exploration or ventilation merely leads to defensiveness and further entrenchment of negativity.

Attachment research shows that it is only when the attachment dynamic is quietened that a child can return to exploratory play and learning. Anna expertly identified the approach–avoidance dilemma that David and Denise were trapped, in which any attempts at intimacy were met with increased anxiety and so further rebuff. The guiding precept here is 'before beginning the chase, first create a Secure Base'.

Conclusion

Thomson raises Winnicott's political-existential question: 'we are poor indeed if we are only sane' (Winnicott, 1964, p. 10). A vital component, as society and the health care it provides becomes increasingly fragmented and instrumentalised, is *the uniqueness of secure connection*. Marital and family love and continuity form the bedrock of this counter-instrumentalist principle. Stripped of its ironic cynicism, George Bernard Shaw's aphorism that 'love is a gross exaggeration of the difference between one person and everyone else' (Shaw, 1908, p. 32) is profoundly true. The fact that IAPT and NICE now recognise the role of couple therapy in depression suggest that change is possible. Whether this is a straw in the wind, or an early building block towards more humanistic healthcare remains to be seen.

Notes

1 In an interesting, and for psychoanalytic practitioners disturbing example of brand triumphalism, psychotherapy is now often equated with CBT, just as vacuum cleaners are described as 'Hoovers', or sodas with 'Coke'.
2 Aka 'purchase', either themselves or via a third-part funder such as the NHS, a 'service', increasingly provided by profit-oriented private companies.
3 Ironically, this was Bevan's mantra for care from the NHS. Today's medicine is increasingly de-contextualised – socially (doctors know little of their patient's social circumstances) and developmentally. Decisions about health care are decided in a 'big data' utilitarian framework, rather than a focus on the individual and her stage in the life (and death) process.

References

Coan, J.A., Schaefer, H.S., & Davidson, R.J. (2006). Lending a hand: social regulation of the neural response to threat. *Psychological Science*, *17*(12): 1032–9.
Dicks, H. (1993). *Marital Tensions*. Hove: Routledge, 2016.
Holmes, J., & Slade, A. (2017). *Attachment in Therapeutic Practice*. London: Sage.
Johnson, S., Makinen, J., & Millikin, J. (2001). Attachment injuries in couple relationships: a new perspective on impasses in couple therapy. *Journal of Marital and Family Therapy*, *27*: 145–55.
Shaw, G.B. (1908). *Getting Married*. Sioux Falls, SD: Nuvision, 2008.
Winnicott, D.W. (1964). *The Child, the Family, and the Outside World*. Harmondsworth: Penguin, 1991.

Chapter 7

Mentalization-based couple therapy

Viveka Nyberg and Leezah Hertzmann

This chapter describes a model of mentalization based treatment for couples (MBT-CT) developed at Tavistock Relationships. We would like to express our thanks to all our colleagues who have taken part in the MBT-CT workshop over the past five years, both for their enthusiasm for the idea of developing a service for couples who otherwise can be hard to engage and for their dedication in developing and applying this model of intervention. Our special thanks go to Amanda Cuthbert who generously contributed the case vignette that follows, and to the couple who consented to their experience being published.

> Carrie and Nick were seen at Tavistock Relationships for mentalization based couple therapy. The couple sought help when they became concerned about their behaviour and its impact on their four young children. Carrie and the children were living separately from Nick as a result of this concern.
> Carrie has a strong claiming style. She appeals to me to understand that she is 'obviously' furious when Nick gives the children the fizzy drinks that she forbids. I do not know why this is 'obvious' and I ask Carrie to say more. I feel positioned as a sort of fellow good parent who knows this. Carrie is appealing to me to agree with the idea that there is a good parent and a bad one: the claim is that the bad parent is undoing the work of the good parent. She is accusing Nick and sounding increasingly angry. Nick sits in silence pinching his lip. He then tells me that the row erupts at home when Charlie, their eldest child, 'tells mummy' that daddy has been giving them fizzy drinks and that it is supposed to be 'their secret'. He suggests to me that this is why her rage is 'obvious'. I am struck by his appeal to me too: to understand why Carrie is fuming.
> The beginning phase of MBT-CT involves identifying the moments of emotional arousal between the couple that are most intense. This is the affect focus for the work. There were pressing difficulties: Carrie was being evicted from her home and Nick was concerned about the mental well-being of one of their children in particular. In this first session, however, the couple began the heated row above. The 'fizzy drink argument' that erupted between them, they told me, was typical. As I listened, I

experienced a deep fearfulness in myself that was beyond the difficulties they were describing to me.

The process of eliciting the detail of the row in the session engaged the couple, eventually becoming a little more able to think. We identified that Carrie felt disappointed in Nick as a parent, and he expressed a feeling of being unimportant when she was raging. Each had the idea of the other as 'rigid and immovable'. Each recognised, too, a withdrawal from the other into a 'lock-down' state to cope with the intense anger that they experienced. The aloneness and isolation that the couple felt in living apart was striking, but both partners wanted to avoid the children being affected by their 'door-slamming' arguments.

Together we agreed a focus for the remaining sixteen sessions that captured the pattern of relating between the couple, and the emotional intensity of the affect focus: that the experience of seeing the other as rigid and demanding elicits angry feelings, which in turn is associated with being treated and seen as 'unimportant'.

The middle phase of the work was a process of exploring the way this clinical pattern of relating was repeatedly enacted in the couple interactions. We used the affective template we had formulated together to guide the exploration of the explosive angry outbursts. Nick discovered that Carrie's rules helped her to calm down, and his idea about being unimportant was a surprise to Carrie. Carrie accepted that the children missed out on 'messy play' because she was preoccupied with controlling the anger she felt towards Nick. The 'rules' were constricting and seemed to demand too much of her and the children.

There were also clinical enactments, for example when Nick did not attend for three sessions. It was as if the therapy had become a too rigid demand on the couple. Working alone with Carrie, I had both of them in my mind and the template of the agreed focus still made sense. She expressed fear and anxiety as the main feelings which underpinned her angry outbursts: perhaps the children were burdened by keeping secrets? Perhaps Charlie was angry, or worse, did not feel important to his mum and dad? There were links in her mind to her family of origin and her own experience of being a child in relation to her own parents, but our focus stayed with the present difficulty in regulating intense emotion.

Nick returned with an ankle injury linked to over-training, and we used that session to explore the way he had withdrawn from sessions when his own anger felt explosive. He used a deactivating, self-soothing activity that was an attempt to feel stronger. He made the link with feeling unimportant to me and I 'rewound' the couple to think about the session when he felt this way. He pinched his lip and remembered feelings of being left out. This phase of the work was about marking, recognising and differentiating feelings in the 'fizz' of heightened arousal and the flatness of avoided experience.

The ending phase brought a resurgence of conflict. Carrie wanted more sessions and Nick was struggling to attend. He brought somatic complaints and worries about their child who was 'naughty and sad' at school. The couple giggled about an idea that their behaviour had been so bad that they would not be welcome to stay after twenty sessions. The shared nature of their feeling 'unimportant' surfaced during these last weeks, and they both expressed sad and disappointed feelings.

The 'fizzy drinks argument' had lost its toxicity. Rather, it had functioned to point towards the shared unconscious experience of the couple. Perhaps 'their secret' from me was a shared vulnerability. Nick was encouraged when he connected Carrie's 'rules' to the kind of lock-down that he recognised in himself. He recognised the impact of his own anger when he saw her as rigid and he did not feel so isolated from her. For Carrie, 'the rules' softened, and she risked co-parenting more confidently, using agencies to help.

In the course of the intervention Carrie and Nick became better able to apprehend their own intense feelings *in vivo* in the sessions, and they developed an increased reflective capacity. As the therapist, I was left wishing for more time, while at the same time being satisfied with a model that increased the couple's capacity to understand one another better from the inside, and to parent more effectively together.

There is a need for specific interventions and services for challenging populations of couples and parents who are unable to engage with traditional psychodynamic or psychoanalytic therapy models. This population of couples will often present with a history of conflictual relationship problems including domestic violence, histories of mental ill health and substance misuse. The narratives of the couples are often incoherent, accompanied by sudden outbursts of anger directed in an accusatory manner towards the partner, the therapist and sometimes towards clinic staff. These are couples who in the context of an intimate adult relationship, are particularly vulnerable to affective dysregulation. Many of the couples are known to child protection services, mental health services, or are attending anger management programmes for domestic violence. The clinical vignette illustrates one such couple where there was concern that the difficulties the parents experienced in regulating their emotional outbursts were also having a destructive impact on their children.

Over the past decade, Tavistock Relationships (TR) has developed a number of mentalization-based treatments (MBT) for couples and parents (Hertzmann, et al., 2016, 2017; Target et al., 2017). The mentalization-based treatment for couples (MBT-CT) emerged out of TR's 'Parenting Together' programme, which utilised an MBT model to work with separated parents who were in conflict about their children (Hertzmann & Abse 2009, 2010; Hertzmann et al., 2017). The models are firmly rooted in a psychoanalytic understanding of complex relational dynamics, an understanding which has been harnessed and developed by TR over the past 70 years (Morgan, 2018). MBT-CT is integrated into TR's range of services, and the treatment model offers up to 20 joint, weekly therapy sessions for the couple (Nyberg & Hertzmann, 2014).

This chapter examines how MBT-CT and a psychoanalytic understanding of the couple relationship interact theoretically within the area of highly troubled couple relationships, with a focus on key psychoanalytic concepts: containment, projective identification, transference and countertransference. Space precludes a fuller exploration of how the two models understand the origins of trauma. Couples treated in MBT-CT, however, have generally suffered early traumatic experiences and deprivation, including separations, abandonment, emotional and physical abuse.

Although the theoretical basis for understanding the couple relationship is grounded in an understanding of the unconscious interaction between the partners, in adapting this to an MBT intervention we are careful to adhere to MBT principles and structures. The relationship between MBT-CT and a psychoanalytic understanding of the couple relationship may potentially appear like an unlikely 'relationship' between two mis-matched partners. The MBT model, however, has for its therapeutic focus a relational approach, and it can be argued that the model by definition is applicable to couple relationships who present in what we describe as 'being on the borderline' (Nyberg & Hertzmann, 2014).

The use of the term 'borderline' in relation to couples does not necessarily refer to a diagnostic group but rather describes the mental functioning of a group of couples whose thinking and emotional experiences become greatly disorganised within an intimate attachment relationship. The couples are understood as being on the 'borderline' in the way they are, for example, emotionally 'balancing' on a border between phantasy and reality, between dysregulation and stability, or between rigidity and flexibility. In the tradition of psychoanalytic couple psychotherapy, the guiding principle of the work is that any pathology is shared between the couple (Abse, 2006, 2013).

Although couple psychoanalytic psychotherapy provides opportunities to foster mentalization, this is not its primary focus. An important area of overlap between MBT and psychoanalytic couple psychotherapy is the focus on the patient's mind in the context of a relationship with another person, whether with the therapist or an intimate partner. It is this inter-relational focus which we believe contributes to making the combination of these two models especially helpful with couples on the borderline.

Mentalization-based treatment (MBT) is a form of psychodynamic psychotherapy which has been developed and manualized by Peter Fonagy and Anthony Bateman (Bateman & Fonagy, 2012, 2016). It was originally designed for individuals with borderline personality disorder (BPD). In the course of the past decade the use of the MBT approach has widened and is now used in a variety of settings, as well as within different modalities, including short-term interventions. It is being applied to a range of diagnostic categories such as depression, eating disorders, addiction and trauma (Bateman & Fonagy, 2012).

Containment

The adult intimate couple relationship can be conceptualised as an emotional container for the two partners, and it is often when the relationship has failed to function as a psychological container that a couple will look for help. One couple, attending a first consultation, describe how the state of their relationship feels like 'being in a house where the roof had fallen in'. In itself, this description indicates a couple capable of a degree of mentalizing and symbolic thinking as they can conceptualise the emotional state of feeling trapped under dangerous circumstances. Nevertheless, the image speaks to the terror of being ensnared in an intimate relationship where the containing function is missing. The example with Carrie and Nick illustrates how for some couples an argument about fizzy drinks can be experienced as if 'the roof falls in' in the way it stirs up unmanageable feelings around the couple's different ways of parenting. When the internal space to manage and contain is absent it leaves 'people with no choice but to use the external space they live in ...' (Ruszczynski, 2012, p. 141). Whatever the presenting problem, individuals within a couple relationship are often seeking help to address overwhelming anxiety, or unbearable psychic pain. It is not only that the couple have difficulties, but that their central problem is being unable to find a way to talk about them (Morgan, 2018).

The aim of MBT-CT intervention is to enable couples increasingly to be able to regulate the affect between them, as well as within themselves, so that the relationship can be experienced as a potentially containing and benign resource rather than as a state which threatens the stability of their minds. In the overlap between MBT-CT and a psychoanalytic understanding of containment, it is evident that when someone is feeling contained this in itself fosters mentalizing. Conversely, when it is missing, the couple's joint affect dysregulation disrupts any potential containing function that the relationship might offer. If emotional states are contained the couple is able to think differently, and if they can think differently the couple may also be more contained. Although old wounds and traumatic experiences cannot be undone, the adult couple relationship holds within it the possibility of a different experience, and this speaks to the potentially benign cycle that may develop in a couple relationship, and the centrality of containment in understanding the couple relationship.

A person's facility to provide containment relies in part on the capacity for curiosity about other's mental states, to 'read' one's own and others' psychic processes. A mind which is characterised by a limited capacity for containment will also manifest a deficit in curiosity, as well as being unable to provide containment for levels of anxiety aroused by the attachment and proximity in an intimate relationship. This can lead to the development of a more fundamentalist state of mind where perceived solutions are often omnipotent and where differences between the partners challenges certainty and hence are perceived as a threat. In psychoanalytic theory this state of mind is understood as being characterised by unconscious paranoid–schizoid anxieties (Klein, 1946). When a couple is able to challenge and dislodge some of their fixed *ideas* of who the other partner 'ought' to be, and instead can be *curious* about the other, this provides the basis for a relationship which potentially offers emotional containment.

Bion argues that emotional experience is at the centre of the processes of mental growth and development (Bion, 1967). His representation of the nature of communication between infant and parental object is also a central tenet in the early theoretical foundation of MBT (Fonagy et al., 2004). Fisher (2014) explores this process through the lens of the adult couple relationship and suggests that 'emotional experience that contributes to growth is an emotional experience that can be thought' and that 'thinking feelingly about a loved object can also be dominated by a wish to control or destroy it' (p. 7).

Within the MBT model, the idea of fostering safety, which is based on the concept of a secure attachment relationship with a therapist, is essential in providing a relational context in which it is possible for a patient to explore the mind of another. The clinical vignette illustrates how the clinician's ability to 'set the frame' and to agree an affect focus for the work acted as containment for the couple's dysregulated states of minds. As this relationship is experienced as increasingly secure it also modifies the mentalizing capacity and the patient is encouraged to confront more difficult and negative feelings. In order to do this the therapist continually monitors the level of emotional dysregulation between the couple and towards the therapist. In a couple intervention, much of this work takes place through focusing on the couple's relational experience where feelings of distrust are likely to dominate.

The MBT-CT therapist is continually alert to the fact that a therapeutic intervention may potentially destabilise both the couple's mentalizing capacity and their relationship. It is important to consider how a therapeutic intervention 'lands' with the couple unit, not just how it is experienced by the individual partners. In individual therapy the primary relationship is between therapist and patient, while in couple psychotherapy the partners bring their shared relational dynamic right into the session by virtue of the live interaction in the room. The aim is to enable partners to differentiate more clearly between self and other in order to gain some understanding of the partner's mind as different, and capable of holding a separate set of thoughts and feelings. The therapist's ability to maintain a 'couple state of mind' is of central importance. This refers to the clinician's capacity to hold the relationship between the partners in mind, where the frame of reference *is* the couple and the relationship they have created together (Morgan, 2001).

The very prospect of being encouraged to enter into someone else's feelings and thoughts can be terrifying for many couples, and the MBT model offers specific techniques for managing dysregulated affect and anxieties. For example, the therapist is encouraged actively to intervene to encourage a 'slowing down', or 'simmering down' of affect in the clinical situation in order that some of the thoughts and beliefs behind the feelings can be articulated. This therapeutic process is illustrated in the clinical vignette when the therapist in an early session was able to identify the way Carrie felt disappointed in Nick as a parent, and he in turn was able to express his feeling of being unimportant when she was raging at him. This validation of their states of mind engaged the couple and they became a little more able to think. 'Empathic validation' in the MBT model (Bateman & Fonagy, 2016) becomes an important technique for managing a couple's anxiety. It is generally harder for an MBT-CT clinician to emphatically validate a couple's shared dysregulation, in contrast to working with individual patients. It requires the clinician to hold the couple in mind, often under emotionally 'stormy' conditions and to endeavour to validate both partners' feelings. It is through the experience of being, and feeling validated that the couple is likely to feel more contained, and hence more available to make use of the therapy.

Projective identification

The choice of an intimate adult partner can represent both a developmental and a defensive arrangement:

> By making such a choice, by creating a marital fit, the couple may be making an unconscious contract for the purpose of development and defence. Developmentally, the attraction ... is toward knowing more about the repudiated parts of the self as located in the other, and in doing so becoming more integrated. Defensively, the attraction ... may be an unconscious shared collusion to retain certain splits and projections in a shared defence against shared anxieties.
>
> (Ruszczynski, 1993, p. 204)

The unconscious dynamic between Carrie and Nick is perhaps illustrated when towards the end of the intervention they were able to share the experience of feeling unimportant, rather than this emotion having been held and expressed solely by Nick. Rather than this particular emotion becoming potentially explosive in their arguments, the sharing of the experience of being unimportant meant the unconscious projective system lost some of its negative impact on the couple dynamic.

The psychoanalytic concept of projective identification was first introduced by Klein (1946) and the theory explained how, at the very the beginning of its development, the infant deals with unmanageable primitive bodily and mental states, particularly anxieties, by unconsciously splitting them off and projecting them into the primary object. In essence, projective identification involves an unconscious interactive process between two people, denoting a psychological mechanism whereby a person strives for emotional balance by engaging in a particular kind of projective psychic action. It describes a phenomenon which happens in close relationships, such as between mother and child, or between partners in an intimate relationship, where parts of the self are unconsciously thought of as being forced into the other person. The recipient of the projections often has the experience, whether consciously or unconsciously, of feeling manipulated by the other person. Although all couples do to some extent make use of projective identification, couples on the 'borderline' are by definition more disposed to make use of primitive defence mechanisms like denial and splitting. They tend to be more heavily reliant on projective mechanisms and projective identification in its more malignant form, which of necessity is manifested in the therapy therefore making the therapists' task particularly challenging. This can be observed in the clinical vignette where both partners initially locate their own rigid expectations and assumptions into the other, while preserving a view of themselves as being 'in the right'.

Couple psychotherapists are highly attuned to the way couples will appear split in their affect, for instance where one partner presents as extroverted and social, while the other presents as more withdrawn and even depressed. In its more extreme form it can be observed in a relationship which is characterised by marked 'up' or 'down' dysregulation. This dynamic is illustrated in the case vignette when Nick did not attend a number of sessions, but was able on his return to mentalize that he had withdrawn from sessions when his anger felt explosive, as if his experience of anxiety took the shape of a retreat into a withdrawn state, apparently devoid of feelings. In this kind of clinical situation the other partner may then increasingly express an uncontained agitation of affect in an attempt to make contact with the partner who is experienced as unavailable. When this type of split presentation manifests excessively it creates difficulties, as it is hard to 'read' someone's mental state if the person presents as emotionally unavailable. With couples on the 'borderline' it can present as an insurmountable difficulty: for example, when a partner who down-regulates and presents as cut off from affect might respond to his partner's expressed dependency needs by 'stonewalling', or even with contempt.

Sometimes psychoanalysis has viewed a patient's external acting-out as an expression of unconscious aggression or envy. This is challenged by the MBT model where hostile behaviour or actions are instead understood as an attempt to *restore coherence* to the person's self-experience or 'self-survival'. Rather than enactments being perceived as a manipulation they are understood as attempts to restore an *illusion* of self-coherence. Within the couple relationship confusion may occur between one person's intention and the other person's experience of feeling controlled or manipulated. From the perspective of the MBT-CT clinician this distinction is very helpful as it offers an understanding of the couple dynamic without the risk of inappropriately apportioning blame or attributing malevolent motives to one of the partners. The couple dynamic can instead be understood as an attempt to protect fragile selves against overwhelming anxiety and internal threats of psychic disintegration. This is demonstrated when Nick discovers that Carrie's 'rules' actually help her to calm down. He is able to understand that, however annoying he finds her rules, it helps to protect her from anxiety that otherwise she might experience as unmanageable.

Hewison (2014) distinguishes between normal and pathological projections in couple psychotherapy, whereby projections become pathological when they distort the nature of the person onto whom the projections are being put. With couples 'on the borderline', distortion of self-experience is a regular occurrence. In the vignette this is illustrated when Nick is able to connect his experience of Carrie's 'rules' with his own reaction of going into a kind of 'lock-down' state. As he was able to recognise the impact of his anger on his own mind when he perceived Carrie as rigid, this meant his self-experience is less distorted. In turn this meant Carrie's self-experience could be adjusted, and her rules could become softer.

With another couple treated in the MBT-CT model, one partner presented with having a recent psychiatric diagnosis of bi-polar disorder while the other partner suffered from depression. In the course of treatment, it became evident that the 'craziness', which was also part of the depressed partner, was to a degree projected into the partner who suffered from a bi-polar disorder, who in turn had a valency for identifying with the projections. During the therapy some of these distorting manifestations within the couple dynamic could be mentalized and challenged with the help of the therapist. The effect was that the couple relationship became a bit less split in its presentation and a more empathetic relationship developed. Excessive use of projective identification can lead to confusion and a loss of sense of self, as well as exacerbating an extreme rigidity in character where artificial boundaries are created between subject and object. This is a situation where a couple can develop an almost delusional certainty that they 'know' what is in the partner's mind.

We find that a clinical appreciation of the couple's projective system is invaluable within the MBT-CT model because it encompasses a dynamic understanding of the relationship the couple unconsciously creates together, and often enacts. However, couples 'on the borderline' generally do not have the reflective capacity to make use of interventions that address unconscious functioning, or to make links between past experiences and the present. Although Carrie attended a few sessions on her own in the middle of the intervention, and links were made in her mind with her own family of origin, the therapist demonstrates how, even when Carrie attends by herself, she stays with the agreed focus on the couple's present difficulty in regulating intense emotion.

Transference

Transference refers to the unconscious repetition in the present of a relationship that was important in a person's childhood. Within the MBT model, it is generally understood that the therapist does not actively interpret the transference relationship as doing this can potentially be destabilising for a patient because it can activate the unconscious in a way which can induce a more turbulent state of mind in the patient. In our experience this can be especially damaging for a couple whose relational dynamic is already very reactive.

Instead the therapist might make a light touch reference to the transference in the context of mentalizing a specific state of mind in relation to the therapist, or how the patient might imagine the therapist's intention. For example, the therapist might explore with the couple the origins of an argument during the preceding week. In this situation, the therapist will first of all recognise and validate the significance and impact of the argument, but might also, if appropriate, add a tentative comment that the conflict might in addition be related to an upset about the therapist having had to cancel the previous session at short notice. The intervention would be tentative, since the MBT-CT therapist would take care to leave room for the couple to disagree.

Rather than being presented with a separate transference interpretation, which the couple could experience as the therapist attempting to put something of his own agenda into the couple's minds, the transference is put in a mentalizing perspective. This also has the potential for the couple to extend their understanding of what has been happening to *their* minds. With couples who have severe difficulties in regulating affect, the transference is in the first instance used to inform the therapist's understanding, and then, if appropriate, to make 'transference-informed' interventions. This is different from the function of transference in psycho-analytic psychotherapy, where it is more likely to be used to interpret the patients' unconscious phantasies in order to promote insight. MBT-CT does not prioritise insight, but rather curiosity about mental states in self and other and how these can drive behaviours in relationships. The 'mentalizing of the transference' can present an alternative perspective on a particular event, with the idea that there is more than one version of a shared couple experience.

The idea of transparency in the treatment situation is fundamental to the MBT-CT model, and this extends to the way transference is used. For example, should it transpire that the therapist makes a mistake, or an inaccurate comment, this is then accepted by the therapist as her own contribution. Rather than this being considered as a blunder by the therapist, it opens an opportunity for a mentalizing alliance between the therapist and the couple where they might be able to understand together how the 'mistake' came about. This kind of exploratory work in the transference can also mirror different avenues for the couple to mentalize around their own 'mistakes' in less defensive ways.

Countertransference

It is generally recognised that the therapist is vulnerable to reflective enactment when working with this particular patient population. The ability to tolerate powerful affect is a necessary prerequisite for couple therapy, and it is not uncommon in this kind of situation for the therapist to get drawn in and enlisted by one partner to offer explicit advice on how to manage the other partner's difficulties or symptoms. Working with couples on the 'border' can produce extreme countertransference responses which the therapist will have to manage.

The couples will often present a particular challenge for clinicians to hold on to a 'couple state of mind' without being pulled into taking sides.

When projective identification is the primary mode of communication between the couple it has enormous potential to create confusion and turmoil in the consulting room, which can generate an experience of chaos and acting out behaviour. It is perhaps realistic to articulate the possibility that most couple therapists working with severely dysregulated couples will sooner or later enact in the countertransference. We are not suggesting that this is done in a 'bad' or unethical way, rather it is more likely to be expressed as a temporary exasperation in the face of either being bombarded with hostility and a feeling of being helpless and useless (Nyberg & Hertzmann, 2014). In the clinical vignette the clinician exemplifies this in describing her initial experience of 'a deep fearfulness' that went beyond the difficulties the couple were bringing. The therapist is recognising that affect is unconsciously projected by the couple, and then responded to in her own state of mind.

The MBT model, while warning of the danger of unacknowledged countertransference, emphasises that, should the MBT therapist be feeling lost, not knowing what is going on, the therapist is encouraged to share this experience of not-knowing with the couple. This is done in a way which takes care not to burden the patients with the therapist's own feelings. This therapeutic stance means that the couple's wish for an all-powerful therapeutic encounter is implicitly addressed, and the potential hazard of an investment in the therapist's omnipotence is reduced. This kind of response can also function as a kind of mirror for the couple, where they can observe how someone else deals with difficult feelings.

In essence, the countertransference and any potential enactment must be marked as an aspect of the therapist's mind, rather than attributed to the couple. At the same time, the clinician lets the partners know that what they say and what happens in the session will evoke a state of mind in the therapist, in a similar way to how one partner in the relationship will evoke and stimulate mental processes in the other partner. This is the arena in which much of the therapeutic work takes place in the MBT-CT model. It is not just the therapist who may be struggling with feelings of rage and hatred, but this may also be part of the couple's own inter-transferential experience within the couple dynamic.

Psychoanalytic theory differentiates between a *concordant* and a *complementary* countertransference. The distinction is based on the specific identification the therapist makes with the patient (Racker, 1957). The *concordant* identification results from the therapist's identification with the patient's ego, superego and id, while the *complementary* identification is produced by the therapist's identification with the patient's internal objects. Complementary identification occurs in a process whereby the patient experiences the therapist as an internal object and, as the therapist feels treated like the internal object, the therapist also unconsciously experiences the object as his or her own. In other words, the therapist may identify with the object's experience towards the patient as a child, with the risk that the therapist will unconsciously enact this experience in relation to the patient. Racker's distinction between different types of countertransference and his understanding of the origin of complementary identification is proving helpful in understanding the MBT-CT therapist's often powerful countertransference experience. This understanding is not used in order to make an interpretation about the partners' states of mind, but rather as an instrument to understand the extent of the trauma the couple bring to the therapy and the kind of affect this generates.

Working with couples in MBT-CT there is an appreciation that perhaps not all emotional identifications are based on projections. Nevertheless, we find in working with couples on the borderline that an understanding of the projective system, both between the partners and between the couple and the therapist, is a precondition for fully appreciating the countertransference and for being able to process the experience. The greatest pitfall in couple therapy with borderline couples, is when the countertransference remains unprocessed and out of awareness (Abse, 2006), and particularly when the complementary countertransference remains unacknowledged by the therapist. Having a first training in a psychodynamic or psychoanalytic psychotherapy provides a good 'grounding' for the handling of difficult countertransference feelings, and guides the way the couple therapist makes use of mentalization-based interventions within the MBT-CT model.

The challenge of mentalization-based couple therapy

Working with couples in this context can be extremely challenging for clinicians. The issues and difficulties that they present with can easily instil a feeling of helplessness. These couples' valency to receive each other's projections mean that some of their most powerful and difficult mental contents are projected in to others with intensity and force. These projections then land and take root in fertile territory, which, because the structure of each partner's internal world and unconscious couple fit, match closely the shape of the other's projection. Mutually receiving the other's projections and then conforming to that same projection contributes to the problems with emotional regulation which are so characteristic of the difficulties facing these couples on the borderline.

In our experience, therapists often experience powerful countertransference reactions to the work that can hinder their ability to remain steady and thoughtful in the face of the hostility, hatred, and violent projections between the partners. This may, in turn, lead to unconscious enactments by the therapist, which sometimes manifest as a wish to retaliate, or to withdraw from the work in hand.

We have found that a strong theoretical model is crucial to helping professionals understand couples' experiences because this can enable them to work with the intensity and texture of feelings. Many services find it hard to engage or maintain seeing both partners in treatment together and end up seeing them separately. In our experience, and as documented elsewhere (Hertzmann et al.,

2016, 2017; Nyberg & Hertzmann, 2014), the therapeutic model needs to be able to withstand the intensity of these kinds of feelings and support the therapist's capacity to mentalize, so that couples can reflect on their experience safely, thereby challenging the tendency to default to frightening and dysregulated states of mind.

In short, the challenges of working with couples on the borderline are significant. The clinical presentation and the difficulties that this population of couples are struggling with, in terms of the emotional dysregulation and its deleterious effects, cannot be underestimated. They are in extreme states of mind, with feelings of anger, hostility and loss. Specifically, the structure of the MBT-CT treatment – with its focus on mentalization, affective states and emotional dysregulation, the attributions and intentions of the other, the crucial focus on each other's mind and experiences, combined with attending to the unconscious world of the couple relationship – provides a powerful therapeutic amalgam that can target specific areas of couple relationships to effect change.

References

Abse, S. (2006). When a problem shared is a problem …whose illness is it anyway? *Psychoanalytic Perspectives on Couple Work*, 2: 65–79.

Abse, S. (2013). Further thoughts on 'When a problem shared is a problem … whose illness is it anyway? *Couple and Family Psychoanalysis*, 3(2): 179–187.

Bateman, A., & Fonagy, P. (2012). *Handbook of Mentalizing in Mental Health Practice*. Washington, DC: American Psychiatric Publishing.

Bateman, A., & Fonagy, P. (2016). *Mentalization-Based Treatment for Personality Disorders; a Practical Guide*. Oxford: Oxford University Press.

Bion, W.R. (1967). *Second Thoughts*. London: Heineman.

Fisher, J.V. (2014). Poetry and psychoanalysis, twin "sciences" of the emotions. Republished as: The evolution of the analytic process: poetry and psychoanalysis, twin "sciences" of the emotions. *Couple and Family Psychoanalysis*, 4(1): 5–21.

Fonagy, P., Gergely, G, Jurist, E., & Target, M., (2004). *Affect Regulation, Mentalization and the Development of the Self*. London: Karnac.

Hertzmann, L., & Abse, S. (2009) Parenting together – from conflict to collaboration. The review. *Conflict Resolution Quaterly*, 144: 48–9.

Hertzmann, L., & Abse, S. (2010). *Mentalization Based Treatment for Inter-Parental Conflict (Parenting Together). A Treatment Manual*. London: Tavistock Relationships (unpublished).

Hertzmann, L., Abse, S., Target, M., Glausius, K., Nyberg, V., & Lassri, D. (2017). Mentalization-based therapy for parental conflict – parenting together: an intervention for parents in entrenched post-separation disputes. *Psychoanalytic Psychotherapy*, 31 (2): 195–217.

Hertzmann, L., Target, M., Hewison, D., Casey, P., Fearon, P., & Lassri, D. (2016). Mentalization-based therapy for parents in entrenched conflict: a random allocation feasibility study. *Psychotherapy*, 53: 388–401. doi:10.1037/pst0000092

Hewison, D. (2014). Shared unconscious phantasy in couples. In: D.E. Scarff, & J.S. Scharff (Eds.), *Psychoanalytic Couple Therapy*. London: Karnac.

Klein, M. (1946). Notes on some schizoid mechanisms. *International Journal of Psychoanalysis*, *27*: 99–110.

Morgan, M. (2001). First contacts: the therapist's 'couple state of mind' as a factor in the containment of couples seen for consultation. In: F. Grier (Ed.), *Brief Encounters With Couples*. London: Karnac.

Morgan, M. (2018). *A Couple State of Mind*. London: Routledge.

Nyberg, V., & Hertzmann, L. (2014). Developing a mentalization-based treatment (MBT) for therapeutic intervention with couples (MBT-CT). *Couple and Family Psychoanalysis*, *4*: 116–35. Retrieved from http:karnacbooks.metapress.com/content/P3736153R565573X

Racker, H. (1957). The meanings and uses of countertransference. *Psychoanalytic Quarterly*, *26*: 303–57.

Ruszczynski, S. (1993). Thinking about and working with couples. In: S. Ruszczynski (Ed.), *Psychotherapy with Couples*. London: Karnac.

Ruszczynski, S. (2012). Personality disorder: a diagnosis of disordered relating. *Journal of Couple and Family Psychoanalysis*, *2*(2): 133–48.

Target, M., Hertzmann, L., Midgely, N., Casey, P., & Lassri, D. (2017). Parents' experience of child conflict within entrenched conflict families following separation and divorce; a qualitative study. *Psychoanalytic Psychotherapy*, *31*(2): 218–46.

Commentary on Chapter 7

Stanley Ruszczynski

The authors set themselves a formidable task. Their chapter 'examines how MBT-CT (mentalization-based treatment for couples) and a psychoanalytic understanding of the couple relationship *interact theoretically* within the area of highly troubled couple relationships' (my emphasis). They then write that they will approach this task by focusing on 'containment, projective identification, transference and countertransference', concepts referring to interpersonal dynamics, which are central to understanding the therapeutic encounter. Such a focus on clinical practice is always the most powerful way of testing theoretical understanding.

With regard to both psychoanalytic and mentalization based treatment, discussion may be had regarding the application of these theoretical frameworks, both designed and developed in relation to an individual mind, to an understanding of a relationship between two minds, for example the couple relationship. However, contemporary understanding of the human mind is that it grows and develops out of relationships, relationships both in the external world and in internal worlds. As the authors write, both psychoanalysis and mentalization based treatment are fundamentally dynamic, relational and developmental in their approach, and are therefore obvious frameworks for offering an understanding of and working with minds in interaction, for example, partners in a couple relationship.

It would be impossible to take up all the ideas in this commentary, but I will comment on a number of issues which interested me, most of which actually demonstrate a more 'easy' relationship between a psychoanalytic approach to working with couples and MBT-CT than the authors seem to suggest, but some of which, in my view, show some differences. I will approach this discussion from a psychoanalytic perspective, the approach with which I am most familiar.

An early assertion in the chapter is that couples with a history of conflictual relationship problems, including outbursts of anger and violence, mental ill health and substance misuse, are 'unable to engage with traditional psychoanalytic therapy models' (p. 3). Such couples, described as relating at a more paranoid–schizoid level of functioning, do, of course, present complex clinical difficulties, and some indeed cannot be held in traditional psychoanalytic treatment, or perhaps in any psychological treatment.

However, psychoanalysis has developed its theory and practice in relation to the dynamics of more primitive mental states, such as those referred to here. This development has often been clinically driven and based on the growing understanding of the unconscious purpose of patients' evacuative projective processes, and their impact on the therapist's affective state.

The clinical difficulty being referred to might now be understood to be the difficulty for the clinician in being in receipt of, and needing to contain and process, this externalisation, through projective and identificatory processes, of patients' unbearable mental states. Clinical attention to this countertransference experience offers the possibility of a containing process becoming available in the treatment, as a result of which, *some* such patients can now be treated psychoanalytically. This clinical development has included parallel developments in psychoanalytic work with couples whose presentation is disturbing and violent. See, for example, recent publications, including Balfour (2016), Grier (2017), Monguzzi (2011) and Ruszczynski (2006b, 2012). Hence, psychoanalysis does offer a method of working with such disturbing couples. Given the complexity and challenge of such patients, it is therapeutically beneficial that there are applications of different treatment models to meet such patients, be they individuals or couples.

Closely related to this is the authors' discussion of containment, a concept central to a psychoanalytic understanding of the functioning of couple relationships, where they describe the overlap between containment, mentalisation and the capacity for thinking. They refer to the importance in the MBT-CT model, of the 'capacity for curiosity about others' mental states' (p. 5). Such a capacity would represent depressive position functioning whereby the other can be recognised as separate and valued, almost a definition of the capacity for healthy couple relating. The alternative, where containment and the capacity for mentalisation is poor or absent, and where acting out takes the place of thinking, is, as the authors write, a more disturbed state based on more paranoid–schizoid position functioning. Here, vigilant suspiciousness will take the place of curiosity, and will undermine any couple's relationship.

The therapeutic issue is how to develop the patient's capacity for thought when, by definition, such functioning is poor. Psychoanalytic practice suggests that what is required is for the clinician to tolerate their countertransference experience, giving the patient the opportunity to be in the presence of an object that can contain and reflect on disturbing mental states. Much practice in MBT is based on this understanding and, together with an equivalent approach in the traditional psychoanalytic practice, gives the patient the experience of being understood, rather than prematurely being expected to understand themselves (Steiner, 1993).

In their discussion, the authors describe a type of couple where it is difficult 'to "read" someone's mental state if the person presents as emotionally unavailable' (p. 9), suggesting that this is 'an insurmountable difficulty' (p. 9). A psychoanalytic stance might suggest that such emotional unavailability *is the person's emotional state*, most likely a highly defensive state in the service of fending off feared, highly intrusive projections or acting to freeze unbearable internal affects. Those couples who experience their partner, and hence their couple relationship, as if totally dismissive of them and their needs are likely to be unconsciously recreating early experiences where they did not feel recognised or validated by their unavailable primary objects. If this can be understood in the therapeutic encounter, especially in the transference–countertransference relationship, it may become potentially available for being clinically addressed.

Related to this, in their discussion of projective identification, the authors suggest a significant difference between a psychoanalytic view of acting out and the view taken by an MBT approach. They write that the MBT model understands hostile behaviour or actions as 'attempts to restore an *illusion* of self-coherence' (their emphasis), whereas psychoanalysis, they write, views external acting out as 'an expression of unconscious aggression or envy' or 'a manipulation'. In my understanding, psychoanalysis sees acting out as an externalisation, through projective processes, of unbearable and unmanageable internal states which have to be psychologically evacuated and located in the other, for the purpose of the psychic survival of the self. This defensive process is likely to have an aggressive or manipulative impact on the recipient, but if this can be contained by the clinician and its defensive function attended to, it may also be considered to be a very powerful form of communication. The clinician managing to survive the hostile experience provides the individuals of the couple relationship with a model, as a result of which they may begin to see the enacted aggression as being fundamentally driven by profound anxiety, which is feared to be not containable by themselves or by their relationship. Both psychoanalysis and MBT approach this therapeutic task by processing this experience and promoting thought and reflection, about the self and the other, which might lead to a reduction in enactment and the beginnings of the experience of relationships as containing.

Discussing transference the authors write that in the MBT model 'it is generally understood that the therapist does not actively interpret the transference relationship as doing this can potentially be destabilising for a patient ...' (p. 9). They go on to say that in the MBT model, the transference *informs* therapists' interventions because in making direct transference interpretations, 'the couple could experience (that) as the therapist attempting to put something of his own agenda into the couple's minds' (p. 9).

If we understand the transference as being the product of the patient's projection of unprocessed or disturbing internal states, then the *timing* of transference interpretations is a crucial consideration in the psychoanalytic clinical encounter.

With patients such as those referred to in this chapter, i.e. patients with particularly disturbed and disturbing internal states, the psychoanalytic clinician would be very thoughtful at the pace with which transference interpretations would be offered. By definition the patient would not be able to take back projected aspects of their internal states which they have to evacuate (including, often, through action) because of the unbearable toxicity of these states. Such patients require initial experiences of the therapist coming to experience and process within themselves the transference–countertransference relationship, resulting in the patient beginning to feel that he is 'being understood', before they may be able to then move to a capacity to 'understand themselves' (Steiner, 1993) which involves taking back those projected aspects of themselves which had been felt to be in need of evacuation.

A premature transference interpretation with such patients would indeed be experienced by the patient as if the therapist was evacuating something of his own into the couple's mind. At its worse, it might be that the therapist is unable to contain the toxicity of the patient's projection and unknowingly enacts a version of the patient's evacuative process by pushing, back into the patient, states of mind which by definition the patient is desperate to get rid of. As the authors write, it is essential that the therapist has a capacity to come to realise this enactment when it happens and have some way of integrating it into the therapeutic encounter.

The question, however, might be how this is to be done. In their discussion of countertransference the authors recognise the ubiquity, inevitability and, especially with the patient being discussed in this paper, the potential toxicity of the affective states generated in the sensitive clinician (i.e. the countertransference). They refer to states of confusion, helplessness, fearfulness, feeling lost and of not-knowing and to, 'sooner or later', enactment or acting out on the therapist's part. This is all, of course, familiar to every clinician. The authors go on to say that in the MBT model, 'the therapist is encouraged to share this experience ... with the couple' (p. 140). In saying this they appropriately, and very clearly, state that this has to be done 'in a way which takes care not to burden the patients with the therapist's own feelings' (p. 140).

I am curious that, in relation to the transference, the idea of 'transference-informed' intervention is promoted rather than directly addressing (when the timing is appropriate) the transference. In the case of the countertransference, however, rather than promoting 'countertransference-informed' intervention (when the timing is appropriate), the MBT model suggests that the therapist's countertransference or enactments be shared with the patient.

The mutual emotional experience of the clinical encounter between patient and therapist, referred to technically as the transference–countertransference relationship, is of course informed in some part by the internal world of the therapist. This will, to some degree, influence the experience of both the transference and of the countertransference. As the authors write, a psychoanalytically informed training offers the opportunity to develop a capacity to be aware of this likelihood and to be able to come to process the transference–countertransference encounter accordingly. In my view, what is most therapeutic is for the patient to experience a clinician who can go on thinking and reflecting on their experiences in the clinical encounter even when 'disturbed' by the encounter. It is likely that the patients referred to in this chapter have been the recipients of unprocessed mental states from their primary objects – a cruel reversal of the parent–child container–contained relationship which is why their capacity for containment is poor or absent. Can we be sure then that if, as clinicians, we share our internal states, that our patients will not experience this as toxic and intrusive and a repetition of such a cruel reversal?

Towards the end of the chapter, the authors differentiate between the psychoanalytic task of promoting insight and the MBT model, which is concerned to develop 'curiosity about mental states in self and other' (p. 139). In my understanding there is no significant difference between these aims if we assume that insight is the outcome of a capacity for curiosity about self (conscious and unconscious) and other. Moreover, curiosity in the self and other results in insight and understanding of the self, including in relation to the other.

I think I have shown in this very brief discussion that there is much theoretical overlap between a psychoanalytic and MBT clinical approach. The challenge, however, for both modalities, is to have a way of thinking not just about a relationship between the minds of two people, but about the 'joint mind' of the couple-in-their-interaction. I am referring to an understanding of the couple relationship as being the product of mutual projective identification which constitutes the unconscious marital fit of the intimate couple relationship, potentially resulting in what Morgan refers to as a 'creative couple' (Morgan, 2005). Every couple has to attend to the triangular interplay between the needs and interests of each of the two partners, and the needs and interests of *their relationship as a couple* (Ruszczynski, 2006a). In this way we can think of the couple relationship *as a psychological object in its own right*. This is reflected in the clinical stance of the psychoanalytic couple therapist for whom *the patient is the relationship*.

Kernberg puts this in a particular way when he writes that the couple acquires 'an identity of its own in addition to the identity of each of the partners'. He describes how, in a healthy relationship, over time, the interaction of couple's superegos results in the forging of what he calls the 'couple's superego', which has the capacity for 'a sense of responsibility for each other *and for the couple*' (Kernberg, 1993, my italics). We might add that this capacity to be responsible is likely to be the product of having internalised the early childhood experience of having been the object of another's concern and sense of responsibility.

In contrast, in less healthy couples, such as those being discussed in this chapter, a cruel sado-masochistic dynamic informs the nature of the couple's interaction and creates both a sense of persecution by the other, and a sense of being caught in a relationship which is not only not containing but actively threatening and violating. Both a psychoanalytic approach and an MBT approach are challenged to contain and mentalize two such disturbed and disturbing minds, unconsciously organised to recreate in others, partner and therapist, toxic and disturbed mental states. When such couples approach the possibility of a therapeutic intervention, what is required is the presence of a therapist who is contained by 'a strong theoretical model ... able to withstand the intensity of these kinds of feelings' (p. 12). The authors of this chapter make a strong case for psychoanalysis and MBT to provide a therapeutic amalgam which can withstand the therapeutic challenge offered by these patients and begin to introduce the experience of thoughtful and reflective containment.

References

Balfour, A. (2016). Transference and enactment in the 'oedipal setting' of couple psychotherapy. In: A. Novakovic (Ed.), *Couple Dynamics*. London: Karnac.

Grier, F. (2017). Psychotic and depressive processes in couple functioning. In: S. Nathan & M. Schaeffer (Eds.), *Couples on the Couch*. London: Routledge.

Kernberg, O. (1993). The couple's constructive and destructive superego functions. *Journal of the American Psychoanalytic Association*, *41(3)*: 653–77

Monguzzi, F. (2011). Anger and aggression in couple therapy: some clinical considerations from an intersubjective perspective. *Couple and Family Psychoanalysis*, *1*(2): 210–21.

Morgan, M. (2005). On being able to be a couple: the importance of a 'creative couple' in psychic life. In: F. Grier (Ed.), *Oedipus and the Couple* (pp. 9–30). London: Karnac.

Ruszczynski, S. (2006a). Reflective space in the intimate couple relationship: the 'marital triangle'. In: F. Grier (Ed.), Oedipus and the Couple (pp. 31–47). London: Karnac.

Ruszczynski, S. (2006b). Sado-masochistic enactments in the couple relationship: the fear of intimacy and the dread of separateness. *Psychoanalytic Perspectives on Couple Work*, *2*.

Ruszczynski, S. (2012). Personality disorder – a diagnosis of disturbed relating. *Couple and Family Psychoanalysis*, *2*(2): 133–48.

Steiner, J. (1993). *Psychic Retreats*. London: Routledge.

Chapter 8

Working with couple violence

Anthea Benjamin, Parmjit Chahal, Steve Mulley and Antonia Reay

This chapter will describe the Safer Families Project (SFP), a programme Tavistock Relationships (TR) has developed in partnership with a London Borough Children's Services Department. Using a mentalization-based approach, SFP works therapeutically with parental couples who intend to stay together but where there is 'situational' domestic violence. As parental conflict can have a profound negative effect on children's outcomes (Woolfe et al., 2003), there is a pressing need for therapeutic interventions to address violence between parents who choose to stay in relationships.

In the UK, domestic abuse is a widespread phenomenon. Thirty per cent of women and 16.3% of men will experience domestic abuse during their lifetimes (Smith et al., 2010, 2011) and one in four children are exposed to domestic abuse (Radford et al., 2011). Domestic abuse usually refers to a systematic form of abuse that includes physical, psychological, sexual, financial and economic control.

In 2014, a London Borough's innovative response to situational domestic abuse arose because existing interventions, whilst effective in some cases, had little impact on curtailing domestic abuse referrals into Children's Services. This finding was supported by the Early Intervention Foundation's evidence review of national and international work in the domestic abuse and violence arena (Guy et al., 2014). In partnership with Tavistock Relationships, the Local Authority's Children's Services senior management team began developing a model of intervention based on a relational understanding of domestic abuse and trauma, described below.

Exploring domestic violence through the context of the relationship dynamic can be misread as 'colluding or detracting from what should be condemned as intolerable behaviour' (Clulow, 2007, p. 21). However, there is a growing argument that, with careful risk assessment, some violent couples wishing to stay together can be helped to understand what is going on between them and work towards the cessation of abuse in their relationship (Humphries & McCann, 2015). There is an argument to be made that failing to offer therapy that focuses on the couple dynamic, neglects and discriminates against women and men who are experiencing violence, yet choose to stay together.

The need for this relational approach is supported by research that shows while women leave abusive partners on at least eight separate occasions, over 50% return to the same partners from refuges (Zosky, 2003). A therapeutic intervention that supports a parental couple to improve their relationship not only has the potential to improve the well-being of the whole family, but may have an effect on their children's future relationships. Research on attachment disorders suggests that patterns of attachment between primary caregivers and their children affect the child's psychological development and goes on to shape how they parent their own children (Music, 2011). If parents are distracted and distressed by unstable and unpredictable couple relationships their minds are unavailable to the developing child who, in turn, is more likely to develop problems with mentalization and empathy, and manage emotions instead through action (Motz, 2014).

Context, research and development in domestic violence programmes

Support for couples where there is domestic violence in the UK typically involves the provision of perpetrator programmes for men and outreach support and refuges for women, although access to these resources has not been consistent or widespread. Much of the thinking in the field has historically been viewed through the lens of hierarchical distribution of power within a patriarchal society. This considers the root causes of intimate partner violence as the outcome of living in a society that condones aggressive behaviours perpetrated by men, while socialising women to be non-violent.

This separated perpetrator–survivor programme is a response to a particularly severe type of violence, characterised by the dominant model of female victim to controlling male perpetrator, what Kelly and Johnson (2008) define as 'coercive, controlling violence'. Whilst this model incorporates important cultural factors affecting gender roles, it can be reductive and does little to illuminate the intergenerational patterns that occur within couple relationships.

Kelly and Johnson (2008) reviewed research into intimate partner violence and argue for a more complex picture. They identify four common types of violence within relationships: 'coercive controlling violence, violent resistance, situational couple violence, and separation-instigated violence'.

'Coercive controlling violence', is typically present in 11% of cases, whilst 'situational couple violence', which Kelly and Johnson describe as 'acts of violence perpetrated by both men and women, where violence is less frequent and does not result in serious injury', occurs in 89% of cases. The violence for this population tends to occur out of anger or frustration rather than as a means of gaining control and power over the other partner.

Olson (2002) estimated that as many as 50% of heterosexual American couples experienced situational couple violence over the course of their relationships. People who engage in situational couple violence tend to be poor communicators who do not know how to manage conflict without resorting to verbal aggression, insults, or physical abuse such as hitting, shoving or damaging property. A key part of the approach of the Safer Families Project is to work with the Local Authority to assess which couples can be identified as experiencing situational violence rather than coercive and controlling violence and are therefore potentially suitable to work with.

This chapter describes a model of therapy which offers the chance for parental couples who have been violent towards one another in the past to begin to work together to contain their feelings, shift their behaviour patterns and be more available to parent their children effectively. The authors will describe the intervention, with an emphasis on the importance of the assessment process, risk management and close cooperation with Children's Services. A composite case study will be referred to throughout to illustrate this way of working therapeutically with couples that have been identified as being caught up in situational couple violence.

Origins of the Safer Families Project

A pilot project was devised, and a multi-disciplinary screening panel was set up, chaired by the Children's Services lead, together with key partners, including representatives from the police, alongside a domestic abuse advisor and a clinical lead from Tavistock Relationships. The panel played a critical role assessing risk and ensuring as far as possible that the right couples were identified for the project. The panel sought to identify couples for inclusion who were experiencing situational violence, and to exclude couples where coercive controlling violence was occurring.

If either partner was considered, by themselves or the panel, to be at heightened risk from participating in violence, or if there was evidence of a pattern of coercion and control, the couple were screened out. Where there were issues of substance or alcohol misuse, these needed to be sufficiently managed for the therapy to be realistic, safe and not pose a greater risk to either partner or children. In regards to mental health difficulties, couples were required to have a sufficient level of stability to safely participate.

The results and feedback from the couples seen in the pilot project were positive and in 2015 the London Borough secured proof of concept, ensuring the continuation of the work. The Local Authority's Children's Services remained the lead agency, undertaking risk assessments, referring potential cases and providing on-going social work support to the families involved. The model asserts that it is essential to have continued monitoring of the safety of the couple, as well as child protection issues throughout the period of couple therapy. Social workers are seen as an integral part of the delivery team. They need to have an understanding of the therapeutic process in order to refer eligible couples, support them to change, and participate in reviewing the work, whilst continuing to hold child safeguarding and domestic abuse protection responsibilities.

Mentalization-based therapy – parenting together (MBT-PT)

Mentalization-based therapy (MBT) is a researched, evidence-based approach, described in Chapter 7. It concentrates on understanding the mental states and behaviours in self and other and is considered an effective treatment for patients diagnosed with borderline personality disorder, with its roots in developmental psychology and social cognition (Bateman & Fonagy, 2016). The model was adapted for parental couples at Tavistock Relationships to focus on co-parenting difficulties and conflicts (Hetzmann & Abse, 2008; Hertzmann et al., 2016). It was further adapted to focus on couple conflict more generally (Nyberg & Hertzmann, 2014) and this adaption was used within the Safer Families Project, incorporating psychoanalytic couple and attachment theories.

MBT-PT is suggested as the model of choice for working with volatile destructive dynamics in parental couples because it both formulates relationships in terms of attachment and focuses on the here and now. This gives the couple and the therapists a means of unravelling couple dynamics, particularly in times of stress or threat, when the attachment system is activated by the presence of a partner or therapist (Motz, 2014). In being supported to become aware of their own mental state, partners can increasingly hold in mind the other, and make more sense of their experiences from a multiple perspective viewpoint.

In the presence of heightened conflicted couple distress, the therapist's own capacity to mentalize can be undermined. An MBT technique that is particularly helpful, both for individual and co-therapists, is to voice out loud their thinking and curiosity about the couple interaction in the room. This transparent mentalizing allows couples to make sense of the material that comes up between them, with the help of the therapist's mind. In offering an alternate view to a couple's entrenched non-mentalizing, therapists model negotiating different perspectives in an intimate relationship. Closely monitoring how couples tolerate this new way of seeing their interaction, therapists move swiftly to validate any new acceptance of different states of mind as opposed to the couple's familiar and rigid system.

A central tension in the work is how to engage couples who have been 'sent' by external public services to therapy because of serious concerns about their relationship and parenting and who may be feeling shamed, attacked and anxious. There is a need to establish a therapeutic alliance to ensure they feel safe enough to bring their relationship difficulties into the room whilst openly acknowledging the need for couple work to stop if safety is at stake. The couple are supported to understand that their therapist is trying to find a shared understanding of their relationship, including the dangerous and destructive parts of it. The mentalization model suggests using empathic validation of the couple's experience at the beginning of the work, to convey understanding and build trust, without compromising the safety of the couple or their children.

Regular group and individual supervision was key to this project. A supervisory culture where 'safe uncertainty' (Mason, 1993) and curiosity about the therapist's role in the therapeutic alliance was encouraged. Within such supervision, therapists' confusion and anxiety, evoked in the countertransference when working with these distressed couples, was processed from different perspectives and aspects such as minimisation of violence and avoidance of shame thought about with the added advantage of a group mind.

When writing this chapter, the children's rhyme, 'There's a Hole in my Bucket', came to mind. It offered a metaphor illustrating a cyclical dynamic that couples within the project often present with, of being in a deadlock, both focusing on the other, and struggling to know what to do to solve the problem:

> There's a hole in the bucket, dear Liza, dear Liza,
> There's a hole in the bucket, dear Liza, a hole.
>
> Then fix it, dear Henry, dear Henry, dear Henry,
> Then fix it, dear Henry, dear Henry, fix it.
>
> With what shall I fix it, dear Liza, dear Liza?
> With what shall I fix it, dear Liza, with what?

Assessment and structure

Following the London Borough's initial panel screening, the Tavistock Relationships team reviewed each referral in supervision, reflecting on the information given, and if necessary, discussing safety issues with the referring social worker. If the team agreed to the couple progressing to formal assessment, they were offered an initial two-hour meeting. Risk will be constantly at the forefront of therapists' minds. At any point in the process, if the risk of harm to the couple or their children is judged to be too high, work will not go ahead and alternative sources of help are explored. Suicidal states of mind, drug or alcohol misuse, addiction and mental ill-health, as components of a couple's history and contemporaneously, are contra-indicators to conjoint work, along with on-going violent and abusive behaviours.

During the therapeutic assessment, the couple are seen individually to complete psychometric questionnaires, a process to be repeated at the end of treatment. The questionnaires, which request detail on levels of conflict, substance abuse and mental states, provide the opportunity to open up exploration around the chronology of violent incidents and each individual's current level of distress. Individual personal and social history and an assessment of a willingness to engage in the project are also explored. This process helps gauge vulnerability within the couple relationship and the possibility of conjoint work adding to this. Therapists probe for a sense of responsibility and concern around the violence, and for the couple's capacity to think about safety. In particular, a curiosity about the impact of their conflictual interactions on their children is explored. An essential assessment question is the couples' ability to talk about their conflict together or if there is fear of further endangering themselves if certain realities are raised in front of their partner.

If the above criteria are met, a second assessment is conducted with the couple. In this, their ability to be in a room together, to think about their relationship and to tolerate the therapist's interventions is further considered, with the therapist openly mentalizing around risk. By listening carefully to the couple narrative and closely observing interaction in the room, a tentative formulation of the couples' difficulties begins to take shape and is shared with the partners together.

The work necessitates therapists holding in mind the relationship as the product of two attachment systems, 'whose partnership reflects their own unmet needs and deepest fears of abandonment ... and loss' (Dutton, 2007), rather than seeing one partner as problematic. The concept of a couple's shared unconscious fantasy and unconscious couple fit, developed by Tavistock Relationships, is useful here. After the second assessment, a decision is taken as to whether the couple would benefit from working with a mentalization-based approach (MBT-PT).

One common challenge of working with couples locked into extreme conflict with one another is their minimisation of the violence, often due to shame or fear. It takes therapeutic skill to communicate to couples that thinking about the violence is in both their best interests, and that of their children. Feelings of blame are constant for these couples as is the fear that they will be judged as 'bad' parents and their children removed from their care. Their idea of what is safe, non-violent behaviour is often at variance with the therapist's and social services' views. Their historical experience of intimate and family relationships may mean pushing, shoving, verbal abuse and intimidation are considered a normal aspect of family life. Motz (2014) referred to this as 'loving and warring'. Attachment trauma (Allen et al., 2008), experienced by one or both partners in the couples in this programme is also a typical component of their history. Its imprint impairs their ability to feel safe in relationships, including within a hoped-for, secure helping relationship with their therapist.

Added to this, the therapist can be identified as part of social services in the couple's mind. This challenge makes crucial the need to identify and contain the therapeutic work as distinct from other support the couple are being offered by social services. This issue is rife with potential boundary issues and confused agendas. New, reality-based thinking about their difficulties in the therapy can be viewed suspiciously by the couple, not least because any risk needs to be shared with social services. Far from supporting them, many of the couples perceive Children's Social Care as having had them under unjust scrutiny because of serious concerns for the well-being of their children. An additional complexity is their own frequent contact with social services as children and the mindset that has developed over a lifetime as to the role of public intervention.

Weaving a way through all of this to reach collaborative, productive working alliances with both the couple and social services, whilst maintaining a containing therapeutic stance, involves a high degree of skill on the part of the therapist.

> Kathy and Joe had known each other for 15 years, and had been in a relationship for ten years. They had two children together, a seven-year-old boy and a five-year-old girl. Kathy's 14-year-old son from a previous relationship, diagnosed as being on the autism spectrum, recently moved out to live with Kathy's sister. The couple's daughter has Down's Syndrome.
>
> Kathy and Joe were referred into the SFP by their social worker. Their children were also subject to a Child Protection Plan. Since their daughter had been born there had been an increase in conflict. Over the past two years this had erupted into violence on a number of occasions. These incidents would often involve the police and both had been arrested on different occasions. The police referred them to social services, who had been working with them on and off for two years. They had both been referred to anger management courses, but had not managed to complete them. One of the first things the therapist noticed was the couple seemed united when attacking and criticising what they considered to be interfering external services.
>
> Due to the lengthy chronology of social service involvement, sent with the referral, the therapist met Kathy and Joe for the first time with some trepidation and curiosity. Even before they entered the room, Kathy made a disparaging remark about social services and the therapist wondered if Kathy was inviting an alliance against the other professionals involved with them. The therapist encouraged Kathy and Joe to share their thoughts on this introduction to another professional in the light of their experience of many 'helping' services before them.
>
> Kathy began a detailed and confusing account of how unfairly they had been treated. She explained that her eldest son had chosen to live with his maternal aunt after accusing Joe of abusing him. Social services had asked Joe to move out of the family home for a number of weeks during an investigation. The couple smilingly dismissed the idea there was any domestic violence between them. They said that they were getting on well but could acknowledge very different ideas about how to parent the children, and that this often led to disagreements.
>
> The therapist began by explaining the boundaries of the work after noticing Joe's body language and lack of eye contact. He seemed uncomfortable but managed to acknowledge 'you lot' as part of the same system that had persecuted him unfairly. The therapist validated the courage it took both of them to engage in the project, especially considering their lack of trust in professionals.
>
> Although the therapist only spent a little of the early assessment and treatment sessions hearing about their early experiences, Kathy filled the

room with her hunger for connection and care. Joe was more wary and ambivalent, telling the therapist that he couldn't see the point in opening up to the pain of the past. The therapist used her countertransference feelings of helplessness to wonder about Joe's withdrawal, and asked if he felt as if sometimes he disappeared from the room when Kathy filled the space with 'preferred non-mentalizing narratives'. Having noticed that her own ability to mentalize was disturbed during these long monologues of complaint from Kathy, the therapist learnt to stop the couple more frequently as it seemed to lessen a shared and accumulating sense of panic in the room. Believing that Kathy and Joe were powerfully communicating something of their own experience of being neglected and traumatised, in stopping the couple dynamic of Kathy dominating whilst Joe withdrew, the therapist noticed her own mentalizing beginning to return.

At an early stage of the work, the therapist explored the couple's reluctance to talk about the violence between them: which they felt was not an issue. Her questioning was met with a shrug but she persisted, including the couple in her thinking, asking them to think about how it could be worked with, as it needed to be. The mentalizing stance of naïve curiosity was helpful: 'It sounds like things are difficult for you at the moment, are you worried about how things are? Other people seem to be worried.' In mentalizing terms, the couple were validated in the difficulty of their position as they saw it. From this stance, the therapist can gently probe for alternative perspectives, retreating to further validation if they are met with resistance, then probing again. This allows highly emotive subjects to be addressed in small steps, as safely as possible.

Kathy and Joe continued to minimise the violence between them in the early therapy sessions but learnt gradually to have more confidence in the containment of the therapeutic space. As the work progressed, Kathy owned a painful sense of shame and failure as a mother, a position she usually defended against by blaming social services for the stress they had put the family under. This felt like a small step towards helping them begin to have a 'parental state of mind' where the couple can remain in their role as parents and be genuinely curious as to their children's experience.

Distressed and preoccupied parents are unable to provide a reflective function to help children develop a sense of their own minds and, at times, the therapist felt torn between empathy for the parents and painful concern for the children. The challenge of working with Kathy and Joe was to keep their children in mind, preoccupied as they could all become with 'the drama' of their couple relationship. This absence was felt despite the therapist occasionally being surprised by a throw away derogatory comment about one of the children from Kathy or Joe.

Therapists actively request detailed narratives of disputes to illustrate how situations between the couple can escalate into violence. Such narratives commonly trace a '0 – 100' experience: one or both parties will describe the initial interactions, often relatively benign and ordinary, and then the final explosive exchange, with little or no mention of the journey from one to the other, the '1, 2, 3 ... 99'. These narratives give the therapist ample opportunity to explore and promote mentalization. If the therapist can question these descriptions with a mentalizing, curious stance they can begin to draw out such details and fill in the gaps.

For instance, when Kathy and Joe arrived for their fourth session, the therapist felt the couple were different in their presentation in some way. They were restless, irritable and not engaging with each other. The therapist commented on this observation, asking if they felt different. It turned out that the previous evening the couple had an argument that had quickly escalated until both were angrily shouting at each other, culminating in Joe throwing the TV remote control across the room and storming out. All of this was witnessed by their children.

In exploring the detail of what happened, it emerged that Joe had been in the lounge looking after their daughter. Kathy had walked into the lounge and offered to help. He got angry and shouted at her and she responded by shouting at him, picking up their daughter and walking out. Neither seemed to have an understanding as to why they were angry. They could admit to both being confused as to how this argument started, as if important details had simply been skipped over. With encouragement, the couple were then supported in giving a moment-by-moment account of what had happened. The therapist was able to process and reflect on what each had said, about their emotional states, and the reactions they had experienced. They were able to track the argument back, considering where it may have started, and why.

Filling in the gaps

This sense of needing to 'fill in the gaps' with specific detailed accounts is a common one when working with highly dysregulated couples. It is a useful technique as it allows the therapist to question assumptions, be curious about thinking patterns, and validate painful emotions and differing opinions. These moments are at the heart of learning to mentalize and the team quickly learnt that concentrating on detail helped to take some of the heat out of couple conflict. If the therapist can maintain their mentalizing stance, support the couple as they retrace their steps, guide the exploration so as to avoid repeating the conflict in an unhelpful way in the session, the couple can begin to learn about their emotional and cognitive responses to one another in the moment, allowing them to develop their own mentalizing skills.

> The couple continued to work together with their therapist and some of their defensive attitudes began to soften. After six sessions and a review, it was agreed to continue with couple therapy. After this negotiation of another six sessions, it was noticeable that Kathy and Joe began to disagree

with each other more openly in front of their therapist. It seemed that they were beginning to trust the therapy space enough to bring their conflict, with less fear of judgement. Kathy described several instances of waiting downstairs to watch a film with Joe, whilst he spent time 'putting the children to bed'. They quickly got into an angry dispute about who did what around the house. The therapist stopped them and reflected back what they heard and wondered about the couple's shared experience of feeling trapped and unappreciated by each other. Both were able to acknowledge that they had grown up looking after others and feeling criticised if they spoke up, or ignored if they did not. There was a sense that in the past and the present, there were not enough resources to go around; if one person was looked after, the other was neglected. Importantly, after this admission of a shared aspect to their difficulties, both of them expressed a wish to have time together as a couple, without the children.

After attending the full twelve sessions, Kathy, Joe and the therapist met for the final review. Kathy reflected that she felt she had learnt new things about Joe which helped her understand him better. She, in turn, had learnt to think more before speaking, as if she had a second voice in her head stopping her reacting so quickly. Joe said that the sessions had given him the opportunity to talk more about himself and his inner world.

In this final session, the couple could tolerate thoughts about anger in their relationship and what it signified. Joe spoke about struggling with powerful emotions that he found overwhelming at times, and which left him worried about what he might do. With their therapist, they had been helped to recognise the pattern of Joe leaving the scene of a growing argument with Kathy wanting to sort things out immediately, leading to explosive arguments. Kathy had said, as a result of understanding that her need for immediacy could make things worse, she was trying to give Joe the space he needed to process his feelings. Joe admitted to trying hard to talk more openly about his emotions and be more vulnerable with Kathy.

The therapist reflected that mental health had played an important role for both of them. Issues around low mood, poor self-worth and anxiety often made things difficult. She identified a number of significant stressors, including money, unemployment, and relationships with extended families, that the couple had to navigate. They agreed with this, allowing both to feel less isolated and alone.

During a home visit a week after the end of couple work, Joe and Kathy's social worker noticed a difference in the family home, and felt that the children were more settled in their behaviour. Just before the final review, the social worker had recommended that the family were stepped down from Child Protection to Child in Need, a significant move forward for them and the family.

MBT formulation

It can be a challenge for therapists using a short-term intervention such as SFP to maintain the focus on the 'here-and-now' when historic material from the clients' family of origin is often close to the surface. For many of the couples, like Kathy and Joe, where SFP is their first experience of therapy, there is not enough time to address the complexity of their histories. SFP therapists try to manage this by framing the limitations of what can be achieved in therapy for the couple. An important part of the framework is to work with the couple to identify relevant and achievable goals.

A discussion about aims for therapy needs to fit with the couple's strengths and vulnerabilities and involve clear and realistic expectations, including thinking about the end of therapy. Couples need support in working towards change to foster a new sense of hopefulness. With Kathy and Joe, one goal was to work towards an increased understanding of themselves and how they affected each other, with the aim of reducing a rapid escalation of conflict based on rigid assumptions about the other person's intentions.

The MBT model for brief intervention suggests therapists and clients collaborate to develop a formulation which links how each partner tends to experience him- or herself in relation to the other and what feelings (characteristic affect) this evokes. The formulation aims to show how a symptom, such as persistent conflict, can be placed in the interpersonal dynamic of the couple relationship. The therapist worked with Kathy and Joe to identify and name a key pattern in the way they related as a couple when under stress, using their own descriptors as far as possible. Kathy and Joe agreed that at times of stress they tended to experience themselves (their 'self-representation') as 'invisible and robbed' in relation to their partner, whom they would experience as 'controlling, humiliating' (see Figure 8.1).

The formulation was used to help Kathy and Joe notice that when they felt ashamed and vulnerable, they could also join together in rubbishing other

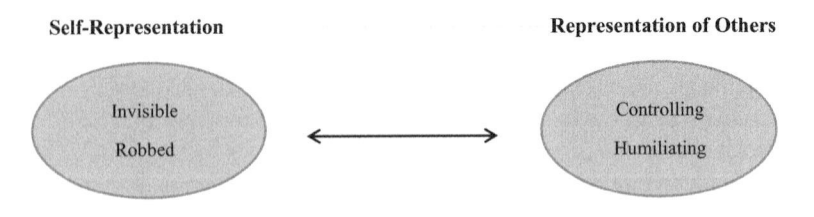

Self-Representation **Representation of Others**

Invisible / Robbed ←——→ Controlling / Humiliating

Characteristic Emotion: Shame

Figure 8.1 Shared formulation

people, such as Kathy's sister or social services. The cost was that it could keep them stuck in an apparently powerless, paranoid and persecuted position where it was hard to take responsibility for making changes themselves or use any help available. In pointing out that it seemed that someone always needed to be rubbished – usually an outside agent – the therapist could wonder if this was a defence linked to fears of being 'rubbish' themselves. Supporting the couple to acknowledge the pattern that each of them could be controlling and rubbishing the other, helped them acknowledge their own anger. The therapist voiced curiosity and explored the children's possible experience of their parents' conflict, wondering if they might similarly feel invisible and robbed of their parents' attention.

Confidentiality

A focus group made up of the London Borough's social workers during the pilot study had identified confidentiality as a major point of interest for them. They agreed that the therapeutic space needed to feel secure in order for couples to explore difficult things without feeling this would elicit an immediate social service response. How to create a different frame around this therapeutic work despite liaison with social services was an intricate task. The effectiveness of any therapeutic intervention is dependent upon clear, safe boundaries that provide a containing therapeutic experience. This is particularly important when working with this client group who are often distrustful of authority figures and professionals.

The first challenge for the therapists was in defining their role within this partnership but maintaining some confidentiality for the couple to be able to make use of the service. Couples are often fearful that if they talk frankly, their children may be removed. The therapist needs to create a sense of safety in the session to allow the couple to 'contain and express' difficult and disturbing feelings rather than 'disavow and project' them (Catherall, 1992) or act them out, either during or after the session.

Couples were free to choose whether they joined the project and they were asked for informed consent for specific material about them to be shared between the two agencies. It was important that the partnership with the Local Authority was explained with transparency, giving the couple a clear idea of boundaries around professional working relationships. However, social workers also expressed anxiety about not knowing the content of the sessions and not being able to use this to facilitate their own work with these families. A further development from the original pilot, SFP included formalised meetings with social workers before, during and after the work. It was made clear to couples that their social worker would be informed if new matters of concern were raised during the sessions. All contact with social services was thought about, both with the couples and in the therapeutic team, prior to any review meetings, provided new safety and risk concerns had not arisen.

Conclusion

The Safer Families Project offers a promising model of working therapeutically with parental couples who wish to stay together, whilst needing support to address the situational violence between them. The participating couples report valuing the experience, describing an increased ability to reflect on their own behaviour and to think about their partner's experiences. There continues to be a reduction in violent conflict for participating couples, who report that they can express themselves to their partner more effectively. Although we must caution that the results achieved represent a relatively small number of couples who have accessed the programme so far, several families have been 'stepped down' from the Child Protection register to Child In Need, following therapy. It must also be acknowledged that this is a short-term intervention for people who tend to have entrenched problems and troubled relationships over years, usually within a framework of historical trauma. Nevertheless, a good experience of brief couple therapy could lay foundations for further work and an important first step for people who have found it hard to trust or use the help offered to them in the past. The project is still in its infancy, it is ground-breaking and controversial work, which forms part of a vanguard of developments establishing conjoint couple therapy for situational violence as a legitimate treatment.

Acknowledgment

The authors would like to thank Jan Irwin, Chair of the London Borough of Harrow Multi-Agency Domestic and Sexual Violence (DSV) Forum, and Children's Safeguarding lead. They are also grateful for the support of Chris Spencer, the Director of Children's Services, and corporate support from the London Borough of Harrow.

References

Allen, J.G., Fonagy, P., & Bateman, A.W. (2008). *Mentalizing in Clinical Practice*. Washington, DC: American Psychiatric Publishing.

Bateman, A., & Fonagy, P. (2010). Mentalization based treatment for borderline personality disorder. *World Psychiatry*, 9: 11–15.

Bateman, A., & Fonagy, P. (2016). *Mentalization-Based Treatment for Personality Disorders: A Practical Guide*. Oxford: Oxford University Press.

Catherall, D.R. (1992). Working with projective identification in couples. *Family Process*, *31*(4): 355–67.

Clulow, C. (2007). Attachment, idealisation and violence in couple relationships. *Psychoanalytic Perspectives on Couple Work*, 3:11–24.

Dutton, D.G. (2007). *Abusive Personality: Violence and Control in Intimate Relationships* (2nd edn.). New York: Guilford Press.

Guy, J., Feinstein, L., & Griffiths, A. (2014). *Early Intervention in Domestic Violence and Abuse*. London: Early Intervention Foundation.

Hertzmann, L., & Abse, S. (2008). Mentalization-based therapy for parenting together: a treatment manual for parents in conflict. Unpublished Manuscript. London: Tavistock Centre for Couple Relationships.

Hertzmann, L., Target, M., Hewison, D., Casey, P., Fearon, P., & Lassri, D. (2016). Mentalization-based therapy for parents in entrenched conflict: a random allocation feasibility study. *Psychotherapy*, *53*: 388–401.

Humphries, J., & McCann, D. (2015). Couple psychoanalytic psychotherapy with violent couples: understanding and working with domestic violence. *Couple and Family Psychoanalysis*, *5*(2): 149–67.

Kelly, J.B., & Johnson, M.P. (2008). Differentiation among types of intimate partner violence: Research update and implications for interventions. *Family Court Review*, *46*(3): 476–99.

Mason, B. (1993). Towards positions of safe uncertainty. *Human Systems: The Journal of Systemic Consultation and Management*, *4*: 189–200.

Motz, A. (2014). *Toxic Couples – The Psychology of Domestic Violence*. Abingdon: Routledge.

Music, G. (2011). *Nurturing Natures: Attachment and Children's Emotional, Sociocultural and Brain Development*. Hove: Psychological Press.

Nyberg, V., & Hertzmann, L. (2014). Developing a mentalization-based treatment (MBT) for therapeutic intervention with couples (MBT-CT). *Couple and Family Psychoanalysis*, *4*: 116–35.

Olson, L. (2002). Exploring 'common couple violence' in heterosexual romantic relationships. *Western Journal of Communication*, *66*(1): 104–28.

Radford, L., Corral, S., Bradley, C., Fisher, H., Bassett, C., Howat, N., & Collishaw, S. (2011). *Child Abuse and Neglect in the UK Today*. London: NSPCC.

Smith, K. (Ed.), Coleman, K., Eder, S., & Hall, P. (2011). *Homicides, Firearm Offences and Intimate Violence 2009/10*: Supplementary Volume 2 to Crime in England and Wales 2009/10 (2nd edn). London: Home Office.

Smith, K., & Flatley, J. (Eds.), Coleman, K., Osborne, S., Kaiza, P., & Roe, S. (2010). *Homicides, Firearm Offences and Intimate Violence 2008/09: Supplementary Volume 2 to Crime in England and Wales 2008/09* (3rd edn). London: Home Office.

Strupp, H.H. (1977). A reformulation of the dynamics of the therapist's contribution. In: A. S. Gurman & A.M Razin's (Eds.), *Effective Psychotherapy. General Psychology Series, vol. 70*. Oxford: Pergamon Press.

Woolfe, R., Dryden, W., & Strawbridge, S. (2003). *Handbook of Counselling Psychology* (2nd edn). London: Sage.

Zosky, D.L. (2003). Projective identification as a contributor to domestic violence. *Clinical Social Work Journal*, *31*(4): 419–31.

Commentary on Chapter 8

Damian McCann

Domestic violence (also termed 'intimate partner violence') is, as we know, a significant and far-reaching social problem affecting a large number of couples and families. Given the nature of the problem, it is not at all surprising that there has been heightened sensitivity within the field as to the most effective ways of intervening in these relationships to manage the risks, ensure safety and obtain positive outcomes. Unfortunately, the push to view domestic violence and abuse purely in terms of a victim and perpetrator divide leaves little room or appetite for adopting a relational perspective on a phenomenon that could ultimately allow practitioners to offer a greater range of treatment options in the service of assisting these couples and families overcoming their adversity.

A recent overview of services for intimate partner violence in Finland, whilst recognising the controversy in offering couple therapy, also emphasises the benefits of working with partners together (Vall et al., 2018). Indeed, there are many accounts of practitioners within the field, both in this country and in the US, working safely and effectively with such couples to help them tackle violence and address important underlying factors that perpetuate the violence whilst ensuring the continuation of the couple relationship (Antunes-Alves & De Stefano, 2014; Goldner et al., 1990; Vetere & Cooper, 2001). Furthermore, Vall et al., (2018), drawing on the work of Karakurt et al., (2016), suggest that couples therapy has a positive impact in decreasing recidivism and, in some instances, is the better treatment option over more standard approaches. Nevertheless, the understandable concerns about safety, together with fears of victim-blaming and the idea of increasing the risk of violence through an intensification of emotions during couple therapy, raises obvious questions concerning its appropriateness and effectiveness for those offering conjoint work.

A key consideration, and one that is fundamental to the development of new approaches within the field, which honours the nature and complexity of violent and abusive relationships, is the recognition that not all violence is the same. Kelly & Johnson (2008), for instance, draw an important distinction between violence and abuse within couple relationships that contains elements of coercion and control from that which is defined as situational couple violence. In situational couple violence, the violence and abuse often involves both partners reacting to particular strains within their relationship, where the flare-ups do not necessarily escalate or involve serious or life threatening injuries and where fear and control is not the primary mechanism driving and directing the relationship. As Antunes-Alves and De Stefano (2014) point out, 'in many couples violence is not a means to control but, rather, as research shows, an ineffective strategy for trying to deal with personal and interpersonal issues' (p. 65). However, this is not to deny that in some instances of situational couple violence, the abuse can escalate to dangerous levels, and so keeping the work under review is imperative to ensure safe and positive outcomes for all concerned. Furthermore, it is essential that practitioners screen for and keep a close eye on coercive controlling aspects of violence, especially since many workers within the field of domestic violence question the very existence of situational couple violence, believing it to be a misguided attempt to conceal the pernicious and dangerous elements that lurk within violent couple relationships involving male privilege and abuse. This notwithstanding, staff at Tavistock Relationships tend to encounter couples seeking help with common couple concerns, now defined as situational couple violence. Indeed, our experience of assessing and working with these couples over many years, has allowed us to develop a way of working with them (Humphries & McCann, 2015). Further refinement of the model, incorporating mentalization based techniques alongside interagency working, is outlined in this chapter by Benjamin, Chahal, Mulley and Reay.

It is testament to the care with which couples are put forward for consideration of the intervention, as well as the comprehensive assessment process that they are required to go through before being accepted into treatment, that Tavistock Relationships and their Local Authority partner were awarded government funding. At the root is an understanding and acceptance that some couples and parents who come to the attention of safeguarding services may not necessarily be helped by a split intervention, reflective of the victim and perpetrator divide. This is because not all couples necessarily define themselves in these terms and, as such, will often be resistant in truly investing in treatments that separate them along these lines. Moreover, the 'Ofsted multi-agency response to children living with domestic violence' specifically highlights a flaw in the thinking that putting an end to abusive relationships by splitting the couple reduces the risk, since, as research shows, this also has the potential to increase it. This is because a failure to fully appreciate the dynamic workings of these relationships, together with the couple's own attachment system, leaves practitioners at the mercy of couples who, despite efforts to separate them, meet with a determination in the couples themselves to remain together. Also, offering separate interventions to partners who are committed to staying together raises important questions concerning the point at which these interventions are felt to have reached the stage where a couple-based intervention could be considered necessary and appropriate. This is not, however, to ignore the dangers that some couple relationships pose a threat to one or other partner as well as to their children, but to appeal for a better understanding amongst professionals within the field that the 'one size fits all' approach is inadequate for the task at hand. Some couples therefore deserve to be considered for the kind of relational intervention offered by Tavistock Relationships and their Local Authority partner.

Generally speaking most researchers and clinicians advocating couple therapy for this population, emphasise particular considerations. For example, Stith et al. (2005) believe that the violence should be low to moderate if couple treatment is considered, and both partners should voluntarily agree to participate in conjoint therapy and have a commitment to remaining together. Further refinement of these criteria extend to the importance of both partners sharing similar views about the nature and incidence of violence, which may offer some protection against attempts to minimise the abuse or to diminish responsibility for it. I found it reassuring, therefore, to have the authors of this chapter outline their approach to assessment, which holds individual meetings with both partners as well as a conjoint session before deciding on the appropriateness of offering the couple intervention. In fact, the system within the Local Authority for putting couples forward for the intervention suggests that there is a robust framework for establishing a secure foundation on which to rest the assessment. This also allows for a meaningful and nuanced conversation between the assessors, the couple and their social worker as to alternative ways of intervening for those couples whom it is felt would not be appropriate for the joint intervention. I believe that this framework militates against professionals unwittingly responding punitively towards couples who fail to co-operate with decisions made on their behalf, thus enacting the very dynamics that operate within these troubled couple relationships. Here I am specifically thinking of mothers finding themselves in situations where they risk losing their children if they remain with their abusive partners. Having both an interagency and multi-disciplinary approach to decision-making about domestically violent couples, who have no wish to separate, enables a richer response to some of the snags within the couple and family system itself that may work against professionals' efforts to help, particularly if it involves attempts to get the couple to separate.

In Vetere and Cooper's (2001) paper outlining their approach to working with couples and parents troubled by domestic violence, they particularly emphasise themes of risk, responsibility and collaboration. In terms of risk, they speak of a continuous programme of risk assessment, whilst also balancing the tension in therapeutic work between 'the responsibility for the violent behaviour on the one hand and the explanation for violence on the other' (p. 383). The purpose of these principles is to ensure an honest assessment of risk together with an understanding of where the couple stands in relation to the violence and abuse that bedevils their working relationship. Collaboration is also an important ingredient, since it speaks to the ability of the parental couple to view professional workers as helpful. They go on to say that 'Previous professional attempts to tell family members to change their behaviour have not always been productive, so, if we cannot establish a context for co-operation through our attention to the therapeutic alliance and our processes of transparent working, we do not proceed' (Vetere & Cooper, 2001, p. 384). It was noticeable in this chapter how, during the work, at least one of the couples was critical of social care's approach to their needs, yet, by closely holding the family's social worker in the treatment framework through regular reviews, the therapists were able to reduce the tendency to split (a particular feature of violent and abusive couples) as well as encouraging and maintaining transparency through the entire process of treatment. In my view, this legitimises the intervention as well as ensuring the safety of the work as the couple is helped towards change.

The application of a mentalization-based approach to working with domestically violent couples seems an entirely appropriate and helpful way of managing the problematic dynamics that operate within these relationships. The authors provide a very helpful description of this approach in action, and the reader will see how the space to think and reflect is created. The technical challenge of working therapeutically with couples in which there is violence and abuse resides in the level of disturbance within and between the partners, as their individual and couple emotional systems are triggered by painful memories, fears of abandonment and frightening reactions. Shared disappointments, frustration and anger are often split between the partners in ways that distort and exaggerate the dynamics between them. Therefore, understanding the nature of their couple fit, incorporating both conscious and unconscious elements of beliefs and behaviour, helps enlarge the field of vision and may assist the couple in understanding the nature and pattern of their relationship over time.

Often the root of the couple's problem will lie in their own past histories brought to life in the present. Therefore, the more able they are to engage with the problematic aspects of these histories within and between them, the more likely they are to feel in charge of the painful and difficult aspects of their relationship. Fonagy and Target (1995) observe that violence is the product of a person's lack of capacity for reflection or mentalization. In other words, 'the lack of a containing function leaves the persecutory and toxic objects in the mind' (Ruszczynski, 2006, p. 115), hence the tendency to blame and the potential for escalation in the violence. Mentalization based techniques are designed to create an increased capacity to manage affective states, precisely in order to allow for a deeper exploration of the underlying issues that often result in the abusive dynamics. The aim of such therapy is to create the conditions for the individuals to understand the nature of their relationship, and to see whether they can become more of a couple in containing and nurturing their relationship for the benefit of themselves and their children. To that end it was noticeable in the chapter how the intervention offered to the couples actually reduced the police call-outs, which may be consistent with Karakurt et al.'s (2016) finding that couple therapy reduces the rates of recidivism. However, although the benefits of offering a couple therapy intervention in the field of domestic violence is gathering momentum, until we have a more secure evidence base supporting such intervention it will no doubt continue to be frowned upon by those firmly wedded to the victim and perpetrator divide.

References

Antunes-Alves, S., & De Stefano, J. (2014). Intimate partner violence: making the case for joint couple treatment. *The Family Journal, 22*: 62–8.

Fonagy, P., & Target, M. (1995). Understanding the violent patient: the use of the body and the role of the father. *International Journal of Psycho-Analysis, 76*: 487–501.

Goldner, V., Penn, P., Sheinberg, M., & Walker, G. (1990). Love and violence: gender paradoxes in volatile attachments. *Family Process, 29*(4): 343–64.

Humphries, J., & McCann, D. (2015). Couple psychoanalytic psychotherapy with violent couples: understanding and working with domestic violence. *Couple and Family Psychoanalysis, 5*(2): 149–67.

Karakurt, G., Whiting, K., Esch, C., Bolen, S.D., & Cakabrese, J.R. (2016). Couples therapy for intimate partner violence: a systemic review and meta-analysis. *Journal of Marital and Family Therapy, 42*(4): 567–83.

Kelly, J.B., & Johnson, M.P. (2008). Differentiation among types of intimate partner violence: research update and implications for interventions. *Family Court Review, 46*(3): 476–99.

Ruszcynski, S. (2006). Sado-masochistic enactments in a couple relationship. *Psychoanalytic Perspectives on Couple Work, 2*: 107–16.

Stith, S.M., McCollum, E.E., Rosen, K.H., Locke, L., & Goldberg, P. (2005). Domestic violence focused couples treatment. In: J. Lebow (Ed.), *Handbook of Clinical Family Therapy* (pp. 406–30). New York: John Wiley.

Vall, B., Paivinern, H., & Holma, J. (2018). Results of the Jyvaskyla research project on couple therapy for intimate partner violence: topics and strategies in successful therapy processes. *Journal of Family Therapy, 40*: 63–82.

Vetere, A., & Cooper, J. (2001). Working systemically with family violence: risk, responsibility and collaboration. *Journal of Family Therapy, 23*: 378–96.

Chapter 9

Working with the fractured container

Avi Shmueli

The 'fracture' of divorce

Eggs, and in particular the egg shell, has been called 'nature's ceramic' because of the immense forces it can bear (Hahn et al., 2017). An avian egg can withstand a well distributed force of 5000 Newtons when this is applied along its main axis, as demonstrated when trying to squeeze a raw egg by hand. Nevertheless, a focus, or 'point load', can lead to a fracture originating from the inner surface of the egg shell; effectively the shell fractures from the inside out. This makes perfect sense given the inherent hope that an egg will give rise to a chick that can then break out from inside the shell.

Similarly, the couple relationship can act as a container capable of withstanding the enormous pressures that can arise in the tension between psychological development and psychological defence that inherently exist within it. As with every container, the forces brought to bear may be overwhelming and the resulting fractures can have significant effects. When considering couples, these effects may include separation and divorce, and there is very little doubt that such effects are highly stressful; divorce as a stressor is rated only second to the death of a child and higher than imprisonment (Holmes & Rahe, 1967; Rahe et al., 1970).

Shmueli (2012) illustrated why this is so through conceptualising the changes that occur for each partner into three separate but interdependent domains. The first of these was termed the Environmental Domain and comprised the very conscious and tangible factors involved in divorce, such as change of home, issues of contact with children, finances, the legal process, and changes of routines. The second was termed the Preconscious Normative Domain because it contained the responses that every individual would be expected to experience, such as bereavement reactions, although expression of these may not be directly observable to either the individual affected or others close by. The third was termed the Unconscious Idiographic Domain and was considered to be the realm of individual psychopathology. It is the realm that comprises what is unique to each individual and therefore makes each individual's response to separation and divorce unique. As such, it has a powerful influence upon both the Preconscious Normative and Environmental Domains. Like the eggshell, the fracture begins from within and moves to the surface. The high impact and stress of separation and divorce arises from change occurring in each of the domains, and doing so simultaneously.

The work of Tavistock Relationships in relation to divorce and separation has done a great deal to identify and describe the nature and types of fracture that can be observed. Results from a study of family court welfare work (Clulow & Vincent, 1987) can be seen as differentiating between three types of divorce according to the kind of rupture in the projective system of the couple. The 'shotgun divorce' described a process of re-introjection that occurs for one partner and not the other, resulting in unsustainable tension prompting her or him to leave suddenly and to the complete surprise of the remaining partner. The 'longlease divorce', in which one partner retains a proprietorial sense of ownership over the absent partner, echoes Freud's (1917) failure in mourning in its refusal to accept change. The 'nominal divorce' refers to a process in which a physical separation is attempted to achieve a psychological separation in an otherwise fused couple relationship.

Such processes, and the extent of change involved, are inevitably accompanied by high degrees of uncertainty and pressure evoking regressive states of mind (Shmueli, 2012). This itself may give rise to pressure for either instant and/or highly concrete solutions intended to manage or displace distress. Vincent (1995) noted implications for practitioners in describing how couples unconsciously may attempt to force therapists into different roles, omnipotent ones such as the judge who can adjudicate between them and the magician who can solve everything, or impotent ones such as the servant who has no power or volition of their own. Projective systems of this kind can play out in families in delusional ways where adults think of themselves only as rational parents with no overwhelming psychological experiences of their own and their children as the seat of all vulnerable emotions. When adults unwittingly project their own experiences into their children, who are then treated as their 'representatives', the scene is set for intense conflicts within and between parents being played out in relation to the children whilst not actually concerning them at all (Clulow & Vincent, 1987, 2003; Donner, 2006; Shmueli, 2005).

This chapter seeks to extend the work described through presenting three different examples of working with couples for whom separation and divorce was a real option but had neither been consciously decided upon nor unconsciously determined. That is to say, the partners found themselves in crisis, knew that divorce might occur, but had not consciously decided to divorce or found themselves in a situation where they felt they had no choice but to divorce. In each case, the processes in the projective cycle described above have not led to a changed situation in their relationship. However, it would equally not be possible to state that the couple was intact in terms of containing their experience. These case descriptions are not complete in terms of clinical data or theorisation but are presented to illustrate the nature of the experience of working with couples in crisis, what might best be described as 'working in and with the fracture' of the couple container. Just as with an egg, a force arising from within has caused a fracture that once present cannot be ignored; but the fracture does not indicate precisely what will happen to the egg or its contents.

The silent fracture and the 'usual'

Duncan and Catherine had been in crisis for a while but only realised this following a particularly intense argument regarding their children. They came to therapy knowing they needed to find a way forward for themselves which included the possibility of divorce, but were unclear as to how precisely they had arrived at this point.

They arrived for their session as usual. Unusually however, they were a few minutes late. She used the toilet as usual. He sat on the sofa in the waiting room as usual. Opening the door, the usual scene presented itself. Catherine standing, Duncan looking through a magazine, slightly delaying the withdrawal of his attention from the magazine before looking up. He smiled. Catherine made eye contact, smiled, and said 'good evening'. They both entered the consulting room as usual.

Catherine placed her coat at her side and sat in her usual seat. Duncan sat in his usual chair and arranged his coat around his legs, as usual. There was the familiar silence at the beginning of a session and, as was usual, Catherine looked slightly to her side, towards Duncan, with the usual implicit acknowledgement that they were at their session and with the suggestion that he begin the discussion.

A silence emerged which was gentle and anticipatory. It had been a week since the last session and a great deal can happen in a week. Where would we begin?

Unusually, however, the silence continued. This raised the question of had something happened? It remained possible to investigate this and break the silence by either offering the observation of the continuing silence to the couple or by linking the observation with the question of whether it was an expression of something that had happened. Yet the silence itself was not tense, the air was not for cutting and a metaphorical knife was not available. It did not feel 'right' to say anything and so the silence continued.

By fifteen minutes into the session, Duncan had closed his eyes. He remained still, conveying the sense of an ongoing attempt to concentrate. He was certainly not asleep, and a sleepiness was also not present in the room. Catherine appeared to join him in this activity. With less apparent withdrawal, she too sat quietly with herself clearly in contemplation. The room was therefore silent but not empty. The experience was of being in the presence of a process at work.

By thirty minutes into the session, the silence had itself developed a momentum and inertia. It would take psychic work to overcome this, were anyone in the room to say anything. The silence itself remained non-persecutory but it would quite clearly take more than one utterance to shift the process into something that could be verbalised. It was also quite clear that the silence itself was the session rather than a feature outside of it, or an interruption to an ongoing interaction between the couple.

For 35 of the 60 minutes of the session, Duncan had remained in his position. This was now where he would appear to stay. Catherine looked to him. Her gaze appeared gentle but firm. She appeared to search for contact and persistently so. Somewhat frustrated and possibly distressed, she then looked to me and there was a mutual acknowledgement through eye contact. No words were exchanged but, as it felt at the time, her presence was acknowledged and in doing so, the fact that she was not alone was affirmed. She returned to Duncan and searched for him once more.

Interestingly, throughout the session time did not seem to slow. Quite the opposite, it seemed to pass quickly. By forty-five minutes, the silence continued although it was increasingly changing in nature. There was more tension. Duncan remained in his stance and Catherine had not managed to make contact with him. She appeared more frustrated, somewhat upset, and withdrew into herself and eventually into a semi-present, somewhat sleepy state. There she remained.

At fifty-five minutes, with only a few minutes remaining in the session, and without a word having been said throughout, the question emerged of how to end. Classically it would have been possible to simply say that we had come to time. This would not, however, take account of the fact that the session had been manifestly silent but certainly not empty. Consequently, I said that 'the difficulty we face at this particular point is that we have come to time'. With that, Duncan opened his eyes and Catherine returned to a fully present state. She smiled, and he silently mouthed 'thank you' as they left, as usual.

The most salient feature of the session was not the silence itself. Most important was the sudden and dramatic difference in the couple's manner to each other and seemingly to themselves alongside and in comparison to their 'usual' style and behaviour. The 'usual' was not lost but held in the mind of the therapist allowing two very different and seemingly incompatible styles of relating to be simultaneously present. This incompatibility may be likened to the fracture in the shell of their relationship. Understanding the nature of the fracture would involve understanding more about both Catherine and Duncan through the lens of psychoanalytic theory.

Understanding the 'fracture' in psychoanalytic theory

Central to understanding the fractured container is a recognition that the couple fit (Mattinson & Sinclair, 1979) has effectively faltered whilst each individual's attempt to communicate and convey meaning to the other continues. The understanding of the 'here and now' (Ruszczynski, 1993) in the consulting room becomes an equally weighted combination of both couple phenomena and individual communications not necessarily connected to the couple projective system. In these circumstances the assumption that the consulting room provides the setting for the transference of an integrated and intact, even if misshapen, couple container can no longer beheld. Therefore, the difficulty consequently posed is that regarding the manifest content of the couple's narrative as representing the shared unconscious narrative is open to challenge. The presence of the fractured container calls for a greater working understanding of the link between conscious and unconscious material.

In one of the milestones of the 'quiet revolution' of their work (Fonagy, 2005), Sandler and Sandler (1984) put forward a model of the mind which incorporated a developmental perspective and combined both Freud's topographical model and his later structural model. The topographical model outlined the functioning of the systems Unconscious, Preconscious, and Conscious, operating under primary and secondary processes. The structural model highlighted the agencies of the Id, Ego, and Superego. The first censorship barrier of repression lay between the systems Unconscious and Preconscious, and remained always impenetrable. It was relaxation of the second censorship barrier between Preconscious and Conscious, at times of sleep or in free association, that allowed access to the derivatives of the system Unconscious to be observed in the system Preconscious. The multilayered meanings of manifest symptoms and statements could then be gradually discerned in the work of therapy.

Sandler & Sandler (1984) noted how the understanding of the system Preconscious had waned and the term 'unconscious' had begun to be incorrectly used to cover all material that was uncovered, resulting effectively in a two-level topographical working model used in clinical practice comprising the systems Conscious and Unconscious. The system Preconscious was rarely mentioned, whilst theory dictated that this system was the site of analytic work.

They attempted to respond to this through presenting the concepts of the past unconscious and the present unconscious using a 'three box' model. The first 'box', or system, contained within it aspects of very early development, including aggressive and sexual impulses, and was never accessible to consciousness. Representations in this system were dominated by childhood theories and could be thought of as the 'child within the adult' (Fonagy, 2005). External stimuli evoked powerful unconscious fantasies rooted in the past. The second box/system was also unconscious, and its contents very subject to censorship. The equivalent of the system Preconscious, it was oriented to the present rather than the past and allowed for the creation of conflict solving compromises, thus facilitating adaptation. Consequently, current or present unconscious fantasies might be modified in response to external stimuli: self and object representations were then modifiable through new experiences. Whilst the first two systems were unconscious and tolerated contradiction, the third box/system in the model was conscious and, as with Freud's models, operated on the basis of logic, secondary process, and was subject to the norms of society. Shame and humiliation were paramount influences within this system.

Overall, the past unconscious of the first system comprised the continuation of past in the present with no seeming need for adaptation. However, the present unconscious of the second system comprised the here and now adaptations to the difficulties triggered in the first system and was more amenable to interpretation. The idea and technique of interpretation from surface to depth comes alive in this model, and the implications for working with the transference can be considered as closer to the clinical reality met in the consulting room.

What may be seen with couples are attempts by each partner to actualise (Sandler & Sandler, 1984) present unconscious fantasies in the attempt to stabilise any disturbance from past unconscious fantasies, given that both are simultaneously present. Interpretations provided by the therapist are essentially aimed at the present unconscious fantasy, for the couple and for each individual. Whilst modifications to past unconscious fantasies are not theoretically possible, modifying present unconscious fantasies are possible, although the introduction of these modifications may challenge and overwhelm the couple relationship as a container. Put simply, the fracture may arise from the non-alignment of present and past unconscious fantasy, the necessary primary process functioning in the present unconscious bursting outwards from within and placing excessive force on the 'shell' that is the couple container.

For Duncan and Catherine, the fracture took place between the intensity of the present unconscious and non-verbal functioning and the more familiar and 'usual' functioning. Both could be discerned in the room, although this required the therapist to be mindful of the 'usual'. Duncan was 'usually' masterful at attending to the other. He had almost been raised to do this, having had a highly narcissistic father and a mother who, almost in consequence, had been frequently absent. Whilst highly intelligent, his representation of self was intimately reliant upon the representation of the other. He aligned himself to the other as if operating within the fantasy that without the other person he himself did not exist. In consequence, he studiously attended to Catherine and, whilst commenting on the absence of time for himself, failed to notice this was the nature of his existence and could not be changed. In a complementary fashion, Catherine appeared highly independent having been sent away from home to boarding school when very young. Successful, she could spend hours in her office working on her own, apparently without need of anyone else. For her, the other did not truly exist. Manifestly each was highly role responsive (Sandler, 1976) to the other, and this was their 'usual' manner of functioning. Theirs was a slow burning developmental crisis, increasingly brought on through having provided a nurturing environment for their children, who, now grown up, had left home.

The fracture presented itself within the silence, quietly dramatic, and within the 'usual' manner of their presentation. Whilst usually using his words to fill the session with meaningful discussion, Duncan unusually remained himself, almost against his will, but also at times making a determined effort to do so.

Catherine's behaviour, in seeking him and then withdrawing in distress, could almost echo her early experience, but seemed to evidence a now more conscious recognition that there was an object to relate to in the room with her. For both, the here-and-now non-verbal functioning in the session conveyed their very different respective fantasies, alive and present, and within the context of their 'usual' functioning.

For the therapist, it was crucial that the simultaneous duality of fantasies could be held in mind. In order to do this, the therapist had to be able to bear the silence, bringing to it both a developmental perspective and some prior knowledge regarding the topic of silence. It is an understandable expectation that once a couple enter the consulting room they begin to talk both to each other and to their therapist. Indeed, relational models of functioning actively favour engagement and mutual exploration (Little, 2015). For the therapist, especially those in training, silence can carry the anxiety that therapy is not happening. The process of expressing internal experience in words is fundamental to psychoanalysis. From the perspective of classical theory, the unconscious is not a verbal system and verbalisation of experience is the evidence that affect has been properly bound. To put it another way, a concept has been found to contain the experience, and therefore expression through non-verbal behaviour becomes unnecessary. This would comprise part of Freud's dictum on the aims of the 'talking cure', namely that 'where Id was, there shall Ego be' (Freud. 1933, p. 80). The use of language is based in a developmental perspective, and Ella Freeman Sharpe's (1940) eloquent description is worthy of direct quotation:

> When the ego stabilizes the achievement of body-control and it becomes automatic, the emotions of anger and pleasure, which heretofore accompanied bodily discharges, must be dealt with in other ways. At the same time as sphincter control over anus and urethra is being established, the child is acquiring the power of speech and so an avenue of 'outerance' present from birth becomes of immense importance ... the discharge of feeling tension when this is no longer relieved by physical discharges can take place through speech. The activity of speaking is substituted for the physical activity now restricted at other openings of the body, while words themselves become the very substitutes for the bodily substance.
>
> (p. 203)

Silence by the patient was initially conceptualised as a resistance or defence and therefore received little attention in the psychotherapy literature (Zeligs, 1960). Kurtz (1984), however, contrasted the therapist's inflected and uninflected silences, and thus linked silence with countertransference. Inflected silence would be considered part of language, whilst uninflected silence was an indication of what cannot be said at the time. Increasingly, silence in the session has been viewed as an over-determined and 'multi-faceted psychic state serving many mental processes and systems of the mind' Calogeras (1967, p. 541). These would include its service in ego processes such as an unconscious re-enactment, a defensive response to interpretation, and a regression (Van der Heide, 1961). Simultaneously, silence was also viewed as a transference–countertransference manifestation (Zeligs 1960), and as a re-enactment stemming from different levels of development (Arlow, 1961). Silence could have as much meaning as any verbal event in a session, although it would be understandably more difficult to manage and require technical innovation.

For Duncan and Catherine, the silence was a deafening fracture in their couple container. Whilst the fracture was early in developmental terms, it was observably present in the here and now. The therapist was aided by having an underlying theory of unconscious functioning, of the function of verbalisation in both developmental and psychotherapeutic terms, and by a capacity to remain with his observations, both of the couple and himself, through the session. It was hence possible to observe and understand both the fracture presented and the serious threat it posed to the status quo of their relationship.

Fracturing as a form of functioning

It was not so much that David and Sue fought, it was the nature of their fights that was striking. They argued about anything and everything. Recently married, and almost immediately in crisis, they were a young couple who had a relationship weighty beyond its years. Interestingly, personal history was very difficult to obtain from them, and when reported done so out of duty or a response to a direct question, but always with an air of irrelevance. David's parents had been together for years; they had their regular routines and were very happy together. Yet, he deeply loathed himself, although he only mentioned this in passing. Sue's parents had each suffered quite significant trauma from which neither had fully recovered and they appeared to lead separate lives. She tried to understand them but also avoided them.

The sessions took on a particular style. Seemingly pleased to attend, they reported on the week that had been since their previous session. Their aim, it seemed, was to examine where each had felt let down in their interaction and thus implicitly work to make the following week pleasurable. Overall, this process led to two different outcomes, and the couple oscillated between these outcomes both within and across sessions.

When events had 'worked', this heralded declarations of love and dedication. These then either gave way to complaints or moved straight into fighting. The couple fought in a particular way, usually beginning with what appeared to be a small difference which then took on huge proportions. David would shout at Sue, often saying 'Oh my God, do you not see . . .' whilst Sue would struggle to state her own point of view whilst experiencing tremendous pressure to assume total responsibility to accept what had gone wrong. The emotional force of the arguments tended to outweigh the content. Yet, for all his shouting, David would look down after his tirade, and it was possible to discern the appearance of a small smile. Sue would look dejected but resigned to the ongoing difficulty.

For a brief period, the feeling would emerge that the relationship was a disaster, unworkable, unsustainable, and broken. They wondered what 'to do', and felt they should get divorced. It was all very painful and very uncertain.

Then, of course, there was the possibility of next week.

David and Sue were not a 'cat and dog' couple (Mattinson & Sinclair, 1979). They did not fight within an understanding that they would remain together. David and Sue had trial separations, followed by reunions, followed by the resumption of their fights. The fracturing for this couple was almost immediate and ongoing. Taking into account his observations, the very 'here and now' quality to the couple's presentation and interaction, and the seeming irrelevance of history, the therapist realised that what was being observed was a couple enacting a core complex fantasy. Central to the concept of the Core Complex (Campbell & Hale, 2017; Glasser, 1979) is the oscillation between two states. The first, a merging with the object so as not to experience any frustration, but resulting in the dissolution of self. The second, the murder of the object as an act of survival, but resulting in complete abandonment. This oscillation is dampened down through sadism: the object is relied upon to meet the subject's needs, but treated cruelly so as to deny any sense of dependency on and therefore threat from it. David's smile clearly conveyed that, for all his seeming distress, the intense and sadomasochistic pattern of this couple's ongoing crisis was necessary for his psychic equilibrium.

Their relationship was dominated by aggression, which in core complex functioning is mobilised as a protective response. In describing the early developmental nature, or depth of this experience, Glasser calls on Freud (1915) in pointing out that it is the object of hatred that is the source of unpleasurable feelings rather than the experience itself. Crucially, whilst acknowledging Kleinian formulations of early object relating, he does not view aggression as fundamentally destructive. He points out that the core complex involves a failure of ego perceptual functioning and illustrates this through a simple but acute example. He notes that 'a man who is furious with his car because it will not start on a cold morning, needs to be able to know that he does not want to destroy the whole car but rather its non-startingness' (Glasser, 1979, p. 284). For David and Sue, the establishment of a couple relationship that could be experienced as a psychological home for each of them seemed to be experienced as a 'non-starter', so it was viciously attacked. They relied more on their conscious knowledge that they were married and that the experience 'should' be better than that which they were having. The only exceptions to this were holidays, periods of time in which everyday reality and its demands was removed and the fulfilment of wishes became paramount.

For David and Sue there appeared to be an absence of perceptual identity (Sandler & Sandler, 1984), that is, the everyday experience of seeing and perceiving what you believe is the case. What they saw in their own marriage seemed to powerfully clash with the unconscious phantasies each had regarding relationships. Furthermore, the lack of reference to personal histories for each was an important indication of where the fracture lay. For David, his parent's relationship appeared uncomplicatedly good. They had been married a long time and were very happy. There appeared no thoughts regarding this and no reference to it in trying to address his own marriage. For Sue, the parental relationship appeared overwhelmed by undefined trauma to a point that it was difficult to imagine her parents as being in a relationship with each other. It could therefore be hypothesised that for David and Sue the differentiation between past and present unconscious fantasies became rather blurred and undefined. This would imply that for each, the unconscious fantasy, whether past or present, was dominated by earlier and childlike notions. This would then clash with what each actually perceived, resulting in the experience that their very perceptions threatened their underlying phantasies. Between them, David and Sue managed to create a relationship which fundamentally threatened each of them. Yet to leave the relationship would require a withdrawal from an external reality that would leave them exposed to an even greater adherence to early unconscious fantasies.

It was possible to view David and Sue's pattern of interaction as following Core Complex functioning, fracturing resulting from the moment when perceptions met both past and present unconscious fantasy. It was only possible to speculate on the nature of past unconscious fantasy: how David might not feel that he existed in his parent's seemingly perfect relationship, and how Sue could not maintain a separateness from her parents underlying trauma. Yet together, the present shared unconscious fantasy operated according to the core complex, resulting in a process of living in a fracture which, while necessary for their psychic survival, made the possibility of development extremely limited.

The psychotic wavelength

Aye and Bee were both self-employed and struggled. Theirs was a competitive business in a profession where success was not gained easily. With hard work, the couple were able to make enough money to sustain themselves.

Over time, Bee became increasingly successful whilst Aye continued to work as before. There developed a point at which the distinction between them was neither transient nor deniable. Bee was more successful than Aye and this introduced tension between them. They sought couple therapy, which proceeded for over a year. From their account of this, the couple therapist appeared to emphasise Aye's envy of Bee's success. Aye admitted this, but the admission did not ease the tension between them. They ended the therapy. Bee suffered, and finally stated that the relationship could not continue: they had to separate and divorce.

They sought further consultations. Aye became livid, describing anger sufficient to melt those parts of the body which conveyed identity, namely the face and fingertips. Bee was alarmed, worried and especially so as, even at this time, their relationship was not without mutual concern and care. Aye's presentation at times suggested a severe breakdown. The consultations continued alongside negotiations between them to divide up their joint assets. These negotiations became bogged down and entrenched, and they resorted to lawyers. The therapist reported two countertransferential aspects: first, he felt the extreme nature of the impact of the aggression being described; second, and as if an aside, he had a heightened awareness of Bee's sexuality. Whilst this was a feature of the experience, it also seemed dissonant with the situation at hand and the therapist wondered whether this was a personal response to Bee rather than countertransference.

As the consultations continued tensions remained, although Aye's anger began to abate. There came a point at which Aye reported contemplating becoming employed rather than maintaining self-employment. In a moving sequence, Aye reported the extreme experiential difficulty of 'working for the man'. At this point, and trusting in his counter-transferential experience, the therapist pointed out the confusion for Aye between 'the man' and Bee. It was a short, and essentially descriptive intervention. By the next session, Aye had suggested to Bee that lawyers were predominantly unnecessary and that the negotiations could be resolved between them.

It may not have gone unnoticed that this vignette was written in a manner specifically avoiding language that would assign gender to either Aye or Bee. For this couple, the fracture occurred because the difference that emerged between them in terms of business success allowed for the emergence of Aye's profound past unconscious fantasy regarding the peril's and torture of dependency. This was expressed both in the initial destruction of identity, and then in the statement of 'working for the man'. Felt intensely and concretely, the fantasy was very present but could not be fully expressed because it would clash directly with perceived sexuality and gender. Bee was not a man, and yet for Aye, the experience was precisely that of relating to 'the man', that is, an object that was very powerful and upon which Aye was dependent. For Aye, the clash between fantasy and perception was such that it could not find room within the couple relationship, and a fracture ensued. Aye's attempt to convey the fantasy of being in service to a demanding and unrelenting object was undoubtedly related to personal history. However, in the here and now of the couple relationship, the accommodation of Aye's powerful and intense fantasy would require Bee's temporary repudiation of a profound identification regarding her sexuality. The fracture in the couple's relationship seemed to arise from there being insufficient room for the fantasy of Bee as 'the man' alongside the reality of her sexuality and identity. An additional and retrospective insight was that the work of enabling the expression of Aye's fantasy of working for 'the man' was facilitated by the therapist's awareness of Bee's sexuality. This awareness allowed for the duality of sexuality and fantasies concerning dependency to be simultaneously but independently present in the consulting room.

The case of Aye and Bee highlights the manner in which an unconscious fantasy can emerge for couples and represent an aspect of functioning that has been very powerfully psychically split off and at odds with the couple's established everyday routine functioning. Its appearance can initially appear akin to the development of a psychotic illness because it cannot be sufficiently represented in the 'here and now' of conscious psychic functioning. However, being able to conceptualise these elements as part of a 'here and now' present unconscious fantasy, operating under primary process, allows an attunement to the psychotic wavelength (Lucas, 2009). This allows the form and meaning of the fantasy simultaneously to become known and elucidate the fracture in the couple relationship. As with all clinical work, but particularly when working with divorce and separation, it is important to distinguish between psychotic processes that can occur as part of a regressive phase in development, and psychotic states which encapsulate breakdown.

Conclusion

This chapter has described different aspects of understanding and working with the fractured container in couple relationships that can become manifest when partners consider the possibility of divorce. Couples present themselves for help at a time when the container is already fractured rather than under strain. Central to the argument has been asserting the value of considering the duality of present unconscious fantasies and past unconscious fantasies, maintaining a link between the two whilst also factoring in external reality. A fracture can occur at the juncture between any of these sites when all three can no longer be mutually accommodated. Taking account of such fractures can aid therapists when working in situations where personal histories (for example, David and Sue) and aspects of time (for example, Duncan and Catherine) are not necessarily available, both literally and psychically, to be worked with.

It is one of the beautiful and frustrating aspects of psychoanalysis that any clinical situation can be formulated from a number of different perspectives. However, a common thread linking the experience of those going through separation and divorce is the belief that it is fundamentally connected with issues of psychic development. Part and parcel of divorce is the attempt by at least one partner to take a developmental step. As such, understanding couple functioning in situations of divorce is no different from understanding couples who present in other situations where divorce is not being considered. However, working with couples who are separating and/or divorcing requires the therapist actively to maintain the capacity for observing, tolerating and making formulations about difficult affects, some of which have been illustrated by the cases described. Under the circumstances of such work, it is easy to forget that the divorcing couple was once a pair of lovers, and that their relationship originally included, even if unconsciously, the hope of resolving their developmental difficulties. The couple relationship, with its projective cycle, respective role responsiveness of each partner and balance between the wish for development and need for defence forms a substrate from which development can occur. The couple who divorce are not a different species from the couple who fall in love. As with an egg, a fracture in the shell can herald the arrival of a chick or it can mark the end of a particular creative endeavour.

References

Arlow, J. (1961). Silence and the theory of technique. In the symposium on the silent patient. *Journal of the American Psychoanalytic Association, 9*: 44–55.
Calogeras, R.C. (1967). Silence as a technical parameter in psycho-analysis. *International Journal of Psychoanalysis, 48*: 536–55.
Campbell, D., & Hale, R. (2017). *Working in the Dark: Understanding the Pre-suicide State of Mind*. Abingdon: Routledge.
Clulow, C., & Vincent, C. (1987). *In The Child's Best Interests: Divorce Court Welfare and the Search for a Settlement*. London: Tavistock.
Clulow, C., & Vincent, C. (2003). Working with divorcing partners. In: M. Bell & K. Wilson (Eds.), *The Practitioner's Guide to Working with Families* (pp. 129–46). Basingstoke: Palgrave Macmillan.
Donner, M. (2006). Tearing the child apart: the contribution of narcissism, envy, and perverse modes of thought to child custody wars. *Psychoanalytic Psychology, 23*(3): 542–53.
Hahn, E.N., Sherman, V., Pissarenko, A., Rohrbach, S., Ferandes, D., & Meyers, M. (2017). Nature's technical ceramic: the avian eggshell. *Journal of the Royal Society Interface*. DOI:10.1098/rsif.2016.0804
Fonagy, P. (2005). An overview of Joseph Sandler's key contributions to theoretical and clinical psychoanalysis. *Psychoanalytic Inquiry, 25*: 120–47
Freud, S. (1915). Instincts and their vicissitudes. *The Standard Edition of the Complete Works of Sigmund Freud. Vol. 14*, pp. 109–40. London: Vintage, 2001.
Freud, S. (1917). Mourning and melancholia. *The Standard Edition of the Complete Works of Sigmund Freud. Vol. 14*, pp. 237–60. London: Vintage, 2001.
Freud, S. (1933). The dissection of the psychical personality. *The Standard Edition of the Complete Works of Sigmund* Freud. *Vol. 22*, pp. 57–80. London: Vintage, 2001.
Glasser, M. (1979). Some aspects in the role of aggression in the perversions. In: I. Rosen (Ed.), *Sexual Deviation* (pp. 278–305). Oxford: Oxford University Press.
Holmes T., & Rahe R. (1967). The social readjustment rating scale. *Journal of Psychosomatic Research, 11*(2): 213–18.
Kurtz, S.A. (1984). On silence. *Psychoanalytic Review, 71*(2): 227–46.
Little, S. (2015). Between silence and words: the therapeutic dimensions of quiet. *Contemporary Psychoanalysis, 51*(1): 31–50.
Lucas, R. (2009). *The Psychotic Wavelength*. The New Library of Psychoanalysis. London: Routledge.
Mattinson, J., & Sinclair, I. (1979). *Mate and Stalemate*. Oxford: Blackwell.
Rahe R.H., Mahan J.L., & Arthur R.J. (1970). Prediction of near-future health change from subjects' preceding life changes. *Journal of Psychosomatic Research, 14*(4): 401–6.
Ruszczynski, S. (1993). *Psychotherapy with Couples*. London: Karnac.

Sandler, J. (1976). Countertransference and Role Responsiveness. *International Review of Psycho-Analysis*, *3*: 43–7.

Sandler, J., & Sandler, A. (1984). The past unconscious, the present unconscious, and interpretation of the transference. *Psychoanalytic Inquiry*, *4*(3): 367–99.

Sandler, J., & Sandler, A. (1994). Phantasy and its transformations: a contemporary Freudian view. *International Journal of Psychoanalysis*, *75*: 387–94.

Sharpe, E. F. (1940). Psycho-physical problems revealed in language: an examination of metaphor. *International Journal of Psychoanalysis*, *21*: 201–13.

Shmueli, A. (2005). On thinking of parents as adults in divorce and separation. *Sexual and Relationship Therapy*, *20*(3): 350–7.

Shmueli, A. (2012). Working therapeutically with high conflict divorce. In: A. Balfour, M. Morgan, & C. Vincent (Eds), *How Couple Relationships Shape Our World*. London: Karnac.

Van Der Heide, C. (1961). 'Blank silence and the dream screen.' In the symposium on the silent patient. *Journal of the American Psychoanalytic Association*, *9*: 85–90.

Vincent, C. (1995). Consulting to divorcing couples. *Family Law*, *25*: 678–81.

Zeligs, M.A. (1960). The role of silence in transference, counter-transference, and the psycho-analytic process. *International Journal of Psychoanalysis*, *41*: 407–12.

Commentary on Chapter 9

Christopher Vincent

Avi Shmueli takes the image of the bird's egg to help us understand his approach to conceptualising and working therapeutically with troubled couples whose future options might include separation and divorce. The egg's shell provides a protected space within which the fertilised ovum develops until the point that the fledgling outgrows its need of the shell and breaks it open from within. However, this healthy development might be harmed by pathological events within the eggshell which results in the shell being fractured prematurely.

This vivid picture draws the reader's attention to a way of viewing couple interaction and couple breakdown. It is a picture that gives prominence to the idea that the couple therapist should be concerned primarily with psychological processes that are generated between the partners of a relationship understood in systemic terms. The therapist tries to understand how a previously functioning interactive system has broken down to the point that the system itself is threatened by the separation of the partners; the containing boundary or 'shell' breaks. Understanding the nature of this fracture is the major theme of this chapter.

Before considering this phenomenon in detail, Shmueli refers to his earlier work (Shmueli, 2012) in order to provide a background context for understanding the 'biology within the shell'. Drawing on the theories of Freud and the Sandlers, he puts forward his own topographical framework involving the Environmental Domain, the Preconscious Normative Domain and the Unconscious Idiographic Domain. These domains of experience combine two interrelated axes. The first involves recognition that experience can be located on an axis between what is shared at a social/interpersonal level and what is private to the individual. The second involves an hierarchical scale of experience: at the apex are experiences that are consciously known about and acknowledged, and there are 'at depth' experiences which are unconscious but have an influence on behaviour. Shmueli argues that it is the third of these domains that is critical in shaping the way that each partnership approaches and manages a separation:

> It (the Unconscious Idiographic Domain) is the realm that comprises what is unique to each individual and therefore makes each individual's response to separation and divorce unique. As such, it has a powerful influence upon

both the Preconscious Normative and Enviromental Domains. Like the eggshell, the fracture begins from within and moves to the surface.

(p. 169–170)

While it is the deeply unconscious individual experiences of both partners that are likely to shape the unique ways that any one couple contemplate a separation, Shmueli points out that their effects will surface at the boundary between preconscious and conscious experience.

The Unconscious – at depth or on the surface?

When I am working with a couple two modes of thinking and working alternate with one another, which I will call 'working at depth' and 'working on the surface'.

Working at depth

When in this mode, I am concerned to understand shared problems from each partner's point of view, and this often holds sway over other ways of thinking and behaving at the initial assessment stage. I will seek to garner histories of the partners before and since they have been together, plus close and detailed pictures of their current interaction with one another both outside and inside the consulting room. This focus on what partners bring to the consulting room implies a receptive and listening stance as I seek to understand interaction 'at depth'.

When thinking of myself operating in this vein I value Shmueli's way of conceptualising layers of experience because it provides a prompt to look behind the manifest content of what people do and say in order to access the unconscious meaning of their behaviour. This working 'at depth', of trying to look below the surface of what is in front on my eyes, can be helpful in gaining an understanding of what has, hitherto, been perplexing. Two puzzling aspects of stuck interactions are commonplace. First, partners are invariably uncertain and confused about what is happening and how to move forward, notwithstanding the fact that ideas about future possibilities are sometimes thought and talked about; 'stuckness' endures, and there is, therefore, an implied wish from one or both partners to expand their understanding and their freedom to act so that decisions can be made about whether the partnership survives or ends. This is important to make explicit because it justifies the couple psychotherapist's stance in focusing on what each partner can potentially take responsibility for and change. For most people, the capacity for change in an intimate adult partnership is strongly but not exclusively influenced by the quality of early childhood experiences, and Shmueli's chapter directs our thinking to take this into account.

The second puzzling aspect about 'stuckness' is that most of the couples I see for whom separation is mentioned are angrily upset with each other, whether the anger is expressed overtly or covertly. I am very often perplexed and bemused by the deadlocked quality of couples who maintain an ongoing fight in the domestic arena yet seem unable either to separate or relate to one another in less angry ways. In my state of not knowing I feel impelled to look under the surface behaviour to find answers. What is the function of the anger in the various forms in which it may emerge? Is it essentially destructive in nature or is it a form of primitive communication (Vincent, 2014)? Is it designed to push a partner away or bring him or her closer, and how does past history answer this question? Does anger, with its concomitant property of certainty about where blame lies, serve to hold fragile egos together which would otherwise fall apart if more uncertain, confused ways of thinking were embraced? Is it a much needed defence against intimacy and/or more radical separation?

Working on the surface

While, at times, I feel it necessary to think of what lies beneath the surface of observable behaviour, I also switch mode (invariably forced to do so by the dynamics of the moment) and concentrate on the 'here and now' of the consultation, convinced that it is only by considering everything that the couple brings into the consulting room, including how their presence elicits responses in me, that I can affect any therapeutic leverage. This is, in some ways, a more complex therapeutic stance than the listening and observing mode mentioned earlier. I see myself as being a more active participant in a three person conversation which is situationally unique and jointly constructed over time. The challenge is to be both a participant in the exchange and an observer and commentator upon it so that learning takes place. This stance was given theoretical support by Joseph (1985) who argued that the transference, understood as a mechanism for communicating to the analyst what the patient is ambivalent about knowing, 'must include everything that the patient brings into the relationship' (p. 447). She adds that how the analyst is made to feel in response to the patient's behaviour is further evidence for understanding and making good use of the transference. On this reckoning I think Joseph would argue that the unconscious is embedded in everything that people talk about, how they talk about it and how they appear and behave. In this sense, the unconscious is not so much hidden as lying around on the surface of experience if only we have eyes to see it. This view involves the theoretical spotlight switching from an exclusive focus on the internal and interpersonal experiences of the couple to an interaction in the consulting room which includes the capacity or otherwise of the therapist to make sense of what he or she sees. In focusing on how therapists discern the unconscious aspects of surface phenomena there can be a recourse to metaphors which convey the trickiness and slipperiness of capturing what tries to remain hidden. For example, Ogden (2012) quotes with appreciation Searles' reference to the natural world in the latter's paper on unconscious identification:

> one can detect ... unconscious identification ... beneath or behind ... something like a sea plant ... (which) ... can be discovered to be flourishing

far beyond and beneath the few leaves that can be seen on the water's surface.

(p. 169)

In the same paper, Ogden uses the metaphor of the Moebius strip, whose inside surface is continually in the process of becoming outside and vice versa, to capture the proximity yet elusive and hidden quality of an unconscious dimension. These two metaphors speak to the experience of sometimes only glimpsing what is unconscious before it slips out of view. Take, for example, the following illustration:

> I had ended seeing a couple after two years of therapy on what was a negative note. They each blamed the other for the problems between them and considered that it was the other's responsibility to change if the relationship was to survive. After some months I was approached by the female partner to discuss the state of their relationship. Over the course of an hour's conversation she conveyed two strong messages. The first was that she continued to believe that her partner was at fault and that he had a personality disorder. In justifying her claim she gave me lengthy details of his contradictory and irrational behaviour that was incomprehensible to her and, she claimed, would be to anyone else. She appealed to me as a reasonable person to support her view. However, she then went on to say that she was a very kind woman who went out of her way to be considerate to other people and, indeed, went out of her way to accommodate the views of others.
>
> In the safety of our consultation there came a moment when she could see the contradiction that these two messages implied. How could she reconcile a belief that she was right with an acknowledgement that her partner might have legitimate points to make? She laughed nervously and became lost for words. In that brief moment she and I both witnessed the potential collapse of a paranoid way of thinking that felt deeply shaming and alarming.

The way that partners talk about events, whether stories cohere and how they induce countertransference reactions can be the complex mix from which an understanding of unconscious meaning is deduced. This way of looking at what couples bring might be thought about as a lateral way of appraising evidence to sit alongside Shmueli's model which gives prominence to a focus on depth.

Concluding thoughts

In responding to Shmueli's chapter I have found myself thinking about some profound questions that go to the heart of couple psychoanalytic theory and practice. I will mention two that concern me.

First, when thinking about models of the mind and models of couple interaction I wonder about their ontological status. Are models of the mind embedded in the neurological structure of the mind or are they essentially metaphors of heuristic value? I tend towards the latter view partly because I use different psychoanalytic models of the mind to explain different clinical phenomena but also because I am part of a postmodern culture that elevates the importance of social diversity and theoretical pluralism (Popper, 2009). These values also influence my thinking about models of couple functioning. While I trained within a therapeutic culture that reflected the wider societal norm of monogamous, heterosexual and developmental marriage, there has evolved in recent decades more varied patterns in the way couples choose to live. For example, marriage rates have fallen overall over the last two decades while cohabitation has increased (ONS, 2018), there is an increasing number of couples who chose to live physically apart but consider themselves committed to one another (Duncan & Phillips, 2010), while some same sex partnerships, whether or not formally recognised in law, are founded on polyamorous assumptions (McCann, 2017). These changes, which reshape normative assumptions about personal boundaries operating between partners and between the couple and wider society, will necessarily influence how couple problems present their difficulties and elicit responses in the consulting room.

Second, when working with very disturbed couples for whom separation is a strong possibility, when do we as therapists choose to 'fracture' our own hope in the couple, as a couple, or do we allow that the loss of hope is an emergent reality for which the couple have to take responsibility? This seems to me to be a profound question with ethical and technical ramifications. Some couples are not healthy couples and involve power imbalances that result in abuse of the weaker partner and children. I wrestle with the worry that, in some situations, by continuing to interpret the mutual projective system I collude in perpetuating unhealthy and dangerous relationships when it may be better for all concerned to relinquish that hope and to acknowledge the reality that the egg must fracture permanently.

References

Duncan, S., & Phillips, M. (2010). People who live apart together (LATS) - how different are they? *The Sociological Review*, 58: 112–34.
Joseph, B. (1985). Transference: the total situation. *International Journal of Psychoanalysis*, 66: 447–54.
McCann, D. (2017). When the couple is not enough, or when the couple is too much: exploring the meaning and management of open relationships. *Couple and Family Psychoanalysis*, 7(1): 45–58.
Office of National Statistics (ONS) (2018). Marriages in England and Wales: 2015. Available at: www.gov.uk/peoplepopulationandcommunity/birthsdeathsandmarriages/marriagecohabitationandcivilpartnerships/bulletins/marriagesinenglandandwalesprovisional/2015 (accessed 13 July, 2018).

Ogden, T.H. (2012). Harold Searles' Oedipal love in the countertransference and unconscious identification. In: T.H. Ogden, *Creative Readings: Essays on Seminal Analytic Works* (pp. 157–77). London: Routledge.
Popper, K. (2009). *The Logic of Scientific Discovery*. Abingdon: Routledge.
Shmueli, A. (2012). Working therapeutically with high conflict divorce. In: A. Balfour, M. Morgan, & C. Vincent (Eds), *How Couples Shape Our World: Clinical Practice, Research and Policy Perspectives* (pp. 137–58). London: Karnac.
Vincent, C. (2014). Getting back to or getting back at: understanding overt aggression in couple relationships. In: D.E. Scharff & J.S. Scharff (Eds.), *Psychoanalytic Couple Therapy: Foundations of Theory and Practice* (pp. 71–80). London: Karnac.

Chapter 10

Living together with dementia

Andrew Balfour and Liz Salter

Emily, whose husband, Harold, was in the more advanced stages of dementia, spoke of how she felt that everyone expected her to be a saint and they were not interested in what she felt about how hard it was. 'No one's interested, they don't know what it is like', she said. Their marriage had always been difficult and, although they had clearly had some good times earlier on and had raised three children together, their relationship had been troubled long before the dementia. As this had worsened, looking after Harold repeated, for Emily, a version of her experience as an only child, when her mother developed profound mental health problems after the death of her father. Then, as now, she felt left alone with a burden, with no one able to understand how difficult it was for her.

In recent months, Harold's dementia had progressed significantly and he responded to the anxiety of not knowing what to do, moments when he was disorientated, by getting angry. For her, it was much like the angry exchanges they had had for years and she retaliated with anger and criticism of him. This was worst at times when he was in a panic and feeling lost.

Their therapist witnessed how Emily would tell Harold things that he could not understand or have the capacity to follow; he would respond by saying he did not know what she was talking about, that she was not making any sense. It was at these times when she was critical or angry and he was at his most vulnerable that Harold became aggressive towards her.

Disagreements and misunderstandings could quickly ratchet up between them. When Harold responded to Emily by saying 'You're not making sense' or 'Do it yourself then', she heard this as examples of his refusal to cooperate, his deliberately being difficult. It took a lot of work for Emily to begin to shift her perception of such episodes and to think about what might be happening in his mind, to put herself, to some extent, into his shoes.

Why does the couple matter in dementia care?

It has been said that the physical and psychological health of older couples can be linked 'for better or for worse'. Spouse's symptoms wax and wane closely with those of their partners, research showing that there are strong associations between depressive symptoms and 'functional limitations' (the physical inability to perform basic tasks of everyday living) between partners in older couples (Hoppmann et al., 2011). This indicates how interdependent emotionally and physically older couples are, and highlights the need for a health and social care system that does not just focus on individuals in isolation.

For couples, the experience of dementia occurs in the context of a relationship that pre-dates the dementia often by the best part of a lifetime, and the pre-existing quality of the relationship affects how the dementia is experienced (Ablitt et al., 2009). People who feel that their relationship has been less satisfying prior to the dementia tend to experience more depression and distress (Gilleard et al., 1984; Knopp et al., 1998), greater strain (Morris et al., 1988a), and more emotional difficulties in response to the challenges of caring for their partner. Emotional factors are of crucial importance and the carer's experience of loss of intimacy and understanding of their partner with dementia has been found to be one important issue (Morris et al., 1988a, 1988b). Loss of intimacy is associated with carer spouse depression, and low levels of positive interaction between the partners in the marriages of people with dementia predict the move to residential care (Wright, 1991, 1994). Norton et al. (2009) found that closer relationships between carer and the person with dementia are associated with slower decline in Alzheimer's disease, and this effect is highest for couple relationships, highlighting the importance of our finding ways to intervene clinically to support such couples.

Whilst dementia impacts upon the couple's relationship in terms of diminished companionship, communication and intimacy (Evans & Lee, 2013), some studies have emphasised what might also be held onto, giving examples where feelings of belonging and reciprocity within close relationships in couples living with dementia were sometimes possible to maintain (Hellstrom & Lund, 2007; see Wadham et al., 2016 for a review). Research has also shown that, if couples can find ways of maintaining continuities in their lives together and find new ways of relating to one another in the context of dementia, this may help them to adapt to the challenges of the illness (McGovern, 2011). 'Couplehood' has emerged as a term in the literature to describe the key elements in the relationship which dementia impacts on, including the partners' experiences of intimacy, trust and support. Whilst partners' of people with dementia's experiences of losing 'couplehood' were connected to separation and the sense of being alone (Forsund et al., 2014), couples' experiences fluctuated, with recovered moments of connectedness, reciprocity and interdependence which contributed to their sustaining a feeling of togetherness.

Research shows the importance of a sense of inter-connectedness in the couple relationship in dementia and the value of understanding and validating the shared experiences of both partners in order to support this. There is a profound need for such a 'relationship focused' approach which reconceptualises dementia as a condition that affects *relationships* rather than individuals alone (Henderson & Forbat, 2002; McGovern, 2011). Such an approach 'offers more hope than focussing exclusively on cognitive decline, which is of crucial importance given the intense distress, despair and hopelessness that such couples can face' (Wadham et al., 2016, p. 471).

The Living Together with Dementia intervention

'Living Together with Dementia' (LTwD) is a structured approach to working with couples where one partner has a dementia, which draws upon psychoanalytic thinking and therapeutic methods developed in working with parents and children which emphasise observation and use video as part of their focus. These include Parent–Infant Psychotherapy (Baradon et al., 2005), Video Interaction Guidance (Kennedy et al., 2011) and the Relationship Development Intervention (Gutstein, 2005) (an approach to working with children with autism and their parents) as well as techniques from couple psychotherapy. The LTwD intervention uses everyday domestic activities of life as opportunities for shared endeavour and involvement for the couple. The focus is upon the emotional meaning and potential of these everyday activities to support inter-dependency between the partners (what Uchino et al., 1994, called 'cohesion'), and so to address some of the relational impacts which are identified by dementia research as linked to negative outcomes for both partners. Our aim is to support couples as much as possible to maintain, or recover, the protective aspects of their relationship, which research indicates are to do with emotional contact and understanding, shared activity and involvement as well as the overall quality of the relationship. The intention is to hold the couple, for longer, in a position where they are in emotional contact with one another and to give them tools which help to counteract the pressure towards withdrawal between the partners, which is so often associated with dementia.

Video approaches have been found to be very powerful in work with parents and children, helping to promote change and new understanding. They have the tremendous advantage, given the nature of the cognitive deficits of dementia, of not relying on linguistic and symbolic communication. Through use of video it is possible to work with couples with dementia across a range of stages of the illness to promote change through shifts of awareness. We work alongside the couple, engaging them in working together on carefully selected activities highlighting and supporting moments of emotional contact between the partners, and engaging the person with dementia in activities that they can still manage with the support of their partner. This involves carefully structuring the activities, so that they are broken down into manageable tasks, and, depending on the capacity of the partner with dementia, helping the carer spouse to learn to function as a guide, enabling their partner to be as involved as they are able to be. The intention is to maximise the extent to which activities are shared, rather than, for example, taken over by the healthy partner. It is the process of the shared activity rather than the end-goal that is important, and the extent to which mutuality and emotional engagement are maximised. If the couple can be helped to think about their everyday activities as opportunities for becoming more involved together in this way before the dementia becomes too advanced, this may be protective and give strategies and understanding that can be helpful later on in the illness.

In addition, the theoretical framework draws upon the model of couple psychotherapy developed at Tavistock Relationships (see Chapter 1) in order to conceptualise how the partners in the couple may affect one another in conscious and unconscious ways, focusing on the interactional field of the relationship. Whilst the partner with dementia may be the identified patient, this approach seeks to understand the dementia also as a shared problem, which will be experienced in a way that is particular to each couple, based upon their shared histories and the underlying dynamics of their relationship. In the course of the work, the therapists need to ask themselves, how are the couple functioning at the moment and the therapeutic task is to explore the main issues facing the couple. What are the points of maximum pressure and what kind of support will help them; what aspects of the couple's relationship provide resilience? Although couple therapists will be trained to think with couples in this way, we believe that a range of professionals would be able to apply this approach in their own settings, by using the manual for the intervention with training and supervision. The goal is not to train people to become couple therapists or to make 'expert' formulations; the important thing is for the person working in this model to hold a position of curiosity, an interest in thinking about what behaviour or feelings may mean. It is the act of showing curiosity and interest which we see as the central element, in order to model for the couple the idea that there is something to think about, that both partners' experiences are meaningful and worthy of attention. The following case example illustrates how such an approach can create the conditions for a discussion which has much deeper emotional significance for the couple.

> Jack and Mavis were watching a video of their attempt to sort out the videos in a display cabinet. Soon after the video clip began, both partners laughed and the therapist stopped the tape and asked them about this. Jack responded, saying that he thought that Mavis was 'peeved' because he was not sticking with the task. The therapist asked her what she thought Jack had been feeling. Mavis said that she thought he felt parts of his life were being thrown away. The therapist picked up this comment and repeated it, asking Jack if this was right, that this was how he felt. He said: 'It feels like that ... yeah ...' And he then talked about how he used to go to the cinema every Saturday morning as a boy. Mavis chipped in, reminding him of the name of the cinema when he struggled to recall it. He had seen all of these people – Laurel and Hardy – all the old classics, the ones on the videos ...
>
> After a few more minutes, Jack took the initiative and asked Mavis what she was feeling. She said, 'I thought you are not going to give in, no matter

how I tried to help you, you were fighting me ... That's what it was, a fight ... a quiet fight, but still a fight.' He agreed with this and went on to describe how the mess in the cabinet was what in Yiddish they call a '*bouja*'. The therapist asked what this meant. 'A big mix-up', he said. Mavis commented, 'that's what your mind is sometimes, isn't it?' Jack agreed and then there was a discussion of how what was happening was a good example of the difficulty of helping each other with the '*bouja*', the difficulty and confusion of the memory loss, and it could turn into a battle. Mavis went on to say that it did not use to be like that. 'Everything used to be organised but now we keep not being able to find things. If anything happened to Jack, I wouldn't know where to start, to sort it all out. My mind, at the moment, is quite tidy ... but this morning I had such a shock. I lost my purse.' And then Mavis described how she had become very angry with him. 'I felt such an idiot myself and then I let him have it full blast – two guns ... which is a shame and I do feel sorry'.

It was possible for the therapist to explore this with them – how it seemed that Mavis could try to keep her mind 'tidy', but when she lost her purse it felt as though she were becoming forgetful too, that the dementia was overtaking both of them. This was frightening for her and she became angry and attacking of Jack. Mavis said: 'It is like a precipice, and I can't afford to lose my mind or my memory because I am fighting for the two of us – and that is what it boils down to, because I have no one to rely on, you know, if I go down'.

Recognising the emotional challenge facing the carer partner

Whilst research indicates the importance of the inter-connectedness of the couple and the capacity of the carer partner to engage emotionally with their partner with dementia, the challenges of the situation raise the question of what supports may be needed to survive an experience that does not contain the hope of the carer–cared for relationship in early life. Having emotional contact with fragmented experience is very difficult, and it is understandable that carers who are themselves less contained may be less able to tolerate emotional contact with the person with dementia.

Whilst there is a great deal of awareness in terms of the needs of mothers with new-born babies for help and support in combating post-natal depression, there is relatively little research or clinical interest in the needs of the caring relationship at the other end of the lifespan. Pilot work in developing this approach indicated the tremendous challenge that 'going on being interested' and emotionally available within the relationship presented to the partner without dementia (Balfour, 2014, 2015). In developing the model, this drew attention to the importance of considering not only the impact of dementia on couple attachment, but also of recognising the emotional challenge of the situation facing the carer partner.

Clinically, there is an additional element that has been important in developing the intervention model: the psychoanalytic understanding that it is very difficult for someone – a carer partner in this example – to take in and think about the experience of someone else if they themselves are not feeling understood and 'taken in' emotionally. Therefore, the approach also includes separate space, outside the joint work, for the carer partner to have their feelings listened to by the therapist – based on the understanding from mother–infant psychotherapy that 'the mother whose cries are heard hears her infant's cries' (Fraiberg, 1987). This is a crucial dimension of the clinical approach – not simply to exhort the partner without dementia to think more closely about what is happening in their partner's mind, but for the clinician to think with them about their own feelings in order that, once they themselves are feeling better understood they are more able to 'think their way' into their partner's experience.

It is important not to gloss over the challenges of the situation or idealise what is possible. The carer partner may have all kinds of feelings towards the individual with dementia apart from compassionate ones, such as resentment or hatred. These feelings might arouse tremendous guilt or anxiety, and there may be a great need for help with this. And yet approaches to interventions with carers generally do not address this more difficult area.

One man we worked with said:

> There are all these images everywhere of rosy carers on all the leaflets – but it's not like that ... I hate her a lot of the time and it's shit– and it's like no one can tell the truth – how shit it is, and the resentment ... What do I do with that?

If we think about the concept of projection, we might recognise how difficult the task of sustaining emotional contact can be under such circumstances. People often lack a way of thinking about or making sense of such feelings, particularly of guilt and shame, and have no one to talk to about them. This highlights the importance of the carer partner having the opportunity to speak without fearing being judged. For them to be able to use the therapist in this way, as someone able to acknowledge, take in and understand feelings that they may be very ashamed of having, may be a huge thing in itself.

Addressing changes in the couple's relationship

If things previously have been good enough, the couple living with dementia are losing a relationship that has contained them and in which they have provided containment[1] and intimacy for each other. In a relatively healthy adult relationship where projections[2] are not too fixed, partners may be able to act as containers of difficult feelings for one another in a flexible way. In a relationship where one partner has dementia, the burden will increasingly shift to the partner without dementia to act as container for their spouse. This can result in significant changes in the dynamics of couple functioning. Carer partners, particularly men, often speak of this as a 'reversal' of how things had been before:

> It used to be me who was the one who was more shut down. Now it has switched around and she is the one who is more like I used to be ... now we are crossing over into opposite places.

But as the dementia progresses, it may not simply be that patterns get reversed or amplified, instead there may be a whole sea change. As the person with dementia deteriorates, not only are they unable to offer containment for their partner as they might once have done, but they may also be projecting something persecuting into them. So it may become a very literal coming true of the situation of a loss not simply being experienced as an absence, but instead as living in the presence of something persecutory. The carer partner may increasingly be needed to be the container in the relationship, but they are likely to be filled with their own fears and anxieties and so it may be very difficult for them to take in their partner's projections or state of mind. One can see that the stage is set for a potentially difficult situation. The presence of a third containing figure, a therapist or a counsellor who the carer partner is able to talk to about the reality of their feelings, who is not going to judge but who will listen, can be very helpful. The model is akin to a Russian doll: the person with dementia contained by their partner, who is contained by the therapist, who themselves has the containment of supervision. The important thing is 'containing' the 'container', so to speak.

We have found that a protective factor for the couple is the carer's continuing capacity to be interested in what their partner with dementia is feeling and the ability to see meaning in their behaviour. To this end, an important element of our approach is supporting the carer partner to establish and sustain this state of mind. What we find helps with this, as we have said, is if they themselves have the experience of someone trying to understand how they feel and how they see things. Once this is established, when the carer partner starts to feel 'taken in' emotionally, they may be more able to allow themselves to think about their partner's experience. Linked to this, another important factor is the couple's ability to observe and think about their relationship with one another. Although the extent to which this can be shared will depend on the capacity of the person with dementia, we have seen the importance of helping the couple to notice and reflect on their engagement together, particularly moments of responsivity and pleasure in their interactions, which can be captured visually in the video recordings taken during the work and which we now discuss in more detail.

Using video

> Mary had been caring for her husband John with dementia for several years at home. She had been able to ignore the extent of his difficulties by

carrying on as usual, attending to her outside interests and classes, leaving him at home and never really talking about his dementia, even with their adult children. However, recently John had had a fall whilst she was out and been taken to hospital. He was discharged home but Mary started to become very anxious about being trapped. She found it difficult to sleep, and was getting more irritated with John and by the limitations his condition imposed on her. She tried to manage things by keeping a diary, with their daily timetable written down, so that John knew what was happening. But he was unable to hold events and time in his mind and this infuriated her. She felt he was doing it deliberately to spoil her plans.

Mary was disappointed when we showed the couple the first video we had made of them at the start of our work together. This was a recording of them washing up. When we discussed her feelings with her, it became clear that Mary had been hoping for something rather miraculous: that they might get back to a place before John had dementia – when he was very much the partner who took the lead in the family. This was a central theme, and exposed just how much things had changed since his dementia and how self-reliant she had to be now.

The second video we made a little later in our work was of them looking at some photographs together. Mary had been complaining about how John did not listen to her and that whatever she did, it made no difference. John was in his own world, she said. On the film, she was showing him photos in quick succession and he could not keep up with her. At the next visit we showed her the film separately first, and then with John. This was to allow her more space and less distraction, so that she might be freer to notice her reactions and to think with us. In the video it was clear that John was watching her and following her with his eyes, as they looked at the photos. We stopped the film and asked her what she had noticed and she said she could see John looking at her. Mary became upset and said 'he looks really lost'. These visual moments captured on film helped her attune to John and see his vulnerability, softening some of her irritation with him.

In an individual session, Mary voiced her painful feelings and uncertainties about the future, as well as how embarrassed she could sometimes feel to be seen in public with John, and she could begin to acknowledge how lost she felt too. For his part, John expressed very poignantly an awareness of being close to dying and his concern for Mary's future. Mary was very touched by his consideration of her and this helped her feel more in contact with the 'old John', the man she had known for so many years. As the visits continued, Mary also made more emotional contact with her children who became more involved. At the final meeting, she said she felt that she was more realistic about their situation and able to enlist help and local support; she recognised, as she said, that she was doing her best and now felt less guilty than she had before.

The aim of using video is to help couples become observers of themselves and their relationship, with the focus on finding meaning in everyday things. Whether we work with the couple together reviewing the video, or the carer partner alone, has varied case by case. Where the dementia is advanced, we may be more likely to do this with the carer partner alone.

We have found video to be a powerful tool in helping couples to observe what is going on between them, to get them into a state of mind in which they are able to stand back and begin to question, or become interested in, why things are happening between them in the way they do. The activities we video can seem mundane and every day, but being able to find new meanings and ways of thinking that are grounded in the couple's daily living is very important. Things can easily become very calcified between partners: he or she perceived as simply like that leaving nothing to be thought about, but the video can allow things to be noticed and seen afresh in a way that is powerful and can support change.

The intervention is manualised, and there are step by step instructions for the therapist to follow. The essence of the approach is that we say something like this to the couple: 'We want you to work together as a team. Can you think of something that needs to be done around the house – e.g. cleaning the fridge – something that feels natural'. The approach is structured, focusing upon techniques for enabling greater contact around the everyday activities of life and, as part of this, trying to enable the couple to think about their feelings. It is important that time is spent with each of the partners individually, so that there is the opportunity for feelings and thoughts which may be stirred up by the activities, to be expressed and thought about. Here the hope is that if the partners are more contained, they will have less need to recourse to defensive withdrawal or acting out their anger and frustration.

The therapist goes through the video interactions looking at moments of contact between the partners, as well as points of frustration or difficulty. Noticing something with the couple, however mundane, that is difficult for them to see when they are otherwise immersed in their experience, can help them to step back, observe and think about themselves and their relationship:

> Before the visit, Barbara the carer spouse, had said on the telephone that there was no point in going ahead with the intervention as her partner Ray did not really do anything his memory loss was too bad and he had totally withdrawn. However, when the therapist showed her the video and highlighted examples of her partner's competence she was taken by the examples of his capacity. The video captured how she had moved away from her familiar, memory-testing interaction with him (she had tended to question him in a rather 'school mistressy' manner) to using declarative comments. For example, on the video there were instances of where, instead of testing him with questions about what he remembered, she shows him a picture and says to him 'these are old buildings that were

near your parents' house'. She supplies the context and her personal memory. He then supplies an association to it and a memory of his own, and they are both in more emotional contact with one another. This was something that the therapist had been working on with her; using the video clip she was able to show Barbara how effectively she was putting it into practice, and how much Ray was responding to her. This helped her to change her mind: she re-engaged and became very interested in the process, seeing the therapy through to its end some months later.

We have focused on the positive responses of the couple but it is also important to explore more negative feelings:

> Another video, this time of their clearing the fridge together, captured a moment when Barbara expressed frustration. In one part of the activity things become more difficult when Ray's role is to put things back into the fridge. Watching the video, her tension is evident from the outset. The therapist is careful to show the positive interaction first, and then Barbara's moment of frustration: in the corner of the screen she can be observed putting her hands to her head in a manner that reveals her rage and frustration. She is asked what she is feeling. The ensuing discussion is helpful and links to mourning the man she used to have as well as her ability to focus on what she does have with him and what is possible now.
>
> She described how she was frustrated about the fridge and also other things, such as his complaints about his tinnitus, and her frustration with him felt at times to be like a terrible noise between them. But the opportunity to think about it seemed to lead to a softening between them and evident shifts in their relationship. He was a man whom she had described as often hidden behind a book, shut off and withdrawn, and at this point in the therapy she said he was emerging more. On one occasion, she spoke of how she had noticed that he does come out into the kitchen now, asking if there is anything he can do? She said he had never done this before, and she thought he was making a link with the work that we had been doing. This seemed to help her to tolerate the difficulties and her frustrations with him. Towards the end of the therapy Ray talked in a way that seemed linked to a restoration of greater intimacy and a sense of being more contained by her and by the therapeutic work. Here, Ray seems to be communicating something about this:

> I have moods – particularly when my tinnitus is bad. She treads softly around me – she doesn't say anything. She is quietly responsive – I am a lucky man. My memory is not so good. She helps me, she's my rock. I do fear the couple being broken . . . not staying . . . that it will come to that.

Taken together, the examples discussed in this chapter illustrate how emotionally interconnected partners can be and the value of their being helped to hold on to emotional contact and meaningful interaction with one another, though the movement of the dementia is towards progressive loss of this. This loss is a central part of the experience of the illness, and increased emotional contact can be painful and challenging. However, the clinical experience described in this chapter suggests that, if supports can be put in place to help couples manage this it can be very important in terms of the quality of their lives and their resilience, in the face of the challenges of dementia.

Concluding thoughts

Unfortunately, Ray's fear that they, as a couple, might be broken up is not unfounded. Whilst the option of residential care is an important one, the evidence is that when there is insufficient support and few options for professionals, then premature or unnecessary residential placement may be the outcome (Moniz-Cook & Manthorpe, 2009). We are not suggesting that people with dementia should always be kept at home – many of those with whom we have worked felt that the time would come when they would need to place their partner in residential care. But this can be a very difficult decision which is rife with the potential for guilt and anxiety, and here we are not just talking about the consequences of physical separation. When the person with dementia is admitted into residential care, the experience of their partner can be that it is difficult to have a link and continued role with them, and this can greatly compound the emotional difficulty of the situation for both partners. Services are not, on the whole, set up to take account of couple relationships. Indeed, in some cases where both partners have needed residential care, it has not been uncommon for them to be placed in different homes.

A British Institute of Human Rights Case Study describes the situation of Fred and Mabel who had been married for over 65 years (Sceats, 2008). Fred was unable to walk on his own and relied on Mabel to help him move around. She was blind and used her husband as her eyes. They were separated after Fred fell ill and was moved into a residential care home. Mabel asked to come with him but was told by the local authority that she did not fit the criteria. Speaking to the media, Mabel said: 'We have never been separated in all our years and for it to happen now, when we need each other so much, is so upsetting. I am lost without him: we were a partnership.' This highlights how couples function as a unit: Fred literally leans on Mabel, and he, quite literally, is her eyes. This captures the interdependency of couples, which can be at the physical level, as with this couple, but also at the emotional level, each holding functions for the other that help them to sustain their equilibrium, and, under benign conditions, function better together than either partner could alone.

Particularly in times of austerity a false dichotomy can be set up, between commissioners and managers on the one hand, who are concerned with cost, and clinicians on the other, who are focused on patient well-being and ideals of care. But these positions might come together here, because the older couple relationship can be a tremendous resource, able to provide care that is costly to give in institutional settings. Real support of the resilience of the couple living with dementia depends upon recognising the emotional challenges these couples face and avoiding an idealisation of what is possible. To this end, the couple relationship needs to be thought about at different levels – at the policy level and at the level of local service provision. We need our policy makers and local commissioners to act to avoid both the monetary waste that neglect of the older couple entails, but also to address the human cost of this neglect, which is most starkly illustrated in the case of the separation of couples, who may have been together a lifetime, when one or other of them becomes unable any longer to be cared for at home.

We have tried to show that there is a profound need for interventions that support relationships at the end of the lifespan. More particularly, there is a need for our services to become relationship-minded, in order to support the humanity of the individual with dementia and those around them, so that emotional meaning can be held onto within the environment of care for as long as possible. We would all wish for such an environment for ourselves and those we care about. The converse position of lack of support for, or separation from, important relationships, and lack of emotional engagement with the person with dementia, is a situation that we can recognise as profoundly damaging – one of 'society's ills' that needs to be changed. There are signs of progress and after a lifetime of neglect dementia is now centre stage in terms of political and media attention. Our hope is that new ways of working will be developed, such as we have described in this chapter, that will be part of a process of bringing new thinking and understanding to an area of life that has languished largely ignored by our profession and by society at large for too long '... stowed out of conscience as unpopular luggage' (Auden, 1968, p. 860).

Notes

1 The concept of 'containment' (Bion, 1962) is rooted in the earliest relations of infancy. According to this theory, if the mother is able to take in and think about her baby's distress, it can become 'detoxified' and the baby may be able to take back in its emotional experience in more manageable form. As it does so, over time, the range of feelings that the infant can encompass in its own mental apparatus expands and the capacity of the caregiver to take in, think about and give meaning to experience is internalised.
2 'Projection' refers to an unconscious process (or 'phantasy') in which aspects of the self are 'split-off' and attributed to an 'external object' – that is, to another person. In this context, it means that partners attribute to, and see in, the other qualities that are, in fact, aspects of themselves.

References

Ablitt, A., Jones, G.V., & Muers, J. (2009). Living with dementia: a systematic review of the influence of relationship factors. *Aging & Mental Health*, *13*(4): 497–511. https://doi.org/10.1080/13607860902774436

Auden, W.H. (1968). 'Old People's Home'. In: *Selected Poems*. London: Faber & Faber.
Balfour, A. (2014). Developing therapeutic couple work in dementia care – the living together with dementia project. *Psychoanalytic Psychotherapy*, 28(3): 304–20.
Balfour, A. (2015). Growing old together in mind and body. *Fort Da: The Journal of the Northern California Society for Psychoanalytic Psychology, American Psychological Association*, 21(2): 53–76.
Bion, W.R. (1962). *Learning from Experience*. London: Heinemann.
Baradon, T., Broughton, C., Gibbs, I., James, J., Joyce, A., & Woodhead, J. (2005). *The Practice of Psychoanalytic Parent–Infant Psychotherapy: Claiming the Baby*. London: Routledge.
Evans, D., & Lee, E., (2014). Impact of dementia on marriage: a qualitative systematic review. *Dementia*, 13: 330–49.
Forsund, L.H., Skovdhl, K., Kiik, R., & Ytrehus, S. (2014). The loss of a shared lifetime: a qualitative study exploring spouses' experiences of losing couplehood with their partner with dementia living in institutional care. *Journal of Clinical Nursing*, 24: 121–30.
Fraiberg, S. (1987). Ghosts in the nursery. In: L. Fraiberg (Ed.), *Selected writings of Selma Fraiberg*. Columbas OH:, Ohio State University Press.
Gilleard, C., J., Belford, H., Gilleard, E., Whittick, J.E., & Gledhill, K. (1984). Emotional distress amongst the supporters of the elderly mental infirm. *British Journal of Psychiatry*, 145: 172–7.
Gutstein, S., (2005). Relationship development intervention: developing a treatment programme the address the unique social and emotional deficits of autism spectrum disorders. *Autism Spectrum Quarterly*, winter, 2005.
Hellstrom, I., & Lund, U. (2007). Sustaining 'couplehood': spouses' strategies for living positively with dementia. *Dementia*, 6: 383–409.
Henderson, J., & Forbat, L. (2002). Relationship-based social policy: personal and policy constructions of 'care'. *Critical Social Policy*, 22: 669–87.
Hoppmann, C., Gerstorf, D., & Hibbert, A. (2011). Spousal associations between functional limitation and depressive symptom trajectories: longitudinal findings from the study of asset and health dynamics among the oldest old (AHEAD). *Health Psychology*, 30(2): 153–62.
Kennedy, H., Landor, M., & Todd, L. (2011). *Video Interaction Guidance: A Relationship-Based Intervention to Promote Attunement, Empathy and Well Being*. London: Jessica Kingsley.
Knopp, D.S., Bergman-Evans, B., & McCabe, B.W. (1998). In sickness and in health: an exploration of the perceived quality of the marital relationship, coping and depression in caregivers of spouses with Alzheimer's disease. *Journal of Psychosocial Nursing*, 36: 16–21.
McGovern, J. (2011). Couple meaning-making and dementia: challenges to the deficit model. *Journal of Gerontological Social Work*, 54: 678–90.
Moniz-Cook, E., & Manthorpe, J. (2009). *Early Psychosocial Interventions in Dementia: Evidence Based Practice*. London: Jessica Kingsley.
Morris, L.W., Morris, R.G., & Britton, P.G. (1988a). The relationship between marital intimacy, perceived strain and depression in spouse caregivers of dementia sufferers. *British Journal of Medical Psychology*, 61: 231–6.
Morris, L. W., Morris, R.G., & Britton, P.G. (1988b). Factors affecting the emotional wellbeing of the caregivers of dementia sufferers. *British Journal of Psychiatry*, 153: 147–56.

Norton, M.C., Piercy, K.W., Rabins, P.C., Green, R.C., Breitner, J.C.S., Ostbye, T., Corcoran, C., Welsh-Bohmer, K.M., Lykefsos, C.G., & Tschanz, J.T. (2009). Caregiver–recipient closeness and symptom progression in Alzheimer's disease. The Cache County Dementia Progression Study. *Journal of Gerontology: Psychological Sciences*, *64B*(5): 560–8.

Sceats, S. (2008). The human rights act – changing lives. London: Garden Court Chambers. Available at: www.advicenow.org.uk/is-that-discrimination/whatsit-all-about/human-rights-fred-and-mables-story,10059,FP.html

Uchino, B. N., Kiecolt-Glaser, J. K., & Cacioppo, J. T. (1994). Construals of preillness relationship quality predict cardiovascular response in family caregivers of Alzheimer's disease victims. *Psychology and Aging*, *9*(1): 113–20. doi.org/10.1037//0882-7974.9.1.113

Wadham, O., Simpson, J., Rust, J., & Murray, C. (2016). Couples' shared experiences of dementia: a meta-synthesis of the impact upon relationships and couplehood. *Aging & Mental Health*, *20*(5): 463–73.

Wright, L. (1991). The impact of Alzheimer's disease on the marital relationship. *The Gerontologist*, *31*(2): 224–326.

Wright, L. (1994). Alzheimer's disease afflicted spouses who remain at home: can human dialectics explain the findings? *Social Sciences and Medicine*, *3*(8): 1037–46.

Commentary on Chapter 10

Jane Garner

'Remember, I am still me.'
(Alzheimer patient, Scotland)

Currently in the UK, 850,000 people have a dementia. The duration of what is a terminal disorder can be in excess of ten years after diagnosis, leaving patients[1] feeling extremely scared and lonely for a significant part of their lives. The loneliness is not only from social isolation, the kind that may benefit from attending a day centre, but an intense personal aloneness, reflecting a loss of emotional contact and understanding. Some will experience dementia as an indication of failure, and faced with the profound existential threat it represents may experience intense rage against the shame and humiliation they feel it has inflicted on them. When anxiety is too great and overwhelms an individual's defences the reaction has been described as nothing short of catastrophic (Kohut, 1972).

At the same time as coming to terms with illness, dementia sufferers and their carers may be experiencing other potentially difficult aspects of life, such as retirement, death of a parent or problematic family relationships. These normal life events become harder to manage with a diagnosis of dementia in the family, bringing with it seismic shifts in power and dependency. As Balfour and Salter have described, some fear dependency more than they fear death because with dependency may come a change in the hermeneutics of the self and the narrative of an individual's life story.

It is not only patients who fear dementia. Public opinion reflects the view that dementia is one of the worst things that can happen in life, the loss of one's mind and the capacity to remember superseding all other health afflictions (Brunet et al., 2012). The National Dementia Strategy (DoH, 2009) was a welcome attempt to think about attitudes to the illness and to describe diagnostic and management services that might be put in place. Since then, the focus has been on achieving targets to increase the number of people receiving an early diagnosis. However, this has not been matched by attending to the need for post diagnostic support (BPS, 2014). Although having the diagnosis, knowing the cause of your or your partner's difficulties, may help (Evans, 2014), if patients are then left to fend for themselves it is predictable that feelings of panic, anxiety and hopelessness will only increase: as one person said to a GP, 'Oh please, don't say the "A" word', expressing the common fear of Alzheimer's held by so many.

More perniciously, there is a politico-social tendency to view old age, and particularly old age with dementia, as a burden on the state, by which is meant a burden on the (especially younger) taxpayer. Dartington (2010) questions how acceptable it is in our society to be vulnerable. Bell (1996) fears that the ideology of the market, now introduced into socialised medicine, is an attack on human values causing us to see dependency and vulnerability as weaknesses to be despised.

Although on 8 January, 2018, the title of the Secretary of State for Health was expanded to include Social Care (an area of responsibility already in the portfolio), the political response to counter such opinion has been slow. Back in March, 2012, the then Prime Minister, David Cameron, identified dementia as a national priority in 'Challenge on Dementia'. He reiterated its importance in February 2015, which resulted in an improved awareness of the disease. However, in December 2017 Cameron acknowledged that nothing had been done to alleviate the issue of funding social care despite his personal pledge to set a lifetime cap on care costs at £72,000. Prime Minister Theresa May has said that the cap on care costs would be subject to a consultative review, but since then all has gone quiet.

Much is expected of health and social care staff looking after patients with a dementia, where additional knowledge, thinking and experience are required. For example, they need to have professional knowledge of aetiologies, neuroscience, pharmacotherapy, end of life care, legal and ethical issues and how to recognise abuse. They should be able to work collaboratively in multidisciplinary, multi-agency settings, understanding the boundary issues involved in intimate caring tasks and recognising the potential for ageism in services, both in themselves and in their patients.

In its treatment, a broad scope of health professionals tend to concentrate on the multiple disabilities occasioned by a dementing illness, but such a focus can omit consideration of aspects of their patients that remain unaffected by the disease, perhaps particularly their affective lives and relationships. They are not *only* patients, in fact there is no linear relationship between brain pathology, as evidenced on MRI scans, and levels of ability. Whilst an organic aetiology is not in question, other bio-psycho-socio-cultural factors interact to produce the presentation and experience of dementia (Garner, 2018a).

Understanding what a patient is going through is hard. It will depend to some extent on the stage their illness has reached. Whenever that is, the encounter will be with a person who has a life history and a network of attachments and relationships. They will have experienced not only illness but also other losses, regrets, dreams and hopes. Their behaviour will be laden with personal meaning. What may be overlooked in understanding this behaviour is the reality that those with dementia have more in common with those who do not than is often appreciated. This consideration may not lessen the devastating impact a diagnosis might have on patients, but it may influence the course of treatments and therapies they receive.

Nevertheless, old age and dementia attract a set of false beliefs and stereotypes. An important aspect of the work, therefore, is to disentangle these myths and prejudices. The experience of dementia is as wide and multifarious as there are numbers of people with the diagnosis (Jennings, 2014), and perhaps it is presumptuous to assume or to generalise about it. For instance, even in late stages of the disease the ability to make relationships can be retained (Garner, 2004). Certainly, early on it will be possible to discuss the experience of the disease, although subsequently carers may have to rely on piecing together fragmented communications, non-verbal cues, body language signals and the feelings evoked in them by the patient.

Affective memory is retained in dementia far longer than cognitive memory (Williams & Garner, 1998), and high cognitive skills are not necessary for affective tasks. Sinason (1992) describes telling her patient that while his Alzheimer's brain was forgetting some things, other things he himself was forgetting, and that was where they could work together. Forgetting may be about many things other than brain damage (Evans, 2008). Kitwood (1990) tells us that the abilities, skills and mood of someone with dementia are contingent on the attitudes and behaviour of those around them. In other words, the expression of the disease, and the way in which it is experienced is mediated – and therefore capable of moderation – by the reaction of others around the person with the illness, a central point of Balfour and Salter's chapter. As they suggest, the partner of the person with dementia has a vital role in the patient's care. The presence of a partner can act as an anchor of such importance that fear is engendered when she or he leaves the room (Balfour, 2018).

But however willing, loving and helpful a partner may be, it is important to recognise that their life will also have changed immeasurably as a result of the disease. While the death of a spouse has been seen as the most stressful of life events (Holmes & Rahe, 1967), dementia often removes vital aspects of their partner, affecting mutuality in the relationship and robbing a person of their primary confidant. Spouses may minimise the signs and symptoms of dementia in order to protect the self-image of their partner or to stave off the reality for themselves, a denial that can add to frustration in a relationship and may even delay unmasking the condition until after the partner has died. Clinical experience suggests one of the main influences on the grief experienced as a result of dementia is the quality of the premorbid relationship.

Much is written on the burden on carers, but this perspective is not necessarily helpful. Offering the practical solutions that carers seem to be seeking is not always effective, and these are often turned down or are unsuccessful because unconscious factors underlying such practical requests have not been understood. Perhaps the most important implicit request carers make is for someone to understand the experience they are going through; then they are better equipped to understand the experience their partner is going through, a crucial yet neglected dimension of dementia care that the authors address in their chapter.

Not every experience will be negative. The patient may retain a capacity to appreciate their relationship. Indeed, both partners may be able to live in the moment and attain a temporary feeling of success in their activities together. Shared pleasures, music, entertainment, and so forth, may bring to mind forgotten times, supporting the sense of connection that lies at the heart of resilience in relationships.

There is a continuing need for intimate connectedness throughout life. The benefits of a stable and intimate relationship may accumulate over the years. Couples bolster their resilience by having overcome previous difficulties together. When a diagnosis of dementia feels threatening, the quality of the couple relationship may determine not only whether patients remain at home but even whether they remain alive.

Intimacy is about one's innermost self touching and being touched by something meaningful in another (Garner & Bacelle, 2016). How increasing dependency is accommodated in a relationship will depend on past experience of dependency and trust earlier in life. Early blueprints of trust and dependency interact between partners throughout their relationship affecting how they experience stress. In one MRI study (Coan et al., 2006), subjects were placed in a scanner while holding the hand of their partner and instructed to anticipate a mild shock. The results showed that those with 'good' relationships experienced less stress reaction on the MRI measures of arousal as well as better affect regulation/co-regulation than others. Such research indicates the tangible, measurable effects of close relationships on the experience of physiological stress, interlinking it with partner response.

Attachment styles persist over time and may become exaggerated in dementia, affecting behaviour. Unless partners live alienated and separate lives, they will be the first to notice the subtle early changes that herald illness in the other. Help may be needed to avoid them resorting to and relating through splitting power and powerlessness between them. The risk is that the 'able' one, the non-patient, may increasingly take over many functions in the relationship that were formerly the preserve of the patient, and in doing so increase their anxiety. However, if the partner can understand and contain the patient's fears about this, both reap the reward in their relationship (Garner, 2018b).

A continuing sexual life can also be healing to the narcissistic wounds of old age; patients within a sexually active relationship are less likely than others to be admitted to a care home (Wright, 1998). Lipinska (2017) writes:

There is great power and autonomy, control and potency, achievement and self-directed pleasure involved in sex.

(p. 19)

These are aspects of the self that may diminish with dementia. Continuing some degree of sexual intimacy may also be comforting and consoling, counteracting some of the pain and loss induced by the illness.

If patients do require admission to hospital or a residential home, care will always be at its best if staff and relatives work collaboratively. Staff are likely to know more about the neuropsychiatric condition and treatment options than partners; partners will know more about the patient, and will be able to bring in their favourite things: photographs, music, memories and so on. Some will wish to be practically involved in caring tasks; others will need to be reassured about the value of just being there with their partner.

In their chapter Balfour and Salter, while recognising the emotional challenges facing carers and partners, note not only the humanitarian but also the economic consequences of services ignoring the innate resources of couples. They describe an elegant, relational approach to dementia, designed to benefit patients in what may be their most important relationship. They move away from an hierarchical demarcation between carer and patient in favour of a therapeutic model encouraging equal participation and a couple approach that is manualised and open to being used by therapists not familiar with couple therapy. In doing so they provide further evidence that psychological reparative work is possible despite the overtly destructive nature of dementia, and offer a model of practice that can improve the lives of those affected by this debilitating disease.

Note

1 In my response to Balfour and Salter's chapter, the word 'patient' will be used for the person with dementia, with the understanding that not everything about the patient can be attributed to organically determined impairment.

References

Balfour, A. (2018). The fragile thread of connection: living as a couple with dementia. In: S. Evans, J. Garner, & R. Darnley-Smith (Eds.), *Experiencing Dementia: Psychodynamic Perspectives from Observation, Theory and Practice*. London: Routledge.

Bell, D. (1996). Primitive mind of state. *Psychoanalytic Psychotherapy*, 10(1): 45–7.

British Psychological Society (BPS) (2014). *Clinical Psychology in the Early Stage Dementia Care Pathway*. London: British Psychological Society Publications.

Brunet, M., McCartney, M., Heath, I., & Tomlinson, J. (2012). There is no evidence base for proposed dementia screening. *British Medical Journal*, 345: e8588.

Coan, J., Schaefer, H., & Davidson, R. (2006). Lending a hand – social regulation of the neurological response to threat. *Psychological Science*, 17(12): 1032–9.

Dartington, T. (2010). *Managing Vulnerability: The Underlying Dynamics of Systems of Care*. London: Karnac.

Department of Health (DoH) (2009). *Living Well with Dementia: The National Dementia Strategy UK*. London: DH Publishing.

Evans, S. (2008). Beyond forgetfulness: how psychoanalytic ideas can help us to understand the experience of patients with dementia. *Psychoanalytic Psychotherapy, 22*(3): 155–76.

Evans, S. (2014). What the National Dementia Strategy forgot: providing dementia care from a psychodynamic perspective. *Psychoanalytic Psychotherapy, 28*(3): 321–9.

Jennings, E. (Ed.) (2014). *Welcome to Our World: A Collection of Life Writing by People with Dementia*. Canterbury: Forget-Me-Nots.

Garner, J. (2004). Dementia. In: S. Evans & J. Garner (Eds.), *Talking Over the Years: A Handbook of Psychodynamic Psychotherapy with Older Adults*. Hove: Brunner-Routledge.

Garner, J. (2018a). Where lies the expert? In: S. Evans, J. Garner, & R. Darnley-Smith (Eds.), *Experiencing Dementia: Psychodynamic Perspectives from Observation, Theory and Practice*. London: Routledge.

Garner, J. (2018b). Can anything good be born of a dementia; potential for reparation? In: S. Evans, J. Garner, & R. Darnley-Smith (Eds.), *Experiencing Dementia: Psychodynamic Perspectives from Observation, Theory and Practice*. London: Routledge.

Garner, J., & Bacelle, L. (2016). Intimacy and sexuality in old age. In: C. Fenieux & R. Rojas (Eds.), *Sexo y psicoanálisis. Una mirada a la IntimidadAdulta* (pp. 141–58). Santiago: La Pólvora Editorial.

Holmes, T., & Rahe, R. (1967). The social readjustment rating scale. *Journal of Psychosomatic Research, 11*: 213–18.

Kitwood, T. (1990). The dialectics of dementia: with particular reference to Alzheimer's disease. *Ageing and Society, 10*: 177–96.

Kohut, H. (1972). Thoughts on narcissistic rage in the search for the self. *Psychoanalytic Study of the Child, 27*: 360–400.

Lipinska, D. (2017). *Dementia: Sex and Wellbeing*. London: Jessica Kingsley.

Sinason, V. (1992). *Mental Handicap and the Human Condition: New Approaches from the Tavistock*. London: Free AssociationBooks.

Williams, D., & Garner, J. (1998). People with dementia can remember. *British Journal of Psychiatry, 172*: 379–80.

Wright, L. (1998). Affection and sexuality in the presence of Alzheimer's disease: a longitudinal study. *Sexuality and Disability, 16*(3): 167–79.

Index

abuse 67, 69, 87, 96, 154, 204; domestic 150, 164, 165, 166, 167, 187; emotional 133; physical 100, 101, 133, 152; psychological 150; sexual 98, 100, 150; *see also* alcohol abuse; couple violence; substance abuse
addiction 121, 133, 154; *see also* substance abuse
Adopting Together Service 53–65
adoption: and conflict caused by differences 60–3; in the context of loss 59–60, 68; effect on couples 53–5, 67–70; improving outcomes for parents 64–5; and pre-existing conflicts around intimacy 63–4; and the problem of disclosure 55–6; by same sex couples 70n2; by single parents 70n1
Adult Psychiatric Morbidity Survey (APMS) 109
affect dysregulation 132, 134, 135
affect regulation 11, 124–5, 134
affective states 142
alcohol abuse 1, 98, 154
anger management programmes 132
antenatal depression 49
anti-depressants 133
anxiety 128, 135; paranoid-schizoid 134
assortive mating 127
attachment 124, 128, 133; and adoption 69, 70; of couples 7 165, 193, 206; difficulties in 51; history of 88; insecure 125; issues in 55; promotion of 107; secure 135; systems 153, 155
attachment behaviours 98
attachment disorders 151
attachment injury 126–7, 128
attachment relationships 124–5
attachment security 41, 43

attachment theory 5, 7, 153
attachment trauma 155
austerity 3, 199

Balls, Ed 2
Bateman, Anthony 133
Becoming a Family Project group 86
behavioural therapies 30, 31, 113, 116; *see also* cognitive behavioural therapy (CBT)
behaviours: abusive 154; of adopted children 55, 69; aggressive 151; attachment 98; of children 40, 51, 53, 86, 87, 110, 126; depressed 87; destructive 19; hostile 137, 146; nonverbal 175; protective 107; sexual 104, 105, 106, 107; sexualized 55; violent 154, 166
bi-polar disorder 138
borderline personality disorder 153
bowel function 100
Breakdown Britain report 2
British Object Relations 5
Brown, Gordon 2

Cameron, David 204
Cameron government 3
caregivers 193–4, 205–6
case studies 8, 31, 32, 49, 53, 67, 109, 152, 199
Centre for Social Justice 2
children 1; adopted 53–65, 67–70; and adoptive parents 56–8; and affect regulation 124–5; behavior of 40, 51, 53, 86, 87, 110, 126; as containers 58–9; difficult 69; effect of parental conflict on 161, 165; effect on couples 39; emotional security of 41, 43; influence of adult relationships on 2, 3, 40–3, 73;

with language difficulties 51–2; matching with adopters 67; mental health of 3, 26; in poverty 2, 3; pre-birth influences on 42–3; with special needs 51–2
classical theory 175
clergy 4
coercion 101, 151, 152, 164
cognitive behavioural therapy (CBT) 5, 116, 124, 127, 129n1
cognitive distortions 98
collaboration 4, 86, 166–7
communication, action as 21–2
'Confide, Avoid, Attack' exercise 75
confidentiality issues 161
conflict: in couples 153, 156–9, 164–8, 184–5; in families 9; around intimacy 63–4; caused by differences 60–3; inter-parental 2, 40, 41, 43; management of 44, 151–2; relationship 4
Conscious system 173
containment 134–6, 145, 195, 200n1
continuous professional development (CPD) 119
control 24, 38, 62, 70, 90, 93, 99, 101, 135, 137, 151, 152, 160, 161, 164, 165, 207; financial 150
co-parenting relationships 9, 40; difficulties in 153; interventions for 45; *see also* parents
Core Complex 177–8
Cost of Family Failure Index 3
counter-instrumentalism 128
countertransference 6, 91, 93, 96, 98, 104, 111, 112, 133, 144, 145, 147, 154, 157, 175, 176, 179, 186; concordant vs. complementary 140–1; in MBT-CT 139–41; *see also* transference
couple attachment 7, 165, 193, 206
couple distress 153
couple psychotherapy 5, 6, 11, 15, 44, 133, 135, 192; enacted nature of couples' presentations 21–2, 24–5; model of 20–1; place of history in 23–5; research study of 8–9; as unique intervention 22–3
couple relationships 73; and adoption 68; breakdown of 49–50; creative 15; curiosity in 26; and domestic violence 164; sexual 95; and shared unconscious anxieties 26; triangular aspects of 43, 148; *see also* couple violence; couples; relationships

Couple Satisfaction Index 117
couple therapy 1, 4–5, 10, 12; assessment and group composition 76–8; for depression 109–22; and domestic violence 166; effectiveness of 30; in groups 71–83; implications for 43–6; improving outcomes of 32; outcomes of in clinical settings 30; Parents as Partners programme 72–5; psychodynamic 29–32, 56; same sex group 80–2; triangular setting of 22, 25, 26; 'Tuesday group' example 78–80; value of 31–2; in the voluntary sector 2, 30; *see also* mentalization based treatment for couples (MBT-CT)
Couple Therapy for Depression 113–16, 121–2, 124–9; and attachment injury 126–7; couples and the system 126; and a fantasy of 'cure' 120–1; funding for training 119; lack of awareness 119–20; outcomes, availability and barriers 118–19; place of in the system 116–17; as a relational approach to treating depression 121–2
couple violence 150–1, 162; assessment and structure 154–8; and confidentiality 161; context, research and development in domestic violence programmes 151–2; filling in the gaps 158–9; MBT formulation 160–1; and mentalization-based therapy (MBT) 153–4; origins of the Safer Families Project (SFP) 152; situational 151, 152, 165
couples: ageing 189–90; changes brought by parenthood 37–40; in conflict 153, 156–9, 164–8, 184–5; and the 'couple state of mind' 20; creative relationships 19–20; disillusionment in 19; experience of loss by 59–60; in a fractured state 171–6, 178–9, 187; history of 23–5; influence on children 40–3; and love, hate, and curiosity 18–19; need for intimacy 17–18; as parents 34–46; reasons for drawing together 16–17; same-sex 90–1; separateness and difference in 18; *see also* couple relationships; parents; relationships
Cowan, Carolyn Pape 10, 73
Cowan, Philip 10, 73
Cowans intervention groups 46
Cuthbert, Amanda 130

dementia 11, 189, 199–200; effect on relationships 190–1; and the Living Together with Dementia intervention 191–3; post-diagnostic support for 203; prevalence of 203; residential care for 199, 207; and the role of the couple 189–91; treatment of 204–5; *see also* Living Together with Dementia intervention
Department for Work and Pensions 3
depression 1, 6, 9, 37, 64, 78, 97, 133, 138, 190; and affect regulation 124; antenatal 49; couple therapy for 109–22, 124–9; developmental origins of 127–8; and the fantasy of 'cure' 120–1; getting worse means getting better 124; postnatal 1, 49; relational approach to treating 121–2
depressive guilt 127
developmental psychology 153
Dicks, Henry 5
disillusionment 19
distance-closeness dilemma 111–12
divorce: longlease 170; nominal 170; shotgun 170; as stressor 169
domestic abuse 150, 152
domestic violence 132, 164–8; programmes for 151–2; *see also* couple violence
dopamine 107
drug abuse *see* substance abuse

Early Intervention Foundation 10, 150
eating disorders 133
ego 175, 176
emotional dysregulation 142
emotional experience 135
emotional security 7
emotional unavailability 145–6
empathic softening 115
empathic validation 136
empathy 151, 153
employment, and parenthood 38–9
enactment 21–2, 24–5, 27n1, 29
Environmental Domain 169, 170, 183
erectile dysfunction 95, 105–6
evaluation 8–10
externalisation 145

families: psychosocial ecology of 46; support for 2–3
Family Action 88
family court welfare work 170
Family Discussion Bureau 4, 5, 7

family justice system 36
family life, five domains of 73–4
family stability 7; and workforce productivity 4
family therapy 1; *see also* couple therapy
fathers: men as 37–8; and the mother-infant dyad 51
feminist policy 2
foetal alcohol/narcotic syndrome 55
Fonagy, Peter 133
fracturing, as a form of functioning 176–7
Francis, Robert 120
Francis Report 120
Freud, Sigmund 8, 22, 31, 35, 42, 95, 121, 170, 173, 175, 177, 183

gender 17–18
group psychotherapy 75, 77; for couples 71–2
guilt 54, 56, 62, 111, 124, 194, 196, 199; depressive 127

health care funding 30
Health Education England (HEE) 119
heart disease 1
housing issues 1

id 175
Improving Access to Psychological Therapies (IAPT) 116, 117–18, 119, 120, 129
Improving Lives: Helping Workless Families report 4
individual therapy 1, 12
infertility 59, 60, 68, 70n2
innovations 10–12
Institute of Human Rights 199
integrated model, for treating psychosexual disorders 98–102\
inter-parental conflict 40; *see also* conflict
interventions: countertransference-informed 147; for couples expecting their first child 46; mentalization-based 141; transference-informed 139, 147
intimacy 206; need for 17–18; *see also* sexual relationships
intimate partner violence 151, 164; *see also* couple violence; domestic violence
intimate relationship distress 114

Jungian thinking 5

Kettering, Charles Franklin 12n10.
Kleinian thinking 5

life-history 127
Living Together with Dementia intervention 191–3; changes in the couple's relationship 194–5; emotional challenges of the carer partner 193–4; use of video 191–2, 195–9
loneliness 1
love 18–19

male privilege 166
manipulation 137
marriage 2; breakdown of 49–50; and postwar trauma and distress 4; societal changes in 187; support for 3; *see also* divorce
marriage counselling and counsellors 2, 4–5
maternal reverie 51
memory 205; *see also* dementia
men: as fathers 37–8; roles and responsibilities of 38
mental health: of children 1, 3, 26; ill 132, 154; of mothers 48–9; of parents 85; perinatal 48–9; problems of 114
mentalization 11, 128; capacity for 145; lack of capacity for 167; techniques 167; transparent 153
Mentalization Based Therapy 11
mentalization based treatment for couples (MBT-CT) 130–3, 151; the challenge of 141–2; commentary on 144–9; and containment 134–6; and countertransference 139–41; and projective identification 136–8; and transference 138–9
mentalization-based therapy (MBT): and confidentiality 161; and couple violence 153–4; MBT formulation 160–1
mentalization-based therapy–parenting together (MBT-PT) 153–4, 167; assessment and structure 154–8; filling in the gaps 158–9; therapeutic assessment 154–5
mentalization-based treatment (MBT) 133, 144
miscarriage 59, 60
models: of couple interaction 187; of the mind 187

mothers: and the mother-infant dyad 51; and parenthood 39; relationship with child 136–7; relationship with unborn baby 42–3; women as 37; *see also* women
mourning 59, 121, 170

narcissistic rage 127
narcissistic relationships 18, 60
National Dementia Strategy 203
National Health Service (NHS) 30, 114, 116, 117, 120, 129n3
National Institute for Health and Care Excellence (NICE) 30, 114, 116, 118, 129
Neonatal Intensive Care Unit (NICU) 51
neurobiology 107–8
neuroscience 5

Oedipus complex 42
oxytocin 90, 107

paranoid-schizoid functioning 134, 144
parenthood, effect on couples 37–40
Parent-Infant Psychotherapy 191
parenting: classes/programmes for 5, 84–5; five sites of conflict 38–9
'Parenting Together' programme 132
parents: and adoption 53–65, 67–70; of children with special needs 51–2; as co-parents 73; divorced/separated 36–7; effect on children 34, 73; improving outcomes for adoption 64–5; influence of others on 35; pre-birth support for 45; preventive help for 45, 50; relationship between 34; relationship with children 85; same-sex 72, 76–82; separated 79–80; *see also* co-parenting relationships
Parents as Partners 71–5; evidence base 85–7; origins of 84–8; research-based determination of content 85; starting up and bringing intervention to scale 87–8
Patient Health Questionnaire (PHQ9) 112, 122n1, 124
patriarchy 2
perceptual identity 177
physical abuse *see* abuse
physical trauma *see* trauma
pluralism 187
postnatal depression 1, 49; *see also* depression

poverty 1–4
Preconscious Normative Domain 170, 173, 183
pregnancy, hormonal changes of 49
projection 200n2
projective identification 136–8, 140, 146
Pruett, Kyle 73, 86
Pruett, Marsha Kline 73, 86
psychoanalytic approach 5, 144, 148
psychoanalytic theory 8, 145, 186–7
psychoeducation 88
psychological division of labour 60–1
psychological well-being practitioner (PWP) 110, 119
psychopathology 169
psychosexual assessment 97–8; homework exercises 101–2
psychosexual disorders 98–102
psychosexual therapy 104–8; assessment of 97–102; behaviour programme 101–2; improving access to 117–18
psychosocial assessment 99–100
psychosocial ecology 46
psychosocial intervention 11

Randomised Control Trials (RCTs) 9, 31, 86, 116
recidivism 167
reflection 42, 73, 109, 146, 167
regression 58, 176
relational dynamics 132
Relationship Development Intervention 191
Relationship Foundation 3
relationships: argumentative 176–8; borderline 133, 137–8, 139, 141–2; conflictual 132, 144; creative 19–20; distressed 1, 32; effect of dementia on 190–1, 194–5; helping 6; highly troubled 144; inter-parental 2, 72–3; mother-child 136–7; narcissistic 18, 60; parent-child 85; stressors to 169; support for 200; troubled 133; unstable 151; *see also* couple relationships; sexual relationships
research 8–10; attachment 128, 151; government support for 9; neuroscientific 107; psychodynamic 31; on support for couples 46

sado-masochism 148
Safer Families Project (SFP) 150, 152, 162; use of mentalization-based therapy 153
same sex couples 90–1; adoption by 70n2
Schoolchildren and their Families Project4 86
self-coherence 137, 146
self-survival 137
separations 133
sex education 105
sexpertise 92
sexual abuse 98, 100, 150; *see also* abuse
sexual health 90
sexual relationships: contentious 92–4; and the couple psychotherapist 95–7; non-heteronormative 92; in old age 206–7; and parenthood 38; problems between couples 99–100, 106–7; problems with 90–1; and psychosexual therapy 104–8; and psychosocial assessment 97–8; same-sex 105; talking about 94–5, 97–8, 102, 104–5; therapists asking about 91–5; unexpressed emotions about 91–2; *see also* intimacy
sexuality 17–19
shame 43, 59, 71, 82, 90, 92, 97, 98, 100, 101, 107, 124, 153, 154, 157, 160, 174, 194, 203
SHAME acronym 38
Sharpe, Ella Freeman 175
silence, of couples in therapy 171–2, 174–6
single parent families 2; adoption by 70n1
social cognition 153
social diversity 187
social workers 4, 5, 152
stress: caused by death of spouse 205; caused by depression 190
substance abuse 1, 98, 132, 154
suicidal thoughts 109, 154
supervision 6, 74, 76, 77, 79, 116, 119, 154, 192, 195
Support for All: The Families and Relationships Green Paper 2
support groups 45
Supporting Father Involvement intervention (SFI) 86–7

therapeutic assessment 154–5
therapists: and confidentiality issues 161; and countertransference 6; in couple psychotherapy 137; and Couple Therapy for Depression 116–17; MBT-CT 135–6,

139, 148–9; mutual emotional experience of 147; point of view of 115; and psychosocial assessments 98, 99; relationship with adoptive couples 70; role of 22–3, 26, 126; working with couples dealing with dementia 197–8; working with couples in conflict 156–9; working with fractured couples 175–6, 180–1, 187; *see also* countertransference

'third position' 20

transference 6, 22, 25, 27n2, 98, 133, 144, 173, 174, 176, 185; in MBT-CT 138–9, 146–7; *see also* countertransference

transference-countertransference relationship 146–7, 176

transparency 117, 139, 167

trauma 133, 150; emotional 100; physical 100

unconscious: anxieties 58; and couple fit 107, 114, 141, 148, 155, 167; and curiosity 148; depth vs. surface 184–6; dynamics between partners 32; fantasies 155, 173, 174, 178–80; functioning model of 173, 176; and guilt 56; influence of 29; past vs. present 173–4, 178; problems between couples 5–7, 58, 61, 90, 92, 95, 97, 99, 111, 138; projection 136–7, 140, 145, 200n2; psychosexual problems 104; reasons for drawing together 15–16; shared anxieties 26; shared narrative of 173; shared worlds of 56, 111, 132, 133, 136, 142, 155; on the surface 185–6; of the therapist 140–1; timeless nature of 35; and transference 138–9

Unconscious Idiographic Domain 169, 173, 183–4

Understanding Society survey 1

United Kingdom, health care funding in 30

United States, health care funding in 30

University of California, Berkeley 46

verbal aggression 152

video therapy 195–9

violent behaviours 154, 166; *see also* couple violence

What Works to Enhance Inter-parental Relationships and Improve Outcomes for Children 10

wicked problems 7–8

women: and hormonal changes of pregnancy 49; as mothers 37; psychic equilibrium during pregnancy 48–9; roles and responsibilities of 38; *see also* mothers